MW00583168

DAVID J. WISHART

The Last Days
of the Rainbelt

University of Nebraska Press   Lincoln & London

Funds for the index were provided by the UNL Research
Council.

Library of Congress Cataloging-in-Publication Data
Wishart, David J., 1946–
The last days of the rainbelt / David J. Wishart.
pages cm.
Summary: "A geographical history of eastern Colorado,
western Kansas, and southwestern Nebraska during the 1890s
drought"— Provided by publisher.
Includes bibliographical references and index.
ISBN 978-0-8032-4618-8 (hardback: alk. paper)
1. Great Plains—History—19th century. 2. Droughts—
Great Plains—History—19th century. 3. Agriculture—Great
Plains—History—19th century. 4. Farmers—Great Plains—
Social conditions—19th century. 5. Human geography—
Great Plains. 6. Social change—Great Plains—History—19th
century. 7. Great Plains—Environmental conditions. 8. Great
Plains—Economic conditions—19th century. I. Title.
F595.W77 2013
978'.032—dc23   2013019313

Set in Granjon by Laura Wellington.

Contents

Illustrations

———•—•———

Acknowledgments

———·•·———

I am grateful to the National Endowment for the Humanities for a Fellowship that allowed me to get this project started, and to the University of Nebraska–Lincoln Research Council and School of Natural Resources for small grants that helped me finish it. I also greatly appreciate the assistance given by Molly Boeka Cannon, who fashioned the maps and diagrams from my own rough copies, and Jessica Ditmore, who produced the final manuscript from my barely legible handwritten pages. Joyce Hurst and Milda Vaitkus, associated with the geography program at the University of Nebraska–Lincoln, helped in many ways too. Thanks also to Bridget Barry for acquiring my manuscript for the University of Nebraska Press and to Joeth Zucco for her meticulous editing. Finally, I'd like to express my gratitude to the Nebraska State Historical Society, which has been my home base for research since I came to the United States in 1967, and to the Colorado Historical Society where, just burrowing around a long time ago I came across the leather-bound volumes of settlers' interviews that made this study possible.

Introduction

--------◆--------

A Ruined Land

In 1899, at the end of a decade blighted by severe drought and economic hardship, J. E. Payne, superintendent of the Agricultural Experiment Station at Cheyenne Wells, made a fact-finding tour of the surrounding plains of eastern Colorado. Payne, a recent graduate of Kansas Agricultural College in Manhattan, drove his spring wagon across thirteen hundred dusty miles of Kit Carson County and what was then Arapahoe County, and is now Yuma and Washington Counties. He interviewed settlers, located the few orchards that had survived the drought, noted the small-scale well and ditch irrigation, and assessed agricultural prospects. Everywhere he traveled, he saw the ruins of towns and an emptied-out countryside.[1]

The semiarid shortgrass plains of eastern Colorado and adjacent southwestern Nebraska and western Kansas, which had been used as open range by cattlemen and sheepherders for decades and as hunting grounds by Native Americans for thousands of years, was rapidly and thickly settled by American farmers, speculators, and town builders from 1885 to 1889. This was (and is), at best, marginal farming land, with annual precipitation totaling less than fifteen inches, and in many years much less than that. It is an austere country of flat uplands reaching to distant horizons, with few trees, and streams that run dry for most of the year, a country of climatic extremes, from smothering blizzards to desiccating summers.

But the settlers were not deterred: for decades they had been assured by scholars, railroad companies, agricultural journals, and state immigration boards that rainfall would increase as farmers planted trees, which would still the hot winds and reduce evaporation, while at the same time returning moisture to the atmosphere through transpiration, causing saturation, and more rain. More plausibly, but still to a degree a fantasy, plowing up the dense prairie sod would allow rainfall to penetrate deeply, so avoiding rapid run-off and evaporation. The stored moisture would be available for the settlers' crops of wheat and corn and would again be slowly returned to the atmosphere, causing more rain. It was only a matter of time, it was reasoned — and widely believed — before the semiarid western plains would be fully farmed without any need for irrigation.[2] The fact that this was the only remaining free, or cheap, land on the central Great Plains only made the apocryphal theories more enticing.

In accordance with this theory, in the second half of the 1880s the plains of eastern Colorado and nearby Kansas and southwestern Nebraska became known as the Rainbelt. This was not in the sense of a natural surplus of rain, the way that Cornbelt denotes a surplus of corn, but in the sense of a deficit just waiting to be corrected. The expectation was that rainfall would be increased through the farmers' own efforts and the land would yield crops as abundantly as the more humid plains to the east. "If we don't have a continuous deluge," the Denver-based agricultural journal *Field and Farm* gushed in 1886, "we will at least have enough rain to get along comfortably."[3]

The settlers trickled into the Rainbelt before the railroads were in place, and flooded in thereafter. The plains of western Kansas and southwestern Nebraska were fully settled by 1886, leaving new arrivals — the "Rainbelters" — to push into eastern Colorado during the last three years of the decade. Because the cattlemen, anticipating the land rush and the end of the open range, had already secured the valleys, the homesteaders were left with the vast uplands, and the dream that rainfall would come to them through their own actions.

The settlers hardly had time to get established before drought and economic turmoil descended and, lacking roots and resources, they blew away like tumbleweeds. An entire layer of settlement was peeled off the land. Many counties lost more than one-third of their population from 1890 to 1900; some lost as much as two-thirds. The 1890 U.S. census population density map had shown continuous settlement across the central Great Plains from the Missouri River to the Rocky Mountains; the 1900 census map showed extensive areas of eastern Colorado designated once again as "unsettled."[4]

The evidence of abandonment was written on the landscape. Payne recalled that eastern Colorado towns like Lansing, Cope, Arikaree City, Thurman, Linden, and Harrisburg had "all aspired to be large cities, county seats, and railroad centers." But without a surrounding farm population to sustain their banks, businesses, and schools, by 1899 they had been reduced to virtual ghost towns. Payne observed that Lansing had "only four cellars to mark its site." Idalia had done a little better, retaining "two stores, two blacksmith shops, a school house, and a few dwellings." At Friend, only one building, a school, was still standing. Cope had kept a store, a school, and a couple of houses. At Arikaree City, the one surviving building was home to a family of four. All that remained of Linden were "a few heaps of earth and a few holes in the ground." There was still a family living at Harrisburg, and also at Thurman, a town that only recently had been the site of two banks and had attracted the interest of two railroads. Payne drove eighteen miles between Cope and Linden, on the divide between the North Fork of the Republican and the Arikaree Rivers, without seeing a single home.[5] Over vast areas, the country was reverting to open range, and the evidence of homesteading was being effaced.

At about the same time that Payne was making his reconnaissance, Willard Johnson, a topographer and geologist with the U.S. Geological Survey, was mapping his way across the High Plains of Kansas and Colorado, clarifying the details of the subsurface reservoir of water that another field geologist, Nelson Horatio Darten, had just named the Ogallala Aquifer. Johnson was also an astute observer of the human landscape and, like Payne, he saw that the area had been the scene of a disaster, an "almost complete depopulation." Johnson concluded that it had been "an agricultural experiment on a vast scale," and it had ended in "total failure."[6]

The drama of the settlement failure was widely recognized. Frederick Jackson Turner, the preeminent western historian of the time (as it would turn out), called it the "first defeat" of the American farmer. Later, geographer Harlan Barrows embellished this epitaph, describing the settlement collapse as the "first great crushing defeat of the American farmer."[7] Coming as it did just after the U.S. Bureau of the Census had officially (and prematurely) declared the frontier closed — "the unsettled area has been so broken into by isolated bodies of settlement that there can hardly be said to be a frontier line" — the failure on the western High Plains in the 1890s had national, not just regional, implications. It was part of a wider "frontier anxiety," the uneasy perception that the era of free land was at an end, and with it everything that had made the United States exceptional, from democracy to social stability. And, of course, it was Turner who codified all this in his famous 1893 paper, "The Significance of the Frontier in American History," a celebration of the frontier as the "crucible" of Americanization, and a lament for its passing.[8]

Yet the drought and associated settlement failure of the 1890s have been overshadowed by the scale, impact, and notoriety of the Dust Bowl of the 1930s, which confirmed the reputation of the Great Plains as America's problem region. In the 1890s there was no Farm Security Administration to sponsor notable photographers to record the misery, as they did so vividly in the 1930s. There was no defining novel like John Steinbeck's *Grapes of Wrath* (1939), or film like Pare Lorentz's *The Plow That Broke the Plains* (1936), to give the drought of the 1890s a mythical dimension. There were no panels of experts like the Great Plains Committee (1936) to study the conditions and recommend future actions. And there was no federal aid, no Works Progress Administration (wPA) to put people to work, no emergency cattle purchases, no payments to list the soil against the prevailing winds, or to retire land from production.[9] State aid and charity notwithstanding, settlers in the 1890s were mainly left to sink or swim by themselves. It's easy to see how it could all be forgotten.

This book is an attempt to bring this period of American settlement and failure on the western Great Plains more fully into historical memory.[10] The first chapter covers the distinctive geography of "frontier zones" and takes American settlement from the Missouri River in 1854 to the western High Plains of Colorado, Kansas, and Nebraska in the mid-1880s. This chapter provides a backdrop to what followed in the late 1880s and 1890s, serving to introduce aspects of the settlement process, such as migration patterns, demography, land laws, speculation, farming adjustments, and persistent delusions that spurred on the westward movement. It also serves to show that continuity rather than change characterized the American settlement of the central Great Plains during the second half of the nineteenth century, even as the physical environment transitioned from almost humid to semiarid.

The focus then falls, more locally and more personally, on the conditions of pioneering in eastern Colorado and adjacent Kansas and Nebraska from the height of the boom in the second half of the 1880s through the depths of the drought and depression of the mid-1890s. This focus is made possible by the existence of a singular historical source. From November of 1933 through the early months of 1934, the short-lived New Deal program, the Civil Works Administration (cwa), operating through the Colorado Historical Society, hired local people to conduct interviews with hundreds of elderly residents of eastern Colorado who recalled their experiences as settlers during the last decades of the nineteenth century. Eight counties on the High Plains of eastern Colorado — Yuma, Prowers, Baca, Morgan, Kit Carson, Sedgwick, Logan, and Phillips — were included in the project. These interviews, which are much more comprehensive than the later wpa interviews and only seem to have been conducted in Colorado, tell the stories of these settlers, revealing who they were, where they came from, how they lived and shaped their landscapes, and how they viewed the entire experience in retrospect.[11]

The format of the interviews varied from one county to another. B. B. Guthrie's interviews in Kit Carson County, for example, seem to have had a template, because the responses covered similar themes, such as the last buffalo, the search for water, the availability of reading material, and the establishment of schools and churches. Velma Hargrove, on the other hand, who conducted the interviews in Sedgwick County, and T. T. Kearns in Yuma County, allowed the old-timers to tell their stories in their own way and wrote them up more as narratives. For all the counties, to varying degrees, newspaper accounts, written reminiscences, biographical accounts, and local census data are interspersed among the interviews. The interviews have yet another advantage as a historical source because the thousands of pages of record include the voices of almost as many women as men.

Memory can be an unreliable source of historical evidence, because it is, by definition, in the present, always on the tip of the tongue, and it comes with the knowledge of outcomes. The past it evokes is far behind, its image dimmed by the passage of time, and sometimes romanticized into something entirely new.[12] Moreover, in this case specifically, the elderly men and women who were interviewed in 1933–34 were not a representative sample of the settlers. They persisted through the hard times of the 1890s, whereas many settlers, maybe most, gave up and left, their stories gone forever. But in combination, the CWA interviews constitute a collective memory of overlapping recollections. Together with other primary sources—land office records, federal and state census returns, the exceptional (though biased) Kansas State Board of Agriculture reports, settlers' journals (especially that of the southwestern Nebraska settler George Washington Franklin), newspapers, accounts of such contemporaries as J. E. Payne and Willard Johnson, historical atlases and photographs, and much more—they help to vivify the past and make it possible to imagine what life was like during the last days of the Rainbelt on the western High Plains in the late nineteenth century.

The Last Days
of the Rainbelt

I

The Approach from the East, 1854–1885

The word *frontier* has fallen into disuse, and for good reason. As used by Turner and other early western historians (and as widely accepted by the general public), frontier connoted a triumphant and ordained American advance into an unimproved wilderness, whereas, to give an example, the Great Plains had been occupied and altered by Indians for at least twelve thousand years. Moreover, those millennia had seen countless Indian frontiers of settlement, as when the Lakotas (or Sioux) expanded westward into the northern Great Plains after 1770, eventually displacing the resident Indians, the Crows, Cheyennes, and Pawnees. Frontier also stood for progress in American minds, a necessary social evolution of (to use Turner's words) "civilization over savagery." To some, it even accomplished the completion of the Creation by making "wilderness" productive and capable of supporting much larger populations than it had in the past. To the United States, this all justified expansion into an already settled land.[1]

But if you shed what historians have called the "wrongheaded baggage" of Turner's provocative thesis — its nationalism, racism, and unsubstantiated theories (all a product of the age) — the idea of the frontier as a place and time, a zone of distinctive geography at the outer edge of American expansion, remains evocative and worthwhile.[2]

Frontier Zones

Here, Great Plains frontier zones are identified as those areas of American (and European) settlement that had recently reached a population density of two persons per square mile. There's nothing original about this: the measurement was also used by the U.S. Bureau of the Census on its colorful maps, and by Turner himself, to locate areas undergoing frontier development. Two persons per square mile (or section) indicated the beginnings of a farming population, of towns that provided them with goods and services, and railroads that connected them to markets. It meant too that counties were officially organized and administered from a county seat (though their boundaries might be subject to adjustment), and that perhaps as much as 5 percent of the land was "improved" by cultivation. Beyond, generally to the west, cattlemen occupied the open range, and rapidly diminishing numbers of Indians struggled to hold on to their invaded homelands and beleaguered lives.[3]

In these frontier zones, landscapes were initially distinctive because they were not yet squared-off by roads, or fenced to any degree, but open country crisscrossed by paths connecting farms to each other and to towns. There was little land under cultivation and, especially on the western Plains, a shortage of wood and water. Again, especially on the western Plains, there was tension between farmers and cattlemen, the latter objecting to the fencing of the range that they had previously used for free. The first, rudimentary generation of homes in the frontier zones were made of local materials, logs and sod, or just dug out of a hillside. The majority of settlers were poor, and many had no farming experience. Most of them were male, though not in great excess, and few were elderly. There was heavy county debt, because counties borrowed lavishly to put in schools, roads, and courthouses, yet they had little revenue — land (as opposed to personal property) was not taxable until the provisions of the land laws had been met and titles, or patents, issued to owners. There were far too many towns, each competing for the farmers' trade, or for a railroad, a land office, or county seat status. Most of the towns were destined to fail. Speculation on rural lands and in the towns was rampant.

Most settlers were only on hand to make money on rising land values, which some did, and moved on. Others failed and moved on to try again somewhere else. These frontier zones were in constant motion, places of chronic impermanence.

The frontier zones could not be occupied by Americans until the land was obtained from its owners, the Indians. Indian dispossession — long ago, way ahead of his time, geographer Carl O. Sauer called this the "dark obverse" of the glorified frontier — was, in effect, the first stage of the American settlement process. That history, which is filled with trage- dy, but also with the eventual triumph of survival, is not the focus of this account. Despite the conflicts, Indian resistance hardly slowed the Amer- ican advance into the central Great Plains. The prevailing American phi- losophy was bluntly expressed by the Commissioner of Indian Affairs, Francis Walker, in his annual report in 1872: "The westward course of population is neither to be denied or delayed for the sake of all the Indi- ans that ever called this country home. They must yield or perish."[4] They did both, and by the time settlers reached the Rainbelt in the late 1880s, Indians were as scarce as the bison they had depended upon.

The Louisiana Purchase of 1803 had established American sovereign- ty over the Great Plains, and the Kansas-Nebraska Act of 1854 brought much of the vast area into the American territorial system. Plains Indi- ans were legally recognized as the original occupants of the land, holding it by "Indian title" until negotiated away through treaties.[5] This was ac- complished quickly on the central Great Plains.

By 1860 the farming Indians of southern Nebraska (Pawnees and Otoe-Missourias) and eastern Kansas (Kansa and Osages) had sold the bulk of their ancestral lands and were restricted to small reservations (fig. 1). They were forced by their dire circumstances to sell. The previous half century of dislocation, famine, and recurring epidemic disease, all brought about by contact with Americans, had reduced their populations by more than one-half, leaving their lands as their only asset. The loss of entire generations of young people, who were vulnerable to smallpox be- cause they had not gained immunity from surviving earlier epidemics,

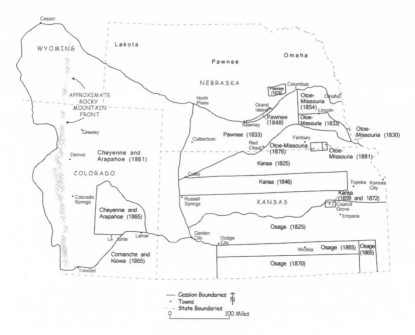

1. Indian land cessions.

was an inestimable tragedy. The loss of old people, because of deterio-
rating living conditions, left holes in the cultural memory, ceremonies no
longer performed, knowledge no longer held. It was not a physical genocide — the United States inoculated Indian children, beginning in the
1830s — but it was a horror, and it lasted a long time.[6]

When the eastern Nebraska and eastern Kansas reservations became
encircled and coveted by settlers in the 1860s and 1870s, the village Indians were excised from their homes, and their place-based histories, and
relocated south to Indian Territory (later Oklahoma). The Osages went
first (1870), followed by the Kansa (1871), the once-mighty Pawnees (1873–
75), and finally the Otoe-Missourias (1876 and 1881). Their former reservations were immediately taken by settlers, and even more so by speculators. The deep-rooted Indian presence in eastern Kansas and Nebraska
never proved more than a temporary hindrance to the advancing waves
of American settlement.[7]

To the west, the Cheyennes and Arapahoes, who dominated the High

Plains between the Platte and Arkansas Rivers, and, to the southwest and northwest, respectively, the powerful Comanches and Lakotas, mounted a more serious resistance to their impending dispossession. As decentralized bison hunters, living most of the year in small bands, they had been afflicted less by contagious disease than the village Indians in their crowded earth lodge settlements. Their horses (the Comanches had five to ten per capita by 1850) gave them mobility, the bison herds — still substantial in the 1860s — gave them sustenance, and their relative isolation from the advancing body of American settlement allowed them a twilight of independence.[8]

But when the railroads breached that isolation, starting in the late 1860s, and the bison herds were reduced to scattered bones whitening the prairie, the Indians' future was foreclosed. The U.S. military, operating out of posts like Fort Dodge (1865), Fort Wallace (1865), and Fort Kearney (1863), which guarded first the overland trails, then the railroads, began to wage total war, attacking Indians in their winter camps when they were immobilized by women, children, and weakened horses. There were massacres, such as at Sand Creek, in southeastern Colorado on November 29, 1864, when Colonel John M. Chivington and his Colorado Third Volunteer Regiment attacked Black Kettle's band of Southern Cheyennes and Arapahoes, leaving more than two hundred Indians, mostly women and children, dead. The clearing of the western Plains through warfare and forced removals to make room for another group of people fits exactly the definition of what is now known as ethnic cleansing.[9]

The area that would by the late 1880s be known as the Rainbelt was officially ceded from the Comanches, Cheyennes, and Arapahoes through a series of treaties in 1861 and 1865 (fig. 1). The Indians were settled on poorly defined, parched reservations in western Indian Territory. This was the prelude to the most serious Indian reprisal against Americans on the central Plains, which took place in Kansas in the fall of 1878, and briefly slowed the westward surge of settlers.

The Northern Cheyennes had been duped and coerced into leaving their homeland in Montana and settling with their estranged relatives, the Southern Cheyennes and Arapahoes, on their reservation in Indian Territory. There were no bison left to hunt there, and the Indians lived on inadequate government rations in a state of near starvation. They were homesick, and malaria and other diseases ran rampant. By August 1878, two thousand of the reservation's five thousand people were ill, and there was only one doctor, and no quinine, on hand. In response, Dull Knife and three hundred followers headed north through western Kansas on their way back home to Montana. As described later (1880) in a Senate report, "their flight was . . . converted into a running fight," leaving more than forty American men, women, and children dead, and more women raped. While condemning these "atrocities," the Senate Report pointed to a failed American Indian policy as the ultimate cause of the conflict.[10]

The frontier was temporarily turned back, as settlers retraced their footsteps down the river valleys. But they quickly returned in even greater numbers. The clearing of the Indians through warfare, treaties, and disease was absolute. According to the 1885 state census, there wasn't a single Indian remaining in western Kansas (nor a single Chinese, because the two peoples, equally disdained, were counted together as one group in the census).[11] The central Great Plains between the Platte and Arkansas Rivers — the spearhead of the American frontier — was completely open for resettlement.

The vacated land was quickly filled with American and European settlers. This rush into the central Plains contradicts Walter Prescott Webb's thesis, presented in his classic study, *The Great Plains*, in 1931. Webb argued that settlers, used to wooded and well-watered environments, lacked the knowledge and means to handle the semiarid, largely treeless, High Plains to the west of the 98th meridian. In Webb's interpretation, the frontier stalled for "the greater part of half a century" after the Civil War at this "institutional fault." Once adjustments were made — Webb stressed such innovations as barbed wire, windmills, and new laws for land and water — settlers were able to move across the 98th meridian and out onto the gently tilted tableland of the High Plains. Webb's thesis, like Turner's, had staying power: in 1954, sociologist Carl Kraenzel, in his

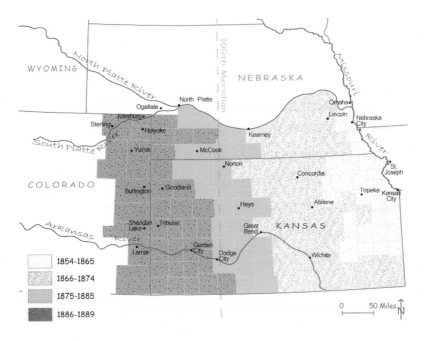

WYOMING

NORTH PLATTE RIVER

100th Meridian

NEBRASKA

MISSOURI RIVER

North Platte

Ogallala •

Julesburg •

Sterling •

Holyoke •

South Platte R.

• Yuma

• McCook

Kearney

Omaha •

Lincoln •

Nebraska City

COLORADO

Norton

Concordia

St. Joseph

Burlington •

• Goodland

Topeka   Kansas City

• Hays

Abilene

Arkansas River

Sheridan Lake •   • Tribune

Great Bend •

KANSAS

• Lamar

Garden City

Dodge City

Wichita

1854-1865

1866-1874

1875-1885

1886-1889

0   50 Miles

N

2. Frontier zones.

Great Plains in Transition, made the same case for a cultural fault line and
a stationary frontier.[12]

But settlers did not halt, perplexed, at the 98th meridian on the central Great Plains. Instead, they rapidly advanced westward during years
of ample precipitation and prosperous economy, only to fall back or else
scatter elsewhere when the rains stopped falling and the nation descended into economic chaos. It was a pulsation, or more accurately, an arrhyth-
mia, marked by sudden rapid movements and periods of hiatus. In this
cycle of boom and bust it was not unusual for areas to be settled by three
or more waves of homesteaders before successful farming took root.

Using the criterion of county population densities of two persons per
square mile, four periods and zones of frontier settlement can be identified on the central Great Plains (fig. 2).[13] In the first period, from 1854 to
1865, settlement was slowed by the Civil War and its violent prelude, the
struggle between pro-slavery and anti-slavery forces in "Bleeding Kansas." Also, with few miles of railroad in place, and with no navigable riv-

ers extending west into the Plains, settlers were tied to the Missouri River, their only connection to markets and supplies.

The pace of settlement accelerated after 1865 in years of good rainfall and rapid railroad construction. Settlers followed the river valleys and the railroads out beyond Webb's iconic 98th meridian. This was down the rainfall gradient, past the twenty-inch isohyet; but no matter, because settlers were assured by scholars and boosters that precipitation would increase as they planted trees and turned over the soil. The boom came to an abrupt halt in 1873–74 with drought, locust infestations, and financial crisis.

The advance continued after 1874, as years of high rainfall washed away the memories of hard times. There was the promise again of a verdant garden to the west where settlers would produce their own climate. "It was almost miraculous," wrote agricultural historian Gilbert Fite, "how a few good rains could change the attitude and outlook of a people in an entire region."[14] Settlers accompanied the proliferating railroads out beyond the 100th meridian, until by 1885 only a band of counties in western Kansas and Nebraska and in eastern Colorado had population densities of less than two persons per square mile (fig. 2).

These counties were deluged by settlers in the final nineteenth-century boom from 1886–89. Settlers located on the uplands, confident that wheat would flourish in the ameliorating climate of the Rainbelt. They endured severe droughts in 1887 and 1890, then again from 1893–96, which also coincided with a deep regional, national, and international economic depression. The settlers kept planting, even after their crops withered in the fields, hoping to recoup their losses in one bountiful harvest. Then they, and the towns dependent on them, failed, leaving the haunted landscapes that Payne and Johnson encountered on their surveys in the late nineteenth century.

Midwest Extended, 1854–1865

The settlers who filtered into Kansas and Nebraska Territories after May 30, 1854, (and a good number who had crossed the Missouri River beforehand and squatted on Indian lands) were drawn mainly from a wide belt in the midsection of the United States, reaching from New York and Pennsylvania to Iowa and Missouri. Ohio was the main state of origin for both territories. It was essentially a latitudinal migration, an orientation that would not change even as settlers moved four hundred miles west across the Plains during the following three decades, though western parts of the belt, such as Iowa and eastern Nebraska and Kansas, would become relatively more important source areas.[15]

In 1860 foreign-born immigrants comprised 22 percent of Nebraska's total population of 28,826 and 12 percent of Kansas' total of 107,204. In both areas, the foreign-born component was drawn mainly from Germany, Ireland, and England. Again, this was a pattern repeated in the Rainbelt thirty years later, both in terms of percent of total population and in their origins (though there was a lot of local variation). The early foreign-born population tended to concentrate in the burgeoning cities of the Missouri Valley (Omaha and Kansas City, Missouri, were both stamped by their Irish and German presence), or else they migrated to the western edge of the frontier, where they often settled in ethnic blocks.[16]

The settlers came into Kansas and Nebraska by water, either by steamboat from St. Louis or St. Joseph (which had the immense advantage, after 1859, of being linked to the east by the Hannibal and St. Joseph Railroad, the first line to reach the Missouri Valley), or by ferry across the river from Iowa and Missouri. As railroads approached from the east after the Civil War, settlers increasingly bypassed the Missouri River route and traveled overland from the railheads to throng the ferries. The ferries in turn would be supplanted in the late 1860s and early 1870s by the first bridges across the Missouri River.

Some of the settlers kept going west from Omaha and Nebraska City on rutted wagon roads that paralleled the Platte on the flat terraces above the river. Others moved up the Big Blue River valley from Kansas to strike the Platte and the main overland trail at Fort Kearney. In the spring of 1856, for example, one Nebraska reporter marveled at the "line of emigrant wagons" that at any time could be seen "winding over the

hills to the west," slicing through the Pawnees' homeland, heading to Oregon or California.[17]

Those who came to stay in Kansas and Nebraska (at least for a while,
because most would soon move on) settled mainly in the aspiring and
competing towns along the Missouri. It was initially unclear which town,
or towns, would capture the trade of the Great Plains and prosper, and
which would be bypassed and condemned to stagnation. The competitors
in Kansas and adjacent Missouri were Kansas City, Missouri (with a population of 4,418 in 1860), Independence (3,164), Atchison (2,616), Leaven-
worth (7,499), and the railhead of St. Joseph (8,932). In Nebraska, Omaha (1,881) and Nebraska City (1,923) vied for control, and for a few years
Council Bluffs, Iowa, (2,011) was also a contender.[18]

The selection of Omaha/Council Bluffs and Kansas City, Kansas, as
the eastern termini of the Union Pacific Railroad in 1862, the accumulating convergence at these points of connecting rail lines to the east, the
commandeering of bridge construction across the Missouri River (completed at Kansas City in 1869 and Omaha in 1872), and the money and
politics that lay behind all the above ensured that these two "Gateway
Cities" would emerge as the main portals to the central Plains. By 1870
with burgeoning trade, manufacturing, and population growth, Kansas
City, Missouri (32,260), and Omaha (16,083) had left their erstwhile rivals
behind.[19]

The letters of Joseph Barker Jr., a young Englishman who represented his family's considerable real estate interests in Omaha in the 1860s
and 1870s, provide a glimpse of what life was like in these bustling river
towns. By 1859 the Barkers had purchased hundreds of city lots, eighty-
four of them located in what would become Omaha's central business
district, as well as a 720-acre farm on the outskirts of town. They bought
much of this land using discounted military land warrants. These were
certificates issued to veterans of various wars that could be exchanged for
160 acres of land. After 1852 the certificates were transferable, and they
could be sold at one-third to one-half of their value and used by speculators like the Barkers to amass large acreages.[20]

The Barkers also ran an import business, shipping knives and cloth from Sheffield, England, where the family was based. Always on the alert for potential profit, Joseph had his finger on the fast-beating pulse of Omaha, and his letters home are filled with ideas for enrichment in the fluid frontier economy.

From its beginnings, following the platting of the site by the Council Bluffs and Nebraska Ferry Company in 1854, Omaha lived on long-distance trade. Joseph Barker characterized the city as "a major wholesale place for the Western Territories." There was substantial business outfitting emigrants who were heading west along the Platte corridor, including miners striking out for Colorado, gold having been discovered at Pikes Peak in 1858. Supplying the Montana mines via the Missouri became a lucrative enterprise after 1862, although that trade was captured by Sioux City, Iowa, in 1868, when the Sioux City and Pacific Railroad forged a more direct link to Chicago, increasingly the main control point for western development. (Barker understood this and took out a subscription to the *Chicago Tribune*.) Outfitting the military for its mounting campaigns against the Lakotas also enriched Omaha, as did supplying reservation Indians with treaty goods such as food and clothing. Serving as the home base for the construction of the Union Pacific was a boost to Omaha's economy in many ways: by 1868 the Union Pacific employed five thousand workers at its shops.[21]

Omaha's wharf—the "very heart" of the city, according to Barker—bustled with activity. Piles of telegraph wire and iron rails and heaps of coal and grain lined the dock, where at any one time four or five steamboats were loading or unloading goods and passengers. Opportunities abounded: Barker claimed that "everyone he knew" had prospered from freighting, government contracts, and "war speculation."[22]

As was typical of the entire Great Plains frontier, there was always a large transient population of young men looking for work. The mobility of the population was frenetic: "People do not stay," Barker wrote, "but they do come, keep the Hotells all crowded, spend money, and travel on." In Sioux City, eighty miles to the north, only 36 percent of the men who were there in 1860 remained in 1870. Turnover amongst laborers and poor people was especially high, whereas teachers, doctors, and others with an investment in the town tended to stay.[23]

Omaha's landscape expressed its frontier condition. The streets were mired in mud in the spring. Most buildings were made of wood, and fires frequently consumed parts of the town. By the mid-1860s some brick buildings were under construction, but the expense of laying the foundations delayed the transition. The cost of living was high, whether for food, fuel, servants, or rent. There was a serious shortage of housing throughout the 1860s, brought about by speculators like Joseph Barker who were holding onto their underdeveloped properties until their values had climbed. Capitalizing on rising land values was a key component of the frontier process across the entire central Plains. It certainly worked for the Barkers, who became one of the richest families in Omaha.

Beyond the Missouri River valley, with its competing towns, settlers extended westward along the Platte and Kansas River corridors. They located at the junction of the wooded river valleys and the open prairies, with timber, shelter, and water below, and pasture above. They avoided wetlands, with their over-enriched soils and association with malaria. They grew corn, as their fathers had done in Iowa or Ohio, and they marketed livestock "on the hoof," driven to the river towns.[24]

There were also thin extensions of rural settlement along all the small tributaries of the Missouri, but only in their lower reaches, because proximity to the river was essential for supplies and markets. This was explained by a certain Charles Robinson in a letter written to a Lawrence, Kansas, paper in 1859. Robinson pointed out that the corn he grew near Lawrence was worth nothing forty miles away at the Missouri River because the transportation costs consumed all the potential profit.[25] Shortage of timber, absence of bridges across small, deeply incised creeks, as well as opportunities to work in the river towns also kept settlers tied to the Missouri River valley.

This was not an unfamiliar environment to settlers who had originated in the Midwest. Rainfall, at about thirty inches a year, was lower than to the east, and droughts were more frequent, as settlers found out in the dry years of 1857 and 1859–60. But the drought hazard was far less than on the western Plains, and in most years crops flourished in the ample rainfall of the growing season and in soils that were rich in organic matter.

This was verdant tallgrass prairie country, with big bluestem on the lower slopes as high as a horse's back, little bluestem farther up, and everywhere, from spring to fall, a profusion of flowering plants. Settlers would have recognized the valley trees too—cottonwood, bur oak, hickory, willow, walnut, box elder, and many more—though the stands thinned to the west, leaving eventually only straggling cottonwoods and willows lining the rivers out onto the High Plains.[26]

The prairie persisted for some time. It was arduous work to turn over the prairie sod, which was densely matted with rhizomes and roots, and land was only slowly put under crops. The woodlands, however, were quickly taken out. As soon as a vicinity had settlers, it also had a water-driven sawmill, and demand for wood for buildings, fences, furniture, and fuel was constant.[27] Obtaining wood remained a problem until the railroads and lumber corporations brought the Great Lakes forests within reach, and even then there was the problem of cost. But, there again, this had been a problem in the Midwest too.

Settlers had five options for staking a claim to a piece of land, options that were still available in the Rainbelt in 1890. The first option was cash, buying already-improved land at market price, which averaged about five dollars an acre around Omaha in 1860. Not many settlers had the wherewithal for this.

Before January 1, 1863, when the Homestead Act went into effect, most settlers filed their claims under the Preemption Act of 1841. This act specified that heads of families (by definition male, unless the man was infirm or deceased) and single men and women over the age of twenty-one who were citizens, or on their way to becoming citizens, were entitled to 160 acres of the public domain at the cost of $1.25 an acre. Settlers were required to live on the land and improve it for twelve months, before swearing that they had followed the letter of the law, paying the two hundred dollars, and receiving a patent. Settlers could expedite the process by "commuting" the claim after six months, paying the two hundred dollars, and obtaining the title. The attraction of this was that once they owned the land, they could use it as collateral and take out loans to invest in machinery and other possessions. Many settlers filed preemption claims by prior arrangement with speculators, with the idea that they would sell them back as soon as they were commuted, or if they were "relinquished" at any time before final proof. In this manner, speculators amassed large acreages to sell at a profit at a later date. The Preemption Act was so riddled by speculation opportunities that it was repealed in 1891.[28]

The other common method of obtaining land before 1863 was through military bounty land warrants, those discounted and transferable certificates that Joseph Barker used to build his real estate empire in Omaha. Like preemptions — even more so, in fact — military bounty land warrants facilitated speculation rather than genuine settlement. They had no occupancy provision and they quickly passed into the hands of wealthy people like Barker, making them even richer.

The Homestead Act introduced the era of virtually free (there was a small filing fee) land for settlers. It gave each qualified adult (the stipulations were similar to those of the Preemption Act) 160 acres, with the condition that the land should be lived on and improved for five years. At that point, settlers filed for "final proof" at the local Land Office, witnesses attested that the land had indeed been occupied and improved, the application was announced in a neighborhood newspaper for anyone to contest, and, after all this, if the application was approved, settlers received their quarter-sections at no cost. As with the Preemption Act, there was ample opportunity for petty speculation. Residency requirements were not taken seriously, and homesteads could also be commuted for two hundred dollars after six months, or relinquished by prior arrangement with a speculator waiting in the wings. Still, the Homestead Act was less subject to abuse than preemptions and military bounty land warrants, and many were gratefully taken by aspiring farmers.[29]

The year 1863 also saw the passage, on June 2, of the Morrill Act, which gave every state thirty thousand acres for each senator and representative they sent to Congress. The sale of these lands would finance the establishment of land grant colleges. States could either receive the actual land, or "agricultural college scrip," which like military warrants were certificates that could be sold on the open market. Again, speculators collected the scrip, paying about fifty cents an acre, and used it to accumulate real estate. In 1868, for example, Joseph Barker acquired a thousand acres along the lower Elkhorn River, just to the west of Omaha, by using purchased agricultural college scrip. As he coyly wrote to his brother in Sheffield, "It cannot be a bad speculation."[30]

Just as Barker's letters provide insights into urban life on this early Plains frontier, so the reminiscences of Even Jefferson Jenkins shed light on living conditions in the rural areas.[31] Jenkins was a lawyer who, in the absence of such work, was reduced to cutting wood for steamboats in Doniphan County, in extreme northeastern Kansas, in the 1860s. Jenkins's account, written a decade later during slack times in his work as a land office agent, evokes "rare scenes of rural loveliness," a lush environment cloaked with valley woodlands and teeming with small game—wild turkeys, pheasants, quail, ducks, geese, and grouse—though the sawmills quickly devoured the trees, and the game was rapidly depleted by hunting. Jenkins also made note of the early evidence of human failure: at least fifteen townsites stood deserted along the Missouri River in Doniphan County, speculations gone wrong, or, in Jenkins's words, "relics of lost opportunities for greatness." The surviving "embryo cities" competed for the trade of the incoming settlers.

These settlers, as Jenkins described them, had been landless in their former states of Illinois, Missouri, Ohio, Wisconsin, and Michigan, and they were attracted by the free or cheap land in Kansas. They pushed west in covered wagons across the northern tier of Kansas counties from Doniphan to Marshall. Each wagon brimmed with furniture, bedding, and children. Typically, a dilapidated chicken coop was attached to the back of the wagon, with the heads of poultry comically protruding. Behind the wagons trailed cows and calves, with a "house dog" bringing up the rear. When a family found a suitable place, they laid a foundation of four logs as a base for a cabin (and proof that the land was taken), then headed to the land office to file a claim. The families slept in their wagons and prepared their meals over an open fire until a rudimentary first home, perhaps no more than a dugout, could be built.

Jenkins characterized the settlers as poor, idealistic, and optimistic, and the same could be said about the Rainbelt settlers a generation later. "Their vision of a new country," he wrote, "was magnified by imaginary guideposts to the future." They were motivated by the prospect of a home and land "unencumbered with debt and mortgage," and they believed that this could be achieved with little labor. They soon found, however, that it took three yoke of oxen pulling a heavy iron plow to break the matted sod, and once the game was gone, meat became a luxury. Jenkins described how a single piece of pork would be rotated around a community to give each family a little flavor to their beans. Though perhaps romanticized, Jenkins maintained that everyone was equal and "mutually dependent" in this frontier setting. The "latch-strings of the cabin door hung on the outside," he wrote, an open invitation to visit. Frederick Jackson Turner would have appreciated this confirmation of the leveling, democratizing effect of the frontier.

Jenkins had his own "imaginary guideposts to the future." Like many of his contemporaries, he assumed that climate would improve as a result of settlement: "The hot winds and droughts that were observed before settlement are things of the past," he claimed, adding, "settlement and cultivation, with tree planting, have removed the cause." Turning over the soil, he explained, allowed rainfall to penetrate deeply, escape evaporation, and gradually replenish streams and springs. More dubiously, Jenkins assumed that the cultivation of trees "contributes materially to the increase in rainfall." Theories linking tree-planting to increased rainfall (and the opposite, linking deforestation to aridity) had held currency since ancient Greece.[32] But on the western Great Plains in the late nineteenth century, almost as a matter of necessity, they hardened into convictions and persisted until eventually disproven in the 1890s by drought and widespread failure.

The First Boom, 1866–1874

With the railroads at hand, and beginning to extend west, and with the Civil War ended, settlers flowed into Nebraska and Kansas after 1865. In June of 1866, from his vantage point in Omaha, James Barker watched settlers "going out all along the Rail Road [Union Pacific] onto the tributaries of the Platt, Elk Horn, and other streams," selecting their homesteads and preemptions wherever there was woodland. Barker was particularly impressed by the "large numbers of Germans from Wisconsin with their sheep and goats" heading to the next free and cheap land. He explained that the market had now come to the settlers: "They now can sell all they raise out west, in the new towns along the tracks and to emigrants passing through."[33]

The Union Pacific followed the Platte River to its fork, then extended due west into Wyoming in 1867, heading toward Utah and the golden spike that connected the first transcontinental railroad two years later. On its way it spawned a succession of "Hell on Wheels" towns at the railhead. These railhead towns briefly flared, until the tracks moved on to another site. North Platte was such a town.

North Platte was laid out in 1866, just in time for the arrival of the Union Pacific construction crews. Within a month, three hundred ramshackle sod, log, and plank buildings, interspersed with many tents, had risen from the prairie, and five thousand people were on hand. Some were Omaha merchants who sold their goods and services to a captive market at successive railhead towns in a rolling economic bonanza. Most were railroad workers (graders, masons, surveyors, and track crew) and the gamblers, prostitutes, and other opportunists who fed off them. There were no churches, no schools, no fire department, and no city government. It was a situation repeated along all the main lines in Kansas and Nebraska in the late 1860s and 1870s.[34]

But by June 1867, the tracks had been laid to Julesburg, Colorado, and

nearly all the people, most of the buildings, and the local newspaper, aptly named *Pioneer on Wheels*, had moved on west. Under the more placid
control of the "better element," North Platte began to build a stable economic base and a solid social foundation of schools, churches, and frater-
nal organizations.

To the south, the Kansas branch of the Union Pacific (after 1869, called
the Kansas Pacific) traced the Kansas River to Ellsworth, then angled
southwest to reach the Colorado line in 1869, and Denver the following year. The Atchison, Topeka, and Santa Fe got a later start (1868), but
quickly extended beyond the settled area, following the Arkansas River
into Colorado in 1872, then on to California (fig. 3).

The rail network thickened in the east, with the Burlington and Missouri connecting Plattsmouth to Kearney in 1872, the same year that the
St. Joseph and Denver Railroad linked St. Joseph to Grand Island, both
bringing south-central Nebraska within reach of homesteaders. The railroads sped up the pace of settlement and allowed settlers to come more
easily from afar. They bridged the distances across the Plains, opening up
the region to commercial farming, and connecting it more tightly to the
outside world, via the Missouri Valley gateway cities.

The railroads also channeled investment directly to the frontier from
the Missouri Valley towns. Omaha's reach westward along the Union Pacific, for example, was extensive. In 1868, Barker and other Omaha business leaders hosted "leading men" from St. Louis, Chicago, and New
York on a "Special Train" to the Union Pacific railhead west of Cheyenne,
Wyoming, the objective being to show off the country and its resources.
Barker characterized Cheyenne as a "little Town," located in a "poor dry
barren place," and completely "run" by Omaha."[35]

All the railroads received construction subsidies from the federal government in the form of land grants, which gave settlers and speculators
another option to acquire land. The details, though not the substance,
of land disposal within the grants varied from one railroad to another.
The Atchison, Topeka, and Santa Fe, for example, was given a belt of ten
miles on either side of the tracks, about 3 million acres in all. The Union

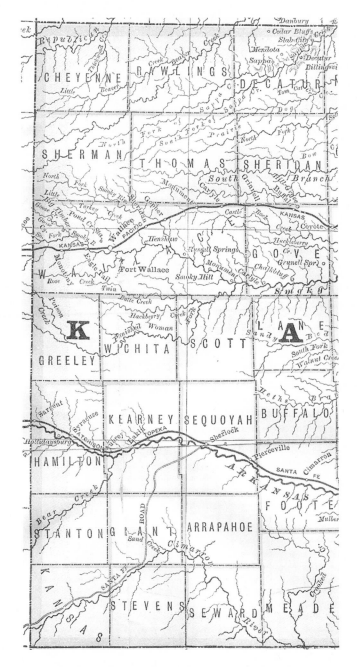

3. Postal map of Kansas, 1876 (detail). Source: *Fifth Annual Report of the Kansas State Board of Agriculture, 1876* (frontispiece).

Pacific's land grant was twenty miles on either side of tracks, amounting to 7 million acres. The Union Pacific and Kansas Pacific land grants extended all the way across Kansas and Nebraska and into Colorado and Wyoming respectively. The Atchison, Topeka, and Santa Fe land grant stopped at the Colorado line.[36]

Within each land grant, the railroads were given the odd-numbered (square mile) sections. The railroads would supposedly pay back their government loans by selling these sections at prices that averaged about five dollars an acre (though, according to historian Paul Wallace Gates, the loans were never repaid in full). The railroads would also benefit, of course, from the increased trade that would ensue as the land was settled. Even-numbered sections in the land grants were subject to entry under the Preemption and Homestead Acts, but only in eighty-acre parcels, and at the cost of $2.50 an acre if preempted (or commuted). Settlers received less land and paid more in order to have access to transportation and connection to markets.[37]

In order to fill their land grants and their boxcars, the railroads became active recruiting agencies, dispatching representatives throughout the Midwest, the eastern United States, and western Europe. The Atchison, Topeka, and Santa Fe was particularly energetic, establishing a land office in 1872 and hiring five hundred agents. Potential settlers could purchase discounted tickets to check out the railroad lands, and if they agreed to buy, the ticket price was deducted from the cost. It was clearly in the interest of the railroads, as well as the states, to broadcast a bucolic image of western Nebraska and Kansas and eastern Colorado, and to stress that agricultural settlement led to climatic amelioration.[38]

The belief that (as Jenkins had argued) rainfall increased with settlement was widely held by the early 1870s. The commissioner of the General Land Office, in his 1868 report, urged the planting of trees on the Great Plains as a means of increasing rainfall. This had already happened in eastern Kansas, the commissioner explained, and there was no reason to believe that it would not also occur on the western Plains. In the absence of reliable climate records (the first widespread systematic measurements of rainfall and temperature were not made until the late 1880s), this theory seemed reasonable.[39] It was also a seductive proposition, a convenient recruiting device for the railroads, a common self-congratulatory theme in each state's agricultural journals, a career-building cause for various experts, and a handy delusion for settlers, who desperately wanted to believe that it was true.

Samuel Aughey, Lutheran minister and professor of biology at the University of Nebraska, was particularly tireless in spreading the good news. In 1873, in an address to the Nebraska State Legislature, Aughey proclaimed: "As civilization extends westward the fall of rain increases from year to year." Aughey explained that the plow was the trigger of change, the cultivated earth serving as a sponge that absorbed the moisture, then released it slowly. Planting trees was also instrumental in the annual increase in Nebraska's rainfall over the previous twenty years, according to Aughey. Aughey's influence was pervasive: he influenced the state's leading agricultural journal, *Nebraska Farmer*, to the extent that hardly an issue from 1878 to 1893 failed to refer to the imagined increasing rainfall.[40]

In Kansas, Richard Smith Elliott, industrial agent for the Kansas Pacific, was every bit as enthusiastic as Aughey. In the 1870s Elliott, who had previously been a farmer, inventor, newspaper editor, and Indian agent, energetically promoted the theory of increasing rainfall to justify railroad expansion. As historian David Emmons put it, in Elliott's thinking "the railroads attracted the people, the people brought the rain, the rain attracted more people." In his *Industrial Resources of Western Kansas and Eastern Colorado* (1871), Elliott expressed his confidence that a "permanent and beneficial change of climate" was moving west with settlement as the land was plowed and shaded by newly planted trees. This would reduce wind speed and evaporation, while at the same time accelerating the return of moisture to the atmosphere. Elliott maintained that bluegrasses of the tallgrass prairie were colonizing westward into the shortgrass prairie. This "substitution of grasses," he went on, was a result of increased rainfall brought about by the planting of trees. The tall grasses in turn would add to the amelioration by diffusing the sun's heat and reducing summer temperatures. Tree-planting was Elliott's main argument, but he was ecumenical in embracing all possible causes: perhaps the increased rainfall was caused by the new iron rails and the "friction of metallic surfaces," sending waves up into the atmosphere as the trains went through.[41]

In his proselytizing, Elliott did his best to dispel the image of the Great American Desert, which clung to Kansas, especially, like a film of dust. Scholars have long argued that this unfavorable image of the Great Plains (a product of Zebulon Pike's expedition in 1806 and Stephen Long's in 1820) was not widely believed in the West, but held mainly by educated classes in the East, who read the newspapers and geography textbooks that had adopted it.[42] But the degree to which the desert image was contested in the promotional literature suggests that it was a real handicap to overcome. Elliott said as much, that the "idea of a desert character of the whole western region held its place in the public mind with a singular tenacity." But by 1873, through the settlers' own deeds, the Great American Desert had been shown to be, in Elliott's words, a "geographical delusion."[43]

Reassured by the prospect of increasing rainfall, settlers moved west along the Platte valley in Nebraska, which had been the main avenue of American expansion since the days of the Rocky Mountain fur trade in the 1820s and 1830s. By the early 1870s, settlers were also advancing up the Republican River valley, even without the presence of a railroad and despite periodic clashes with Cheyennes and Lakotas. The divide between the Platte and Republican remained in the hands of the cattlemen, and therefore sparsely populated. Frontier County, for example, had only two homesteaders in 1872, and no towns.

To the south in Kansas, the frontier line slanted from northwest to southeast, from the 100th meridian at the Nebraska line, to east of the 98th meridian at the boundary with Indian Territory (fig. 2). This orientation reflected the grain of the land, with the Solomon and Republican Rivers being particularly attractive routes of expansion. Settlement was slowed in southern Kansas by the large Osage Reservation, which wasn't opened until after 1870, though squatters were there beforehand.

The homesteaders planted corn as the sod crop as they would do two decades later in the Rainbelt. They cut the prairie with an axe, then folded the turf back over. They also grew spring wheat and potatoes; kept oxen, horses, and mules to pull their plows and binders; raised a few hogs and cattle; and planted orchards. As soon as they owned their land, they borrowed against it and bought the latest machinery. Labor was in short supply on the frontier; hence the need for labor-saving machines. As an unnamed writer in the *Nation* explained in 1868, the farmer borrowed because it was "immensely profitable" for him to do so; it was the way to expand the acreage under crops, the way to grow. But when the crops failed, or market prices plunged, the farmer was left only with his debt, and interest rates of 10 or 12 percent.[44]

Settlers in the central Nebraska and Kansas frontier zone in the early 1870s had one asset that the next generation to the west would not possess, namely the bison. Men went out west in hunting parties from November to April, when the frozen meat could be transported home. They could procure enough meat in a day to last a winter, and also make money selling bison bones (to be used as fertilizer) and hides (which were made into machine belts for industrial production). Much attention has been paid to the causes of the destruction of the great bison herds, from the effects of the long-established robe trade, to competition for forage with horses and cattle, to the spread of bovine diseases, to the so-called hunters on railroad excursions who shot the bison as they stood motionless on the prairie. But the tens of thousands of settlers on the central Plains hunting for their daily food must have had a decisive impact as well.[45]

The destruction was rapid. In Norton County in northwestern Kansas, for example, there were still large herds of bison along the Solomon in 1873. They "remained plentiful" until 1875. By 1876, according to the Kansas State Board of Agriculture, they had "entirely disappeared."[46]

Beyond the valleys, on the extensive uplands, cattlemen used the open range at will. By the early 1870s Texas cattle filled the range. Yearlings and two-year-old steers were driven north each year after 1865 to railhead towns like Abilene and Ellsworth on the Kansas Pacific; Dodge City on the Atchison, Topeka, and Santa Fe; and Ogallala on the Union Pacific. The cattle were either shipped directly to stockyards in Chicago, St. Louis, and Kansas City, or else fattened on the range before being dispatched east as three- or four-year-olds.[47]

Wherever cattlemen and homesteaders came into contact, there was trouble. Counties where homesteaders were in the majority voted for herd laws, obliging cattlemen to keep their stock out of the crops. "It was the only practical thing to do," reported a correspondent from Phillips County, Kansas, because homesteaders lacked the timber to fence their fields. This land-use conflict was repeated to the west in the next few decades, but there was no doubt who would prevail. All the weight of the government's land laws favored the many homesteaders over the few cattlemen, who reluctantly withdrew to the west to avoid paying the taxes of organized farm country and to dispense with the need to confine their cattle.[48]

Just as had been the case in eastern Nebraska and Kansas in the previous decade, the new frontier zone was a ferment of speculation and mobility. Innumerable towns were founded as speculative ventures ahead of the rural settlement that would be needed to sustain them. They vied for choice locations, for railroad connections, for a land office, or county seat status. Far too many towns were established; most eventually failed, with the "inland towns" — those that never secured a railroad — going under first.

The passage of the Timber Culture Act in 1873 gave settlers the opportunity for an extra free quarter-section and opened up new prospects for speculation. The purposes of the act were to get much-needed construction timber on the Plains, and also, following the prevailing theories, to enhance the climate. The act required settlers to plant and nurture forty acres of trees (later, in a concession to reality, reduced to ten) over a period of ten (later reduced to eight) years, before being eligible for title to 160 acres of free land. The settler could then wait another three years before applying for a patent. There was no residency requirement and no problem if the settler already held a preemption claim, a homestead claim, or both.

The act was an open invitation for speculators. Barely a quarter of the timber culture claims in Kansas and Nebraska were carried through to final patent. Settlers could use the 160 acres without paying taxes or rent, or being liable for debt on the land, for up to thirteen years, then relinquish it. It was not uncommon for a timber claim to be taken up and relinquished five or six times before the land was legally owned. This meant that extensive areas in newly settled counties lay unoccupied and uncultivated for many years. Like the Preemption Act, the Timber Culture Act was repealed in 1891 because of its manifest abuses, but for two decades timber claims were the preferred way of holding land without cost on the edge of the frontier.[49]

Mobility, both geographical and occupational, remained a way of life on the outskirts of American settlement. The Kansas historian James Malin, who studied the Great Plains frontier in greater detail, and with deeper insights, than anyone, found that only 43 percent of the farmers in the central Kansas counties of Dickinson and Saline in 1865 were still there in 1870. Whether because of speculative intent, failure, or, indeed, success (they proved up, sold out, and moved on), few homesteaders stayed put. Malin's studies led him to believe that settlers who intended to invest a lifetime in a place were "virtually non-existent."[50] This was only a small exaggeration.

Even Jefferson Jenkins, the woodcutting lawyer from Doniphan County, observed this frontier process from the inside. In 1870 he became the receiver at a new land office at Concordia, Kansas, a three-cabin town on the Republican River in Cloud County. This was the headquarters for the Republican Land District, which had jurisdiction all the way to the Colorado line.

Jenkins found himself in the middle of a land rush. Thousands of settlers, mainly from the Midwest and predominantly men, were moving up the Solomon and Republican River valleys, ahead of the railroads, but no doubt in anticipation of them. It was difficult country to cross. Jenkins himself, on his way to his new post, had to lead his horses one by one across a plank over an incised creek, then disassemble his wagon and carry the pieces to the other side for reconstruction.

The land office opened for business on January 16, 1871. Settlers thronged outside; one particularly determined man had sat with his hand on the doorknob all night long. Lawyers and land agents worked the crowd, selling previous relinquishments or setting up schemes for new ones. Jenkins recorded 180 homesteads and 180 preemptions on his first day on the job.

When the initial rush subsided, Jenkins had time to ruminate about the myth of the Great American Desert. He recalled that in his school days, the Great Plains had been "laid down on the map as a desert waste." But now, he proposed, with the land filling up with settlers who were making their own climate, the Great American Desert had been exposed as a fraud. "It was a mystery to all," Jenkins wrote, "how anyone could have believed in it."[51]

Then, in 1874, the Great American Desert staged a comeback, bringing to an end the first Great Plains boom. The climate reversals began with the hard winter of 1871–72, which was the worst on record for Kansas and Nebraska. The winter of 1873–74 was not much better. Texas cattle, left to fend for themselves on the snow-covered range, died in immense numbers, adding a new layer of bleaching bones to the prairie. This coincided with a deep national (and international) depression brought on in the United States by speculative railroad building, various economic reversals, and the collapse of Jay Cooke and Company, a major banking establishment. Land values and crop prices plummeted. Settlers on the frontier, with nothing to fall back on, were hit particularly hard.[52]

The drought struck in July of 1874, following a warm, wet spring that had promised much for the crops. There was no rain for the rest of the very hot summer. Then, beginning in the middle of July, grasshoppers came down (to use the words of the Kansas State Board of Agriculture) "in numbers so immense as to hide the sun."[53]

The grasshoppers, or, more accurately, Rocky Mountain locusts, came in from the northwest, riding the hot winds. The destruction was most severe in the far-western counties that had received their first settlers after 1870. Just as the settlers' corn was coming into ear, the hosts of grasshoppers descended and within minutes reduced the green fields to "stumpy stalks." In Norton County, Kansas, for example, the crops were "entirely destroyed," and three-quarters of the 750 settlers were declared "destitute." To the south in Osborne County, corn, garden vegetables, fruit, hedges, and trees were eaten, and one-quarter of the settlers gave up and headed back to the "older states." The abjectly poor stayed because they did not have the means to leave. Corn was also a "total failure" in Phillips County where, in the absence of feed, settlers were shooting their hogs. Reports from other western counties in Kansas and Nebraska repeated the same story of destruction, destitution, and out-migration. The degree of destruction decreased to the east, in part because the harvests there were substantially completed by the time the grasshoppers arrived in late August.

Altogether, in twenty-four counties in western Kansas, 12,029 settlers were classified by the state as destitute (from a total of 66,104). The State of Kansas raised seventy-three thousand dollars in bonds to provide wheat to see the settlers through the following winter and seed to get them started again in spring. But each county was left alone to approve additional bonds to aid the destitute, and almost all of them refused to do so because they were unwilling to tax themselves. "Few are able to pay their present taxes," wrote the editor of the *Jewell County Diamond*. He added, "For the county to provide for the needy will put such a burden on it that many of our best citizens will leave rather than bear it." The needy fell back on charity, swallowing their pride as they accepted U.S. Army surplus uniforms and gathered at railroad stations to receive the corn, flour, potatoes, coal, and clothing that were shipped in from the East.

The Rocky Mountain locusts returned in 1875 and 1876 (and multiplied in place from the overwintering eggs and nymphs) but in decreasing numbers. They would come back in subsequent dry years like Biblical plagues, until their extinction in about 1902.[54] The rains returned too,

and by 1875 agricultural expansion and frontier population growth had
resumed. Quickly, the disasters of 1874 were cast as an aberration, rather
than a character trait. In a report to the State Board of Agriculture, J. A.
Anderson, president of the Kansas State Agricultural College at Manhattan, argued that it was the lack of a climate record that had made settlers
overreact to the 1874 drought, because they assumed that this was the rule
rather than a rare exception. On the contrary, he continued, the line of
agriculture and increasing rainfall was extending west, and (again, these
familiar words) the "Great American Desert Theory" was getting "very
thin."[55] With optimism on the rebound, and with railroad construction
recommencing as the economy improved in 1877, the stage was set for the
next advance.

Onto the High Plains, 1875–1885

In this new boom, settlers moved west along the rivers and railroads,
through the dissected country of the Plains border, and out onto the
sprawling grasslands of the High Plains (fig. 4). The High Plains, reaching from about the 100th meridian in Kansas and Nebraska into eastern
Colorado (and north to South Dakota and south into the Texas Panhandle), are the remnant of a depositional surface that once extended from the
Rocky Mountains to the Missouri River. This wide apron of sand, gravel, silt, and clay was laid down over millions of years by streams carrying
eroded material from the Rockies. The surface of the High Plains — geologist Nevin Fenneman, in his influential *Physiography of the Western
United States* (1931), called it "a vast area of phenomenal flatness" — was
resistant to erosion because of its thick carpet of tightly woven sod and
the presence of a hard deposit of calcium carbonate called caprock, which
lies between ten and thirty feet of the surface. Sustained erosion could
only take place at the eastern and western edges of this plateau, as rivers
lengthened headward, cutting into the exposed sides. Beneath the surface, at varying depths, sits the reservoir of the Ogallala Aquifer, its water
moving slowly to the east through the open sands and gravels, and emerging as springs along the sides of valleys where it encounters hard layers of

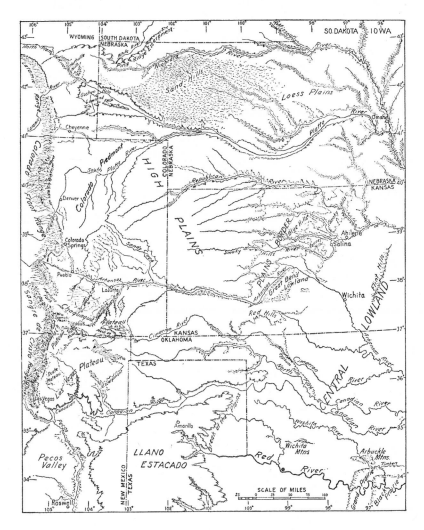

4. The High Plains. Source: Fenneman, *Physiography of the Western United States*, 6.

rock or impervious deposits of clay. These springs also produce erosion and dissection sapping back into the valley walls.[56]

This is very different country from relatively humid and verdant eastern Nebraska and Kansas. Rainfall decreases to about twenty inches a year at the 100th meridian, and to a scant fifteen inches annually at the Colorado state line. Departures of more than 50 percent from average

5. The flat uplands. Source: Johnson, *The High Plains and Their Utilization*, 610.

can be expected in any year; droughts are more frequent and more severe. Moreover, rainfall is localized, often delivered in torrential thunderstorms, so that one farmer's good fortune is another farmer's failure. On the flat interfluves, surface water is absent except for numerous shallow depressions, which hold only ephemeral water after a snowmelt or downpour. Creeks run dry in the summer, or, at least, run silently beneath their sandy beds. Beyond the main river valleys, the country encountered by the settlers was treeless, a level shortgrass prairie upland extending to the distant rim of the horizon, hanging low in the sky (fig.5).

The Kansas State Board of Agriculture, ever an unabashed booster for the state, claimed in its 1886 report that the drought of that year was the first serious one since 1874. The report characterized the period from 1875 to 1880 as an "uninterrupted success," and while it conceded that the 1881 harvest was "a little below expectations," overall the years from 1880 to 1885 were deemed to be an age of "general prosperity."[57] But, in truth, in the west at least, the rainfall over the decade was less reliable than reported, and settlement ebbed and flowed accordingly.

The second half of the 1870s was a time of at least adequate precipitation. In 1876, there was a "large and well-distributed rainfall which resulted in immense crops of wheat and corn" in all parts of Kansas. And the 1878 growing season was "almost ideal," with "record crops." The introduction into Marion County in 1874 (by Mennonites from southern Russia) of a winter-hardy and drought-withstanding winter wheat called Turkey Red, and its subsequent diffusion from farmer to farmer, was a successful adaptation of farming to the central Great Plains. An impressive showing at Philadelphia's Centennial Exposition in 1876—according to reports, the Kansas Building, brimming with the agricultural bounty of the state, was the "best and largest" of all the displays—also drew favorable attention, and dispelled any lingering misapprehensions that this was the Great American Desert.[58]

Many counties in the new frontier zone of western Kansas and southwestern Nebraska (fig. 2) experienced their first substantial burst of settlement in the wet and productive years of 1877 and 1878 (although some had been briefly settled in the early 1870s, before the reversals of 1873–74). James Malin, writing about Edwards County (where he had been raised), noted that the first wave of settlers moved into the sandy country south of the Arkansas River in 1877. Trego County, to the northwest, was settled in a rush in 1877–78 that took all the available public lands. To the northwest again, Hitchcock County, in southwestern Nebraska, was also the scene of a settlers' land rush that drove the cattlemen from the area.[59]

Then, beginning in September of 1879, the rains stopped, and the entire frontier zone experienced a "drouth of unparalleled duration." Much of Edwards County reverted to open range. In Trego County, crops were a "total failure" in 1880. The county seat, Wakeeney, which had been "jammed with people" in the spring of 1879, began emptying out, and was still "going downhill" in 1883. Hitchcock County was stripped of settlers in 1880 and 1881. The cattlemen came back, leaving one settler to ponder "whether or not the raising of grain will ever pay the settlers of the county."[60]

The situation reversed again in 1883–85, which were the wettest years on the short record. A new wave of settlers—in some places, by this time, the third—swept into the frontier zone. By 1885 only the western tiers of counties in Kansas and Nebraska and the counties of eastern Colorado remained unorganized and had population densities of less than two persons a square mile (fig.2).

The map of county population densities, however, hides the linearity of the settlement geography. In the far north, the Platte River valley was the axis of expansion, and North Platte, with a population of 2,540 in 1882, was the largest town in the entire frontier zone. Its numerous frame and brick buildings, and a courthouse that cost twenty-five thousand dollars, proclaimed success. Four hundred workers were employed in its massive railroad repair shops and spectacular forty-stall roundhouse. The town remained an important supply and shipment point for cattlemen and sheep herders who still ranged over the extensive unclaimed uplands to the north and south. And as the land office for Nebraska's western land district, North Platte was also a mandatory stopover to register a homestead or buy a city lot and the last outfitting center for settlers fanning out into the surrounding countryside.[61]

South of the Platte, the land climbs over steep eroded bluffs to a rolling divide that extends for fifty to one hundred miles, before dropping in a series of terraces to the lush Republican River valley. Until 1883 this shortgrass prairie — prime grazing land because the buffalo and grama grasses cured as they dried and preserved their nutritional value over the winter — remained in the hands of the cattlemen and therefore thinly settled. Frontier County, in southwestern Nebraska, had only one town, Stockville, a crude assemblage of shacks, a single store, and about sixty people. Stockville served as a focal point for the cattlemen and a place to keep the county records (in a room at the back of the store). Gosper, the county to the east, had no towns at all, just a few isolated country stores and post offices. Supplies had to be hauled from distant Plum Creek on the Union Pacific.[62]

The area's geography was transformed from 1879 to 1882 as the Burlington and Missouri Railroad was built along the north bank of the Republican. Beginning in Bloomington in December 1879, the tracks were extended through Alma, Arapahoe, and Indianola in 1880; Culbertson in the fall of 1881; Benkelman in the spring of 1882; then on into Akron,

Colorado, and eventually Denver. The completion of the line not only connected places to the Missouri valley gateway towns (specifically Plattsmouth, the eastern terminus), but also opened up the Denver market for Republican valley farmers.

The settlers kept pace with the railroad as it advanced, creating an unfurling landscape of farms and competing towns. After 1883 settlers moved up the north bank tributaries of the Republican, spilling out onto the uplands and forcing the cattlemen to seek more remote refuges to the west. Speculation by settlers and cattlemen alike, aimed at securing the water sources (and therefore the range between), was rife and evidenced by the preponderance of timber claims that were used to hold the land temporarily, until relinquished and reentered as preemptions or homesteads. According to the General Land Office, one small creek running into the Republican near McCook was monopolized by a single cattle company from its source to its mouth. The company, whose owners were merchants in Culbertson, had paid its employees to enter claims all along the creek.[63]

Town-building ventures proliferated along the Burlington and Missouri tracks. The railroad designated a place for a town, then its affiliated Lincoln Land Company bought the site and sold the railroad a hundred-foot-wide right-of-way through the prospective town for one dollar. The land company set about selling the business and residential lots, mainly to native-born Americans, who were preferred for the towns as opposed to Europeans, who were actively sought as rural settlers because, as John Hudson wrote, "They would work harder, complain less, and produce more than anyone else." Townsites in the center of a county were particularly valued because that location increased the chances of being selected as the county seat, a near-guarantee of long-term success. County seat rivalries often simmered for decades, as in Furnas County, where Beaver City and Arapahoe engaged in a competition that began in 1873 and was not decided (in Beaver City's favor) until 1888.[64]

The railroad towns of the Republican River valley, as elsewhere on the Great Plains, were spaced regularly along the tracks, about ten miles apart, each controlling the trade of a section of the countryside. The form of the railroad towns (again, as elsewhere on the Plains) varied from the symmetrical, where the railroad bisected the town and divided the main street along its entire length (for example, Republican City, Harlan County), to the orthogonal, where the tracks crossed the town's streets at an angle, so that there was only one crossing of main street (Arapahoe, Furnas County), to the final iteration, the T-town, where the tracks were at the edge of the site, along with the standardized depot, grain elevator, and lumberyard, and the main street formed the stem of the T (as at Indianola and McCook in Red Willow County). Whatever the specific morphology, the main streets, with their false storefronts looking like stage sets from a western, were crammed with businesses, general stores for sure, but also specialty shops, from boot makers to milliners. In 1883, for example, Indianola, with a population of 350, had fifty diverse businesses providing goods and services to its own piece of the countryside.[65]

Settlers also moved south from the Republican valley into northern Kansas. The nearest railroad to the south was the Kansas Pacific, sixty to eighty miles distant over a flat prairie that was cut into at intervals by broken land along the barely wooded creeks. The tracks of the Missouri Pacific were laid along the Solomon River to Lenora, Norton County, in 1882, but the company ran out of money and that's as far as they got. In 1885, as in 1872, only the Kansas Pacific and the Atchison, Topeka, and Santa Fe crossed all the way into Colorado. All of southwestern Kansas below the Arkansas valley and far-northwestern Kansas above the Kansas Pacific, as well as much of the flat country in-between, was without a railroad, and, therefore, still in the hands of the cattlemen.

The population origins in the northern two tiers of counties in western Kansas reflect the proximity to Nebraska. For the most part, settlers there had not been born in Nebraska, but, for many, Nebraska had been their last place of residence. Decatur County, for example, was settled mainly by Americans who had been born in Iowa and Illinois, as well as elsewhere in Kansas. But Nebraska was second only to Iowa as their previous place of residence. The situation was similar in Sheridan County, just to the south. But in counties three tiers down from the Nebraska line, the Nebraska contingent was much smaller. These counties were within reach of the Kansas Pacific, which channeled settlers west from Iowa, Illinois, Ohio, New York, and Pennsylvania, as well as eastern Kansas. South again to the Arkansas valley and the Atchison, Topeka, and Santa Fe, and the isolated country beyond, and the Iowa and Nebraska components of the population dwindled to insignificance, to be replaced by settlers who had been born in, or who had migrated from, Missouri and other parts of the upland South. These latitudinal alignments were extended after 1885 into the Rainbelt. African Americans, "exodusters" seeking a new Canaan, also moved out of the South after 1877, most famously to the town of Nicodemus in Graham County.[66]

The foreign-born segment of the population was patchy in its distribution, but it was generally less than 10 or 15 percent of the total in most western Kansas counties. Only in a few cases, such as Ellis County, where 1,213 settlers had come directly from Russia by 1885, did foreign-born settlers make up more than one-quarter of the total. At a local scale, however, in some townships along the Kansas Pacific, which actively recruited Europeans for its land grant, more than one-half of the population was foreign-born. It has traditionally been held that foreign-born settlers were less mobile than native-born Americans, that, to use James Malin's words, they "loved the soil for its own sake." But one detailed study of three immigrant groups in central Kansas found no significant difference in population turnover.[67]

The settlers moving into far-western Kansas and Nebraska after 1880 continued to be encouraged by the persistent mythology, kept alive by diverse experts and railroad and state boosters, that they were changing the climate for the better. Although, as the climate record grew, there was an opposing school of thought that settlers should adapt to the semiarid environment, by growing drought-resistant sorghum, for example, the prevailing theory was still that environment was adapting to the settlers.[68]

Samuel Aughey remained an apostle of beneficial, human-induced climate change, writing in 1880 that "as pioneers take up government lands and encroach on the Plains, the line of abundant rainfall also moves west." It was only a matter of time, Aughey reasoned, before the "sufficiently and increasingly moist region will encroach on the dry region until it is entirely crowded out of the state." Aughey now downplayed the role of tree planting, noting that rainfall increases had occurred before many trees had been planted. The agency was clearly, in Aughey's mind, "the great increase in the absorptive power of the soil, wrought by cultivation." Instead of running off the impervious prairie sod into creeks and rivers and away, rain penetrated the exposed cultivated soil, then slowly returned moisture to the atmosphere until, saturated, it yielded more rain. "Anyone can see," Aughey insisted, "that this must make an enormous difference in the moisture of the atmosphere and on rainfall."[69]

Meanwhile, in Kansas, the other early evangelist of "Rainfall Follows the Plow," Richard Elliott, had been fired by the Kansas Pacific when the 1873–74 drought cast serious doubt on the credibility of his theories. But in both Kansas and Nebraska, railroad companies, agricultural publications, university professors, and local newspapers continued to promote the seductive theory. And always the Great American Desert was the blighted image to be countered. In 1883, for example, the *Nebraska State Gazetteer and Business Directory* triumphantly reported that Nebraska had "changed its ancient character — under which it figured so long — of the Great American Desert."[70]

Yet some commentaries in the Kansas State Board of Agriculture reports in the 1880s were becoming more reserved and reasoned than they had been previously, probably due to the irrefutable record of recent droughts, as in 1873–74 and 1879–80. In the 1885–86 report, for example, state meteorologist J. T. Lovewell referred to the "general impression" that Kansas was becoming wetter. But he cautioned that rainfall records had only recently been kept, and were "as yet inadequate to a complete answer." Lovewell agreed that cultivated soil retained moisture better than unturned prairie, and he offered as evidence formerly dry streambeds that now ran with water. What Lovewell was advocating was a more sustained use of the stored water in the soil; he made no claims of an actual increase in the total amount. He also doubted that trees were contributing to increased rainfall, though he did acknowledge their local effects on microclimate.[71]

Although the beguiling theories of increasing rainfall were not dealt a serious blow until the drought of the 1890s, Lovewell's report at least subjected them to scrutiny and emphasized fact rather than fancy. The tree-planting version was becoming less persuasive, in part because so few trees were sprouting on speculative timber claims. And the plow theory was slowly being refined from the myth of increased rainfall to practical implications of preserving moisture in the soil, a transition that would produce the more rational, but still overblown, dryland farming campaign of Hardy Webster Campbell after 1900.

Still, geologist Willard Johnson, working through the Rainbelt in the late 1890s and talking with farmers who had managed to persist, was convinced that settlers did indeed believe that "extensive and persistent cultivation alone, by regulating evaporation, would bring them an equable and humid climate." To believe this was almost a matter of necessity for poor people with few options in life: "The hope had its origin," Johnson wrote, "in the pressing need for another ample expansion of the agricultural area." In Johnson's opinion, advertisement and promotion by railroad companies, town building companies, and agricultural organizations "prolonged and swelled" the boom, but its main cause was the "exceptionally heavy rains" from 1883–85, which seemed to confirm that rainfall was indeed increasing. Moreover, the fertile appearance of the land, which was covered with a "universal green" in spring, suggested a fine soil for wheat. From the start, Johnson wrote, the success of the "agricultural experiment" in the Rainbelt was "taken to be assured."[72] It would take a decade of adversity to persuade the settlers that they had been mistaken.

2

Into the Rainbelt, 1886–1890

There were two characterizations of the Rainbelt in the 1880s. The first was the familiar refrain that rainfall was moving west with the settlers. Hydrologist Frederick Newell, a fervent advocate of irrigation and a skeptic on rainfall enhancement, described what he called "the popular delusion" in this way: "In the extreme east of Colorado settlements have been made by what are called 'rainbelters' who come into the dry country in the belief that the so-called 'Rainbelt' would shift westerly as settlement progressed." The *Colorado Farmer*, also skeptical, ran occasional columns on the Rainbelters and reported in depth on the Rainbelt Farmer's Institute, which was held at Yuma in June of 1890. There was even a town with the hopeful name of Rainbelt, in Meade County, in southwestern Kansas, but it was never more than a rural post office, appearing on the map for only a single year, before dematerializing. "Rainbelt" lives on as a street name in Meade, the county seat, an obscure reference to a largely forgotten past.[1]

There was a second, subsidiary, connotation of the Rainbelt. Willard Johnson, in alliterative language, explained that the cattlemen saw the Rainbelt as a zone in which "desert conditions therein are in a measure mitigated merely," meaning that, in contrast to the truly arid lands farther west, there was sufficient rainfall (and natural forage) on the western Plains to sustain their herds.[2] Whereas the homesteaders — "nesters" to the cattlemen — saw the area in terms of deficiency, a condition to be remedied, the cattlemen saw it as admirably suited to their needs as it was.

The End of the Open Range

The cattlemen's plan for the western High Plains was more realistic than that of the Rainbelters. But it could not possibly prevail at the time because of the national ideology, which promoted the small farmer over the large landowner, or in this case, the large land occupier. It was the same rationale that was used to dispossess the Indians — the cattlemen were not using the land to its fullest, God-given potential. The fact that the cattle business was increasingly controlled by foreign interests, especially English and Scottish, was another strike against it.

Until the settlers descended in great numbers after 1885, cattlemen and sheepherders had the yawning spaces of the western Plains to themselves. There was some irrigated farming in eastern Colorado along the South Platte and Arkansas Rivers, but according to Newell it was small scale, inefficient, and so "recklessly expended" that sometimes the rivers ran dry before reaching Nebraska and Kansas. Moreover, many farmers in these valleys had been "brought to the verge of ruin" by speculators who had sold them worthless water rights to dry ditches.[3] Elsewhere, cattle and sheep, together with countless wild horses, filled the vacuum created by the devastation of the bison herds, thriving with minimal care on the nutritious shortgrass prairie.

The number of cattle on the range of western Nebraska and Kansas and eastern Colorado was remarkable. According to extension agent J. E. Payne, who knew the Rainbelt better than anyone, the tally books of the various outfits in eastern Colorado in the 1880s "summed up to nearly half a million head." John W. Iliff, the "cattle king" of Colorado, ran thirty-five thousand head on nine ranches along the South Platte, with an annual import of fifteen thousand Texas steers. The Keyline Ranch, headquartered near Ovid in Sedgwick County, rounded up more than a hundred thousand cattle each spring from a range that extended from the South Platte to the Texas Panhandle. Mrs. Hans Christensen, who was a young woman in Yuma County in the late 1880s, joked in her 1934 interview that there were so many cattle in the Arikaree valley that "you could hardly see the ground."[4]

Sheep, raised in large numbers for their wool after 1880, when the multiplying railroads allowed access to both the Denver and eastern markets, also covered the range. Judge Irving L. Barker (a rare educated settler who came to the Colorado frontier in 1883 with a university degree) remembered that the Rosckrans Ranch in the Arikaree valley herded seventeen thousand sheep. It was the practice to put them out on the range in scattered flocks of about two thousand each. Of course, the cattlemen and sheepherders (many of whom were Mexican) did not mix easily: the sheep competed for the same grass as the cattle, tramped it down and cropped it short, hastening the deterioration of the range. It was an accepted convention in the Rainbelt that anyone who stopped by a cattle ranch was invited to share a meal; anyone that is, except a sheepherder.[5]

Cattle were trailed up from Texas each year, as they had been since 1865, a two- or three-month haul often involving droves of four thousand head or more grazing their way north at about fifteen miles a day. The cattle trails were continuously displaced westward as the railroads moved ahead, drawing settlers and barbed wire in their wake. By 1885, Dodge City, the last Kansas cattle town to flare, had become enmeshed in this web of settlement, and Kansas had implemented a quarantine law that prevented Texas longhorns, with their latent splenic fever that spread rapidly and destructively to northern cattle, from directly entering the state. Trail City, in Prowers County, Colorado, located where the Chisholm Trail from Texas crossed the Atchison, Topeka, and Santa Fe, became the new buying and shipment point. Reputedly Trail City straddled the state line, with the front doors opening to Kansas, and the back doors to Colorado, confounding the sovereignty of both states.[6]

Joseph Bowles, a longtime Colorado cattleman, whose herds ranged from the South Platte to the Arkansas River, described Trail City as the "toughest town that God let live; nothing there but saloons and gambling houses, hotels and corrals." Bowles and his father would go to Trail City each year and buy up to three thousand Texas yearlings for about eight dollars a head. The cattle were double-wintered on the range, at almost no cost, then sold as fattened steers for as much as forty dollars each and dispatched to the Kansas City stockyards. No wonder English and Scottish investors, with Industrial Revolution money burning in their pockets, invested widely in the lucrative cattle business of the first half of the 1880s. They tended to headquarter their companies in Denver and visited their ranches only at spring round-up (or at other times to hunt), leaving the running of each operation to a foreman.[7]

But increasingly, Texas longhorns were not welcome on the western range. In addition to the problem of splenic fever, their meat was of inferior quality (and only marketable because there was an ongoing nationwide beef shortage). Moreover, they were expensive to ship because their emblematic horns took up so much space in the rail cars (twice as many shorthorns could be packed in). Most important, the Texas cattle and their drovers were increasingly seen as trespassers on the northern range, decreasing the quality of the grass through overgrazing and polluting the bloodlines of their newly acquired herds of Herefords, Shorthorns, and Angus. In a similar manner, Mexican sheep, descended from generations that had subsisted on desert forage in the Southwest and whose wool was thin and wiry, were being replaced by better breeds such as Merinos.[8]

The human imprint of the open range on the landscape of the western Plains was dwarfed by the immensity of the space. The statistician and economist Joseph Nimmo, in his thorough 1885 Treasury Report on the "Range and Ranch Cattle Business," estimated that only 2299, 1669, and 1186 men were employed in the ranching business in Kansas, Nebraska, and Colorado, respectively, a sparse population over such an extensive area. Their settlements were rudimentary. Harry Strangway, an Englishman who had wandered the world before becoming a cowboy in Yuma County, Colorado, in the 1880s, put it this way: "A cattle ranch was a cattle ranch and nothing else." There wasn't a single milk cow or cultivated acre of ground on Strangway's ranch, but there were thirty thousand head of beef cattle. Typically, a ranch landscape consisted of a single

twelve-foot by fourteen-foot log or adobe shack, a cottonwood pole corral fastened with wet rawhide, which tightened as it dried, and a water
source. By the 1880s, perhaps a windmill had been added, providing water to a stock tank.[9]

The range between the water sources was allocated by mutual agreement on a first-come, first-served basis. Newcomers were excluded by per-
suasion or force. Iliff, for example, actually owned only 15,000 acres along
the South Platte, but by controlling the river he had unchallenged access
to 650,000 acres of open range. On the open range, only the sheepherder's cabin and pen and the small winter camps of the cowboys (whose job
it was to break the ice on streams and ponds so the cattle could get water, which they needed every day) stood as landscape evidence of a human
presence.[10]

At first, hardly any of the land was fenced. Judge Barker claimed that
there wasn't a single mile of fence in Yuma County when he arrived in
1883. Joseph Bowles told how he would ride all the way from the Republican to the Arkansas with "nothing in the way of a fence to stop him."
Even along the Arkansas River in southeastern Colorado, where irrigation ditches were dug in the 1880s, there was only one fence between Gre-
nada and Las Animas. The first extensive fences were along the railroads,
because the cattlemen held the railroad companies responsible for stock
killed by trains, and passengers held them responsible for delays as the
herds slowly rambled across the tracks. According to Strangway, the only
plowed land on the eastern Colorado uplands in the early 1880s consisted
of furrows that had been scratched in the earth around ranches in a vain
attempt to forestall prairie fires.[11]

Ranchers did begin to fence their occupied portions of the range in
the mid-1880s, an illegal attempt to lay claim to land in anticipation of
the arrival of the settlers. Fencing the range also saved the ranchers money, because one hand, working year-round, could keep the fence mended, whereas a good number of hands had previously been needed to herd
the unconfined cattle. Joseph Bowles's father, seeking to protect his Herefords and Shorthorns, erected a sixty-five-mile barbed wire fence around

his range, but the federal government forced him to take it down. Similarly, John W. Prowers, in what was then Bent County, was obliged in 1888 to remove a fence that enclosed 75,000 acres. That same year, the government ordered the Arkansas Land and Cattle Company to dismantle a fence that blocked off 627,089 acres of range.[12]

Nor did the local cattle shipment points, specks of places like Akron, Yuma, Burlington, and Cheyenne Wells in Colorado, or earlier, Haigler and Benkelman in Nebraska, add much to the human landscape. They were rudimentary settlements, little more than a windmill, a water tank, a corral and a loading chute alongside the tracks, then a scattering of crude frame buildings and tents. The entire human geography expressed emptiness and impermanence.

Joseph Nimmo's 1885 report was a seething attack on the practices of the cattlemen. Nimmo considered it a "well-accepted fact" that the area with sufficient rainfall for agriculture had "moved westward from 150 to 200 miles" over the preceding twenty years and that, as a result, the days of the open range were numbered. He lambasted the methods that the cattlemen were using to control the waterways and the grasslands "in violation of both the letter and spirit of the land laws"; he resented the foreign corporations and "titled noblemen" who were taking over the cattle business "with no intention whatsoever of becoming citizens of the United States"; and he offered this advice: that "it would be more promotive of the public interests if the lands now held by the Government shall be dedicated to the rearing of men rather than to the rearing of cattle."[13]

Nimmo must have been impressed, then, by the rapidity of the settlement of the Rainbelt after 1885. Johnson described it as an "inroad" of farmers and townbuilders, an "invasion" of the uplands that took the range away from the cattlemen and sheepherders.[14]

Looking back on a transition she had witnessed, Mrs. Artie Richards of Morgan County, in a lecture given to the local Daughters of the American Revolution chapter in 1933, related how the cowboys, "finding it impossible to bluff the settlers out of the country, filed in many cases on the land containing the open waters of the streams, leaving the smooth

uplands for the settlers who came to farm." The cattlemen had to reinvent themselves as stockmen, sedentary landowners who supplemented
the prairie grass with alfalfa, sorghum, and other forage crops. As Lute
Johnson, also an early settler in Morgan County, put it, "the Rainbelt was
moving west, and the cowboys, once as common as field hands, were beginning to look upon themselves as hayrakers."[15]

This transition was also precipitated by brutally cold winters from
1885–88, which persuaded the cattlemen that their herds could not fend
for themselves year-round on the open plains. Hundreds of thousands of
cattle died in the February blizzard of 1886 and the three-day blizzard in
November 1888, drifting south in the hurling wind until trapped against
bluffs or railroad fences, to die there, suffocated by a snow that was, in
one settler's words, "as fine as white flour." Most were not found until the
spring. Glenn Bolander, who settled on "the flats" south of Wray, Colorado, came across thousands of cattle "piled up on top of each other" in the
Arikaree valley. Other settlers to the north of Wray found about five hundred carcasses in a single sand hills blow-out. They skinned them on the
spot and sent the hides east to shoe companies. The coyotes dealt with the
rest. Similar accounts came from all over eastern Colorado.[16]

Even without the blizzards, the nesters, and the deterioration of the
overstocked range, the open range cattle kingdom was finished. By 1885
Texas cattle were being shipped by rail directly to the Chicago, St. Louis, and Kansas City stockyards, bypassing the central Great Plains. The
railroads that had given rise to the cattle trails were now in the process
of supplanting them. "The settler," Mrs. Artie Richards concluded, "had
scored a victory."[17]

Settling the Rainbelt

The settlers took almost all the public domain and railroad lands in western Kansas and southwestern Nebraska in 1884, 1885, and 1886 and
spilled over into eastern Colorado in 1886 and 1887. The tide hit Dundy County, in the southwestern corner of Nebraska, in the spring of 1886,
when three thousand expectant settlers landed at Benkelman. In Sher-

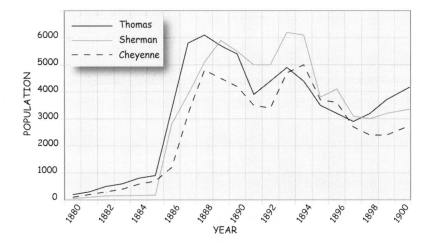

6. Population change for selected northwestern Kansas Counties, 1880–1900.

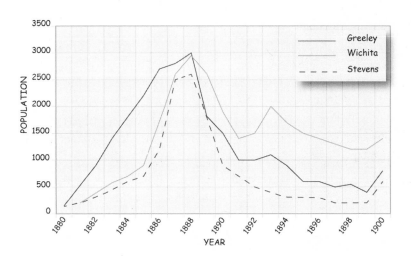

7. Population change for selected southwestern Kansas Counties, 1880–1900.

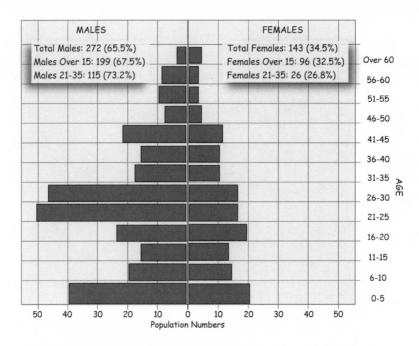

MALES		FEMALES	AGE
Total Males: 272 (65.5%)		Total Females: 143 (34.5%)	Over 60
Males Over 15: 199 (67.5%)		Females Over 15: 96 (32.5%)	56-60
Males 21-35: 115 (73.2%)		Females 21-35: 26 (26.8%)	51-55

8. Benkleman and Haigler Precincts, Dundy County, Nebraska, 1885.

man County, Kansas, population density soared from one person every ten square miles in 1883 to three persons per square mile in 1886, and double that by 1889. All the counties in southwestern Nebraska and northwestern Kansas experienced an abrupt surge in population in 1885 and 1886, which was sustained until 1889 (figs. 6 and 7).[18]

In keeping with stereotype, most settlers coming into the Rainbelt were young, and there were more men than women. The states of Kansas and Nebraska as a whole had more men than women, though not inordinately so (Kansas, for example, was 53.6 percent male in 1885). The male proportion of the population increased to the west, reaching 55 percent or more in the still-unorganized counties near the Colorado line. There were few women in open range cattle county.[19]

The handwritten schedules of the 1885 Nebraska State Census, listing every individual by name, age, and place of birth, and arranged as family units, permit a more detailed analysis of this frontier demography. The

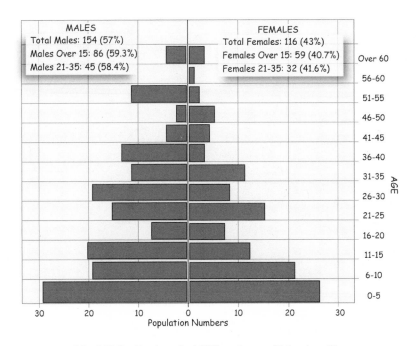

MALES
Total Males: 154 (57%)
Males Over 15: 86 (59.3%)
Males 21-35: 45 (58.4%)

FEMALES
Total Females: 116 (43%)
Females Over 15: 59 (40.7%)
Females 21-35: 32 (41.6%)

AGE: Over 60, 56-60, 51-55, 46-50, 41-45, 36-40, 31-35, 26-30, 21-25, 16-20, 11-15, 6-10, 0-5

Population Numbers

9. North Valley Precinct, Red Willow County, Nebraska, 1885.

farther west you went along the Republican valley, the larger the proportion of men in the population. That proportion was highest in Dundy
County's Benkelman and Haigler precincts, where males were 65.5 percent of the total population, 67.5 percent of the adult population, and 73.2
percent of the twenty-one to thirty-five age group. Comparative figures
for North Valley precinct, in Red Willow County, two counties to the
east and settled a few years earlier, were 57 percent, 59.3 percent, and 58.4
percent (figs. 8 and 9). More of a balance between males and females was
quickly established as a social fabric of churches, schools, and law and order was fashioned, creating a more inviting environment for women and
children. It was often also just a simple matter of a wife and children staying in places to the east with relatives for a period of time, before joining
the husband on the newly established claim.[20]

The census data also show that there was a demographic contrast between towns and rural areas. Some rural areas, like Hayes County (which

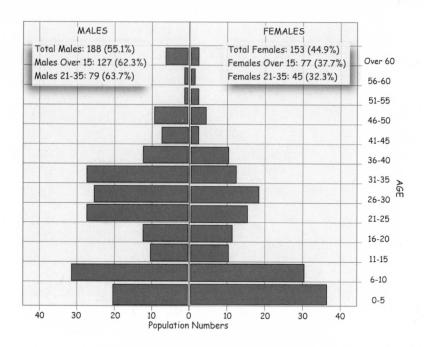

MALES

Total Males: 188 (55.1%)
Males Over 15: 127 (62.3%)
Males 21-35: 79 (63.7%)

FEMALES

Total Females: 153 (44.9%)
Females Over 15: 77 (37.7%)
Females 21-35: 45 (32.3%)

AGE

Over 60
56-60
51-55
46-50
41-45
36-40
31-35
26-30
21-25
16-20
11-15
6-10
0-5

40   30   20   10   0   10   20   30   40
Population Numbers

10. Hayes County, Nebraska, 1885.

was in the middle of its first homesteaders' boom in 1885), had relatively
more women because they were largely settled by families (fig. 10). The
towns, on the other hand—Culbertson, Indianola, Haigler, and Benkelman—had large numbers of single men in their twenties and thirties
who lived packed in hotels and worked where they could as laborers (figs.
11 and 12). Or didn't work, as the case may be, because in Dundy County, for example, most of the laborers reported in the census that they had
been unemployed for much of the previous year.

In all these rural upper Republican River counties, the vast majority of
the women were recorded in the census as "working at home," or as "stays
at home." In the rural areas, a small few were homesteaders in their own
right, by virtue of being single or divorced, or otherwise (because of a husband's frailty or death) the head of a household. Some worked as house-
keepers in the homes of single male settlers.

There were more opportunities for women in the towns, but even there

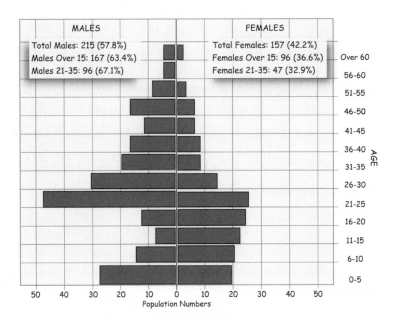

11. Culbertson Village, Hitchcock County, Nebraska, 1885.

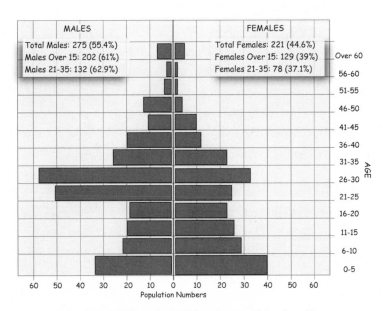

12. Indianola Village, Red Willow County, Nebraska, 1885.

almost all of them were listed as "working at home." Exceptions in Indianola, for example (they can be named because they were so few), included Lulu Hatch, a young waitress from Missouri; Jeanne Miller, a milliner from Illinois; and dressmaker Lizzie Cabrini from New York, all characters in the cast of an untellable story because, other than appearing as a name in the census (and probably on a death certificate too), they are absent from the historical record. Towns also offered more employment opportunities for men, in addition to the predominant category of "laborer." In Indianola, men were doctors, lawyers, land agents, and businessmen of all ilks.

Having settled western Kansas and southwestern Nebraska in a rush, the homesteaders moved on in legions into eastern Colorado in 1886 and 1887, again to the next area of free and cheap land. S. S. Worley, who worked as a locator out of Holyoke in Philips County, remembered that "during the year 1886 it seemed that everyone wanting a home was coming west."[21]

As the land filled up, the local political geography of eastern Colorado was rearranged. The five massive counties that had been created in 1874—Arapahoe, Weld, Egbert, Bent, and Las Animas—were divided in response to the influx of settlers. Logan and Washington were created out of Weld in 1887, and in 1889, Morgan, Yuma, Sedgwick, Phillips, Kit Carson, Lincoln, Cheyenne, Kiowa, Otero, Prowers, and Baca were all organized to serve the local needs of a burgeoning population. Only Arapahoe County, reaching all the way from Denver to the Kansas line, remained undivided because it lacked a railroad in its eastern expanses and had neither the population nor the taxes to support a new county apparatus. The reshaping of Arapahoe County into enlarged Washington and Yuma Counties would not take place until 1904. For the same reasons, and at the same time, three new land offices (Hugo, Akron, and Sterling) were set up in 1890, obviating the need of settlers in eastern Colorado to travel great distances to the Denver (established 1864) or Lamar (1886) land offices.[22]

The pace of the settlers' inroad was dramatic. Worley described the in-migration in this way: "Every train from the east into Denver Junction [Julesburg] brought in would-be homesteaders. Some rode in Pullmans, some in day coaches, some on the bumpers, some in wagons, some on foot — some had money and some had none — all headed for the famous Frenchman Valley, where the land was free, with rich level soil, such as never was seen elsewhere."[23]

Most of the settlers came as far as they could by train, packing "emigrant cars" (just boxcars, really) with household goods at one end, livestock at the other, and beds in between. Elva Sisson of Wray recalled in her 1934 interview that her husband and three other young men came west from Missouri as stowaways in an emigrant car. They had spent all their money shipping farming equipment and household goods and couldn't afford to buy their own tickets. Such "hitchhikers" were commonplace in the emigrant cars.[24]

At the railhead towns, if they had the means, settlers would buy a wagon and a team of horses, some cows and poultry, and provisions like flour, cornmeal, canned goods, and slab bacon. It would be a long time before the first crops came in.

Some settlers, like the portentously named George Washington Franklin, who took out a preemption in Keith County (soon to be Perkins County), Nebraska, in the fall of 1885, came all the way west from Iowa by wagon, a grueling two-week journey that retraced the old Oregon Trail. (Franklin would keep a diary for forty years, a sparse but revealing account, written in a meticulous hand, even between the lines to save the expense of buying paper.) Thomas Jefferson Huntzinger, who came from Indiana to take out a preemption near Akron in 1886, walked in to Colorado from Independence, Kansas. Having established residency on his claim by living there a month, he went back to Missouri by train, bought a team of horses and a double-box wagon, and drove to McCook, where he purchased a plow and provisions. He was then ready to "settle down to be a pioneer homesteader."[25]

A single, vivid image captures the way the land was settled almost overnight. Wallace Hoze Wilcok came west from Illinois to eastern Colorado with his wife and two babies in 1887. Wilcok left his family with his brother-in-law in Benkleman, Nebraska, while he took out a preemption in eastern Kit Carson County. Having staked out the corners of his 160-acre claim, he stood on a rise on his land and saw no sign of human life in any direction. He returned to Benkleman to pick up his family and supplies. When they got back to their new home a week later, Wilcok "counted sixty shacks and dug-outs" from the high point on his property, a new, instantaneous human landscape mushrooming from the earth.[26]

The settlers of eastern Colorado, like those of western Kansas and southwestern Nebraska, were mainly midwesterners who had been born in Iowa, Illinois, Indiana, and Ohio. They had generally moved west in stages, typically spending time as children or young adults in Nebraska and Kansas, before moving on to Colorado. Oliver Graham was representative. Graham was born on a farm near Mattoon, Illinois, in 1872. When he was three his family moved to central Iowa, where they farmed for ten years. They left for eastern Nebraska when Iowa became too densely populated. When eastern Nebraska in turn became too crowded and expensive, they purchased a relinquished homestead just south of Wray in 1886. Graham farmed there on the family land until he was twenty-eight, when he moved into town and became a successful jeweler. The frontier was a place of occupational, as well as geographical, mobility.[27]

Foreign-born settlers, who accounted for 10 to 20 percent of county populations in eastern Colorado in 1890 (with the main component again being German) often came directly to the frontier. Bob Hasart, for example, left Bessarabia (Moldova) in 1889 and landed in Akron, Colorado, three months later. From Akron, he traveled by covered wagon to Idalia, a journey of three days through rain and snow over bad trails, which Hasart remembered as the worst part of the entire trip. He and his sons would eventually own fourteen sections of land. Similarly, Cary Mathias Jacober and his wife came in a single journey from southern Russia to Burlington in 1892, disembarking at the railroad station with only a dollar in their pockets.[28]

Most settlers were poor; that's why they came to the frontier. They couldn't afford to buy or rent land in Iowa or Illinois, but for two hundred dollars they could legally possess 480 acres in the Rainbelt (by taking out a preemption and a homestead sequentially, and a timber claim at any time). There were also a few years without property taxes, a chance to get established. It was their last best chance to make a home, or else speculate on rising land values. They were opportunists with few opportunities.

Some came west for their health. Colorado especially, but the western Plains in general, with their relative aridity and cold, cleansing winters, were prized for their salubriousness. "The climate is good for people with respiratory ailments," the *Keith County News* reported, "and consumption never originates here." Some settlers, like Angelina Fuller of Stratton and Martha Gilmore Lundy of Burlington were "ordered west" to a dry climate on account of their husbands' health. It seemed to work: "We were never sick," Fuller recalled, and her husband "gained in health every day."[29]

Still others, like Nellie Buchanan of Seibert, simply caught "western fever," striking out with no clear destination in mind in hope of a better future. In 1886, Nellie, with her husband and two babies, took the train from Indianapolis to Kansas City, where they were stuck in the snow for a day. They went on to Gaylord (Smith County) on the Rock Island Railroad, where they were again stopped by snow. Nellie was enchanted by the clear blue skies and pure white landscape, and she persuaded her doubting husband to keep moving west. They bought a wagon, a team of horses, and two dozen chickens and kept going. A couple of days later, they came across a sod house, where a desperate man told them: "Go back to where you came from; go back now while you can, for in a year from now you won't have anything to go back with. Go back before you have to starve." Undeterred, they moved on, sheltering the next night from a torrential downpour in an abandoned schoolhouse, with the coyotes howling all around. They homesteaded fifteen miles south of Goodland, with "not a soul nearby, not a house in sight." Nellie's husband worked as a lineman on the Burlington Railroad, while Nellie looked after the homestead, the children, and the cows. They finally moved with his job to Seibert, in Kit

THE CO. SEAT OF YUMA COUNTY,
Situated in the Famous Yuma Valley,
IN NORTH-EASTERN COLORADO,

One hundred and thirty-eight miles north-east of Denver, on the line of the Burlington & Missouri River Railroad. Yuma at 90 days old had a population of over 600 souls, and has enjoyed a steady and healthy growth ever since, and is today the largest, wealthiest and best city between Denver Colo., and McCook Nebraska, a distance of 250 miles.

SITUATED in a new and growing state, whose interests is half agricultural, and the other half mineral. We have incalculable beds of coal, basins of oil, reservoirs of natural gas, Mountains of Iron, and produce more Gold and Silver than the balance of the United States combined. Besides these essential advantages to build up an immense City we have millions of acres of the very best farming land in the world pouring its produce daily into Yuma, the natural market for this vast tract. Draw on your imagination, if you can, and picture in the far west a town where rapid progress seems to cause the eye as it peeps over the morning horizon to stop in astonishment at the improvements of the day before, and you have such a town as Yuma really appears and is to-day.

Yuma being in the midst of the best farming region of the Colorado Rain-belt, and on the main line of the great C. B. & Q. R. R. gives her the advantage of both the eastern and western markets, i.e. Chicago on the east and Denver the natural supply point for the Rocky Mountains and the colony, upon the west.

Yuma School House.

CLIMATE.
The Climate is the healthiest in the world, and the water is soft and pure, cold and clear as crystal.

RESOURCES.
Yuma has no competitor, or rival nearer than 140 miles upon east, and 112 miles upon the west; while there is no point to divide Yuma trade, for 75 miles upon the North and 80 miles upon the South. Think of a thickly settled country of One Hundred and Fifty Five Miles one way by Fifty Seven Miles the other. All dependant upon Yuma for their supplies. Can you imagine the tremendous volume of trade such a territory must afford, and Yuma enjoys?

THE COUNTRY AROUND YUMA.
Is beautiful and just sufficiently undulating to afford natural drainage. And it an ever recurring succession of swales and shallow but gradual dips and basins. Presenting to the enraptured homeseeker, and tourist, an apparently endless yet ever varying scenes of beauty, smiling welcome to the farmer, tradesman, miner, artisan, and all who are seeking new fields, and relief from the over crowded walks of eastern life.

The Soil is Unsurpassed for Fertility.

13. Yuma, Colorado, promotion, between 1890 and 1910. Source: Denver Public Library Western History Collection.

Carson County (probably in 1888). Nellie had hoped this would be "nearer civilization," but instead she found a "dry, shabby place."[30] Like this one, each settler's story was unique in its details, but all were set within a general pattern of migration.

Settlers were also seduced into eastern Colorado by embellished advertising, such as fantastic pictures of Mississippi steamboats on the South Platte. It is understandable that midwesterners, yearning for land, would be attracted by accounts such as the one in the *Wray Republican* on July 12, 1889, which proclaimed the unsurpassed fertility of the soil, a "never-failing supply of good water" (this in a place where there were no "living streams"), mild winters, and temperate summers. In Yuma County, this eulogy continued, "the wealthy find employment for their money and the poor for their hands."[31] An advertising promotion issued by the town of Yuma (probably in about 1890) epitomizes the false images that were issuing from the Rainbelt (fig. 13).

It was common for a husband, like Wallace Hoze Wilcok, to go on ahead of his wife and children, establish a claim, and make a start on farming. James William Cody, who took out a preemption and a timber culture claim in eastern Arapahoe County in the fall of 1889, is another example. Cody had moved from his birthplace of Keokuk, Iowa, with his wife and children to Oberlin in western Kansas in 1884. He farmed there for five years. In the fall of 1889, after selling his proved-up homestead, Cody went on alone to eastern Arapahoe County. He hired a man to help build a sod house and farm buildings and to break some acres of sod so that the ground would be ready for corn and wheat in the spring. In February of 1890 he went back to Oberlin and brought his family out to their new, austere home.[32]

Many times, parents, siblings, and in-laws settled adjacent claims, a complete family transplantation from the old home to the new frontier. This was the case with the Brammeier family, originally from Cedar County, Iowa. Reuben Brammeier came first with his wife and children to a homestead near Burlington in 1887. Within a year, his father, mother, and brothers had settled on neighboring homesteads. Such extended families were a mainstay in the harsh conditions of frontier life.[33]

The geography of the settlement was also shaped by the idiosyncrasies of professional locators, men who were paid to take homesteaders from the train to the hotel to the land office to the claim. Worley was one of these, plying his trade in Phillips County for a good salary of thirty dollars a month. Worley practiced an early form of redlining, sending Germans to the northeast of the county around Amherst, Swedes to the northwest near Fairfield, Americans to the Frenchman valley in the south (the preferred location, even though Frenchman Creek, or the North Fork of the Republican, was generally dry), and Arkansas emigrants to areas of sand hills. Settlers from Ireland and Missouri (a strange and probably derogatory coupling) were "dumped wherever there was room."[34]

The main influence on the emerging settlement geography by far was the railroad. In fact, the surge of settlement into the Rainbelt would not have been possible at all without the unprecedented expansion of the rail-road network from 1885 to 1888. On June 30, 1885, there were 4,168 miles of railroad in Kansas. Only the Kansas Pacific and the Atchison, Topeka, and Santa Fe extended through the western counties and into Colorado. Fourteen counties in southwestern Kansas had no rail lines at all, which prevented widespread settlement. By December 31, 1888, the state's mile-age had doubled, and only five counties, all in the southwestern corner, were without tracks (fig. 14).

Judge James Humphrey, reporting for the Kansas Railroad Commis-sion to the State Board of Agriculture in 1886, was giddy with the pros-pects for economic growth afforded by this "perfect network of rail-roads." He asserted that a "greater number of miles had been built in Kansas than in any other state." He couldn't give an accurate figure, he jested, because the pace of construction was so fast, hardly slowing for winter, that this "would require a fresh census to be taken every day."[35]

Humphrey conceded that railroad construction was more "in anticipa-tion of future growth and development" than to serve settlers who were already in place. And for that reason, he admitted, both freight and pas-senger traffic had been "far below that which was reasonably anticipat-ed." But he brushed any doubts aside, averring that this was always the case in the "western agricultural regions," where it was "impossible to sustain a considerable population without the agency of the railroads." Once the railroad approached, Humphrey effused, "the whole scene is changed, the landscape is quickened with a new life and a marvelous en-ergy, primeval lands become fertile fields, and farms that could be had by settlement and occupancy reach a high value."

In southwestern Nebraska, western Kansas, and northeastern Colora-do, extensions of the Burlington system spanned the spaces between the Union Pacific, the existing Burlington line along the Republican valley and the Kansas Pacific. In one contemporary account the splaying lines were compared to a spider's legs. One leg cut across the flat tablelands of newly created Perkins County through Elsie (five miles from George Washington Franklin's claim), Madrid, Grant, then on to Holyoke and

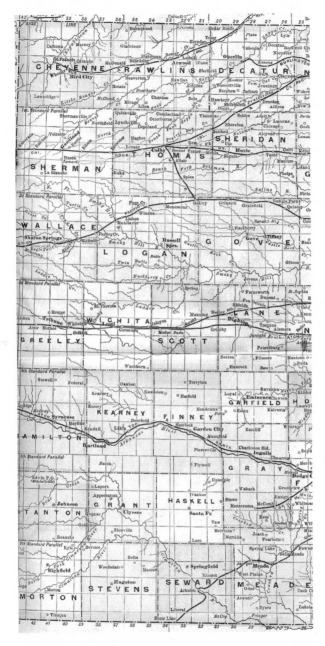

14. Official Map of the Kansas State Board of Agriculture, 1890 (detail). Source: *Seventh Biennial Report of the Kansas State Board of Agriculture, For the Years 1889–90* (backpocket map).

Sterling, Colorado. Another leg traced Frenchman Creek northwest from
Culbertson to Palisade and Imperial, drawing settlers right into the heart
of cattle county.

Almost all the public domain in Perkins County, except for the rolling sand hills in the northeastern quadrant, was taken in 1886 and 1887.
This didn't mean that the land was actually populated, however; most
settlers initially took out timber culture claims, which had no residency requirements, and because only one timber claim was allowed in each
square-mile section, those seeking to speculate in this manner had to keep
moving ahead. Homesteaders and preemptions accounted for the other
claims, whether for speculative or settlement purposes. In eastern Colorado, the fertile loess-covered uplands of the Vernon Divide, south of Wray,
and the Idalia Divide, south of the Arikaree fork of the Republican, were
thickly settled. Anywhere within reach of the two Burlington lines, except again for sand hills country, was taken up in 1886 and 1887.[36]

The Burlington also built a line southwest up Beaver Creek from the
Republican valley in Harlan County, Nebraska, to St. Francis, in Cheyenne County, bringing the northwestern corner of Kansas within reach of
settlers. To the south, Sheridan, Thomas, and Sherman Counties in Kansas were opened up for settlement in 1887 with the extension of the Chicago, Rock Island, and Pacific Railroad, which ran from Norton, through
Goodland, and exited the state at the aptly named Kanorado. The line
continued through Kit Carson County, spawning towns like Siebert and
Burlington. Nearly all the land in Kit Carson County was filed upon in
1887. Extensions of the Kansas Pacific bridged the distances in Rooks,
Graham, Sheridan, and Thomas Counties in northwestern Kansas (fig.
14).

The rail network thinned to the south of the Kansas Pacific, but the
construction of the Missouri Pacific through Lane, Scott, Wichita, and
Greeley Counties, Kansas, then on through Kiowa County, Colorado,
to Pueblo opened up a whole new area for settlement. Still, Kiowa and
Cheyenne Counties remained thinly settled, except along the railroads,
and may not have reached population densities of more than two persons

per square mile until after 1900. Southwestern Kansas, with its intermittent sand hills and scarce surface water, remained outside the railroad grid. With the exception of that area, and adjacent railless Baca County in the southeastern corner of Colorado, all the frontier zone was within thirty miles of a railroad and therefore, depending on the conditions, only a day or two away from a market or supplies. But even dry, sandy, remote, and railless Baca County received an influx of settlers in 1887.[37]

Towns — ports of entry for settlers heading into the Rainbelt — proliferated along the tracks. The Lincoln Land Company was again particularly active along the Burlington lines: Fort Morgan, Holyoke, Haxium, Yuma, Eckley, and Wray were all platted by this Burlington affiliate. Yuma, for example, was initially homesteaded by Ida B. Albert and George F. Weed, a conductor on the Burlington. The couple married (perhaps it had all been prearranged, in order to legally acquire two homesteads as single adults before joining up), pooled their claims, and brought in the Lincoln Land Company to plat and sell the site. The Lincoln Land Company was given every other lot in town in return for its services. The town grew quickly. In December 1885, there were only two small stores, a livery stable, the "inevitable saloon," and a few shacks along the tracks. By the summer of 1886, Yuma had a three-block-long main street lined by a general store, a drug store, five saloons, the Weld Hotel, which doubled as a schoolhouse, and the State Bank of Yuma.[38]

There were many "inland towns" too, distant from a railroad, isolated places like Idalia, in eastern Arapahoe County, with its post office, sod hotel, general store, three saloons, and no residences, because everyone simply inhabited their business. But lacking transportation connections — having to pay the extra costs of time and money just to get to the railroad — these towns were at a great disadvantage, and the map of places was in constant flux, even before the drought of the mid-1890s.[39]

Hoyt, for example, was temporarily an "inland town" in Kit Carson County when it was bypassed by the Chicago, Rock Island, and Pacific Railroad in 1888, which was lured instead to nearby Siebert by the provision of "liberal inducements." Hoyt's businesses — two general stores,

a drug store, a hardware store, and a blacksmith shop—were picked up
and moved by mule teams to the tracks. Similarly, the town of Lowell,
also in Kit Carson County, was left adrift on the prairie when the Chicago, Rock Island, and Pacific Railroad bypassed it in 1888 by locating its
depot a few miles to the west. The "old town," as Lowell was called, was
moved to the depot and rechristened Burlington. This evacuation included the Montezuma Hotel, which was "rolled on skids and poles" by eighteen men and their teams to the new, more advantageous site.[40] In one
way or another, either by moving or dying, the towns were as transitory
as the people.

Julesburg, incorporated in 1887 and connected to the east and to Denver by the Union Pacific's Denver and Gulf line, and Holyoke, founded that same year on the Burlington line, were the main disembarkation
points into what would become Sedgwick and Phillips Counties in 1889.
The rapid growth of Holyoke, based on outfitting settlers heading to their
claims, was astounding (and typical). Within twelve days of its founding,
Holyoke had forty-two buildings under construction. Two months later, the town had three lumberyards, two restaurants, a livery stable, two
banks, two hardware stores, two drug stores, two grocery stores, two bar-
bers, two printing offices, a meat market, a physician, and four saloons.
By the summer of 1888, Holyoke had added another three saloons, another two banks, and its first school and church. By May of 1888, when
it was incorporated (by a vote of ninety-three for and two against), Holyoke's population had soared to seven hundred.[41]

Haigler, in Dundy County, Nebraska, only a few miles from the Colorado line, was the main supply point for Rainbelters moving into Yuma,
Kit Carson, and eastern Arapahoe Counties. Although a village of only
thirty people in 1885 (three years after the Burlington and Missouri had
built through), Haigler's services included a general store, a drug store, a
livery stable, a doctor and an attorney, and a milliner. Even after the Burlington extended west through Wray, Yuma, and Akron to Fort Morgan in 1882, Haigler remained the principal outfitting and service center
for much of northeastern Colorado. This was partly because Wray was

isolated from the main settlement areas to the south on the Vernon and Idalia Divides by steep bluffs, making Haigler more accessible, though seventeen miles more distant. Haigler flourished as a port of entry into Colorado, reaching a population of three hundred by 1890 and offering a diverse array of services to new farmers and surviving cattlemen in a trade area that extended sixty miles in every direction, except to the east, where the larger town of Benkleman took over. By the 1890s, Haigler boasted a four-thousand-dollar schoolhouse, a two-story brick city hall, two churches and two hotels, a doctor who doubled as the station agent, and two loan and trust companies, always ready to provide money and to foster debt.[42]

To the south, western Kansas towns like St. Francis, Jaqua, Independence, Bird City, Kanorado, and Sharon Springs (some of them now long gone) similarly served as staging points for settlers striking farther west into the Rainbelt, at least until more local Colorado towns like Burlington, Cheyenne Wells, Sheridan Lake, and Lamar were well established. Lamar, for example, which was platted in May of 1886 and had a land office three months later, was soon "quite a lively place," according to C. C. Huddleston, who ran the hardware store. Huddleston claimed that by March 1887, there were "16 saloons, 2 dance halls, 75 'gay girls,' and about 100 tin horn gamblers" (though some of these estimates might have been a flight of fancy). Many people, drawn mainly from Illinois and Iowa, were still living in tents that flanked a sagebrush-covered main street. But business was brisk at Huddleston's store, with "lots of settlers' small orders." Small towns like Lamar, Wray, and Haigler furnished settlers with the necessities of life, such as flour, rudimentary clothing, and mail. For more sophisticated goods, such as a superior harness or the latest farming equipment, settlers had to travel farther afield to more substantial towns, such as McCook or Goodland, or else obtain them from a Chicago mail order house such as Montgomery Ward, a business that flourished in the 1890s.[43]

The passage of the front of settlement through western Kansas and Nebraska and into eastern Colorado from 1886–87 can be seen in the rise and fall of land office business from 1880 to 1890. The land office records also confirm that this remained primarily a speculators' frontier.[44]

The west-central land offices at Kirwin and Larned, Kansas, and Bloomington, Nebraska, had seen their peak business in the boom years of the late 1870s, and their numbers fell thereafter. By 1885 almost all the land in the Northwestern District, centered on Kirwin, had been taken, and the Arkansas Land District (Larned) had only claims from the dissolved Osage Reservation left to sell.[45]

The settlers moved on, and new western land offices in Kansas at Wa-Keeney (1879), Garden City (1883), and Oberlin (1883), and at McCook (1882), Nebraska, began their business (fig. 15). In 1883 the register and receiver at the Garden City office reported a "headlong rush of settlers unprecedented in this section of Kansas." "Every train," he wrote, "brought in a crowd of land seekers." In language that recalled Even Jefferson Jenkins's experience at the Concordia Land Office in 1870, the Garden City agent related that "for more than an hour before the office opens a mass of humanity throngs the doorway." From July 1, 1884, to June 30, 1885, the Garden City office filed 2,467 homestead entries (compared to 241 the previous year) and 2,838 timber culture claims (compared to 262 the year before). All the public sections in the Atchison, Topeka, and Santa Fe land grant were taken.[46] Then, just as rapidly, by 1886, their business was done, the land was all claimed, and the first wave of settlers moved on into eastern Colorado, where the newly established land offices at Lamar (fig. 16), and later at Akron, Sterling, and Hugo, began processing claims.

In each district there was a similar sequence of land sales. At first, timber culture claims, ideal small scale speculations, predominated. In the Perkins County township where George Washington Franklin settled, for example, every section quickly had its timber claim, and most were held for five to ten years before being relinquished, generally to a prearranged buyer. As the boom peaked in each district, homestead entries (some on relinquished timber claims) took up most of the business, suggesting a more serious commitment to settlement. Finalized homesteads constituted the main activity in later years, as the pace of in-migration

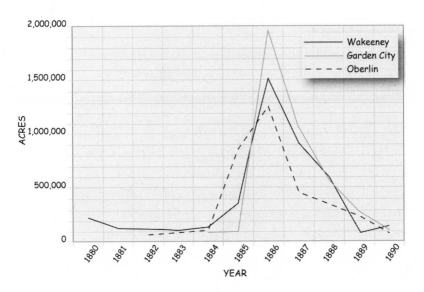

15. Land Office transactions, 1880–1890, Wakeeney, Garden City, and Oberlin, Kansas.

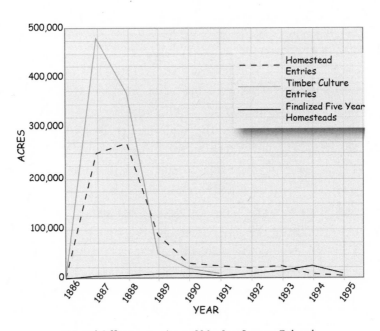

16. Land Office transactions, 1886–1895, Lamar, Colorado.

subsided. It was not unusual for ten or more years to pass before an initial
entry resulted in a final patent, following perhaps four or five commuta-
tions or relinquishments, as settlers came and went.[47]

There were never many successfully completed timber culture claims
anywhere. Their main purpose was petty speculation, and in any case the
stipulation on tree-planting (initially, it might be recalled, the law specified that forty acres had to be put over to trees for ten years) was imprac-
tical in an area where even cottonwoods struggled to survive along the
creeks. If timber culture claims were eventually finalized, it was because
the local land office was lenient in its interpretation of the law. Worley, for
example, looked after his absentee cousin's tree claim in Logan County.
He admitted that he never managed to grow any trees, but the land office
agent agreed to let the cousin "make proof" on the land because of Worley's good faith efforts.[48]

The high degree of speculation in the settlement process was revealed in
an investigation prompted by S. M. Stockslager, commissioner of the General Land Office, in 1888.[49] In a circular dated June 6, Stockslager asked
the registers and receivers at land offices across the country to report on
the amount and types of speculation taking place and to assess what proportion of the settlers were genuine home-seekers. Stockslager saw himself as a reformer. He had dispatched a team of special agents to investigate fraud and inefficiency at the land offices, made the proving-up process
more stringent, and disbarred the "most disreputable and incompetent
lawyers and land agents." It is hardly surprising, then, that all the land office officials reported that attempts to manipulate the laws for speculative
purposes had "greatly decreased" because of Stockslager's efforts. Still, the
reports from the land offices made it very clear that most of the public domain was passing into the hands of speculators, rather than settlers.

The officers at Garden City described the operation of the timber culture laws as "a farce" and estimated that 95 percent of the entries were
fraudulent. Most of the preemption and homestead entries were also for
the purpose of speculation, because they were commuted (after no attempt at the required occupancy) for borrowed cash after six months. "If

good faith means making a home," the Garden City officers continued, "all of these quick, short-term cash entries are speculative."

The response from the Wakeeney office was similar. An estimated 75 percent of the homestead and preemption entries there were made by speculators, as well as the "vast majority" of timber claims. Even if there was general intent to improve a timber claim, it was "nearly impossible" to grow the required acreage of trees, leading to the relinquishment of the claim, and its reentry under another law. And if the full residency requirements for preemptions and homesteads were indeed fulfilled (one year for the former, five for the latter), and title legally obtained, more often than not the land was immediately mortgaged to "some moneyed corporation," then left undeveloped for years until it was profitable to sell. Such idle land was a handicap for newly formed counties striving to generate property taxes to build a courthouse, grade roads, or seduce a railroad.

The same general story came from the recently opened Lamar land office, where again the timber culture act was the agency of most fraud. Only at the McCook land office, an apparent Eden of honesty, did the register report that "entries are generally made by actual settlers who are desirous of making homes. . . ."

The entire illegal process was facilitated by unscrupulous notaries public, who guaranteed settlers success in making final proof on their claims and charged plenty for their services, and nefarious lawyers and land agents, who organized the deals and secured the loans. Every town, especially those with a land office, had its host of agents and lawyers, and innumerable companies were formed in the eastern United States for the sole purpose of issuing mortgages. Typically, according to Frank H. Spearman, a banker in McCook, a farmer would take out a mortgage for a thousand dollars, to be paid back at 10 percent annual interest over five years. Local land agents would take the application for a fee and forward it to the western offices of a New England bank in Omaha or Kansas City, which would send the money to the frontier. There were banks in every western town of any size, but, as Spearman explained, "their combined capital would not suffice to supply a respectable fraction of the de-

mand for money in their territory." Credit, attracted by high interest rates
on the frontier, flowed from east to west over the entire second half of the
nineteenth century. The Great Plains was heavily in debt to the East, especially New York and New England.[50] This wasn't a case of America
being shaped on the frontier, as Turner argued, but of America, already
shaped, being expressed on the frontier.

The reports from the land offices invariably put the blame for speculation on the "unsavory alliance of pretended land attorneys and land
agents who have been practicing their piracies on unsuspicious settlers."
The settlers, however, were not as innocent as suggested, but well aware
of the opportunities for speculation. Glenn Bolander, for example, originally from Ohio, took out preemption and timber culture claims on the
flat uplands south of Wray in 1888. Bolander relinquished his preemption
after almost a year, then homesteaded it, "thus escaping taxes for seven
years." Bolander didn't say what he did with his timber claim, but it probably wasn't much.[51]

The degree of speculation declined as the country filled up and land
values rose, obliging settlers to comply more faithfully with the conditions of the law, or else find their attempt at making final proof thwart-
ed by others who coveted their property. As the officers of the WaKeeney
station put it, "the public domain in this district is becoming exhausted,
and each settler is in a measure driven to comply with the law from fear
of others taking advantage of his failure." For the same reason, timber
culture claims were often relinquished and reentered as homesteads because title could then be finalized in five years (or six months, if commuted), whereas it took at least eight years to own a timber claim. It was important at this late stage to have a legal title, either to hold onto the land
as a home, or to mortgage it, or to sell it.

Under these conditions of rapid settlement and rampant speculation,
the Rainbelt filled up until, by 1888, the frontier zone of two or more persons per square mile enveloped southwestern Nebraska, western Kansas, and much of eastern Colorado (fig. 2). The 1890 federal census map
of population density showed an almost continuous gradient of settle-

ment across the central Great Plains from the Missouri River to the Rocky Mountains. Only the dry heart of eastern Colorado and the tip of southwestern Kansas had not reached a density of two persons per square mile, though some parts may well have done so in the peak years of 1887 and 1888. This was the occasion for the Bureau of the Census to declare the frontier "closed," and for Turner to reach his disturbing conclusion that the conditions and opportunities that had shaped American character and development, and made it all special, were no longer operative.[52]

But the frontier wasn't closed. There remained ample, though increasingly marginal, land that hadn't yet been opened to Americans in Indian Territory, and that remained to be settled on the northern and southern Great Plains. The frontier wasn't even closed on the High Plains of Kansas, Nebraska, and Colorado but was about to be opened up again following the desiccation of the Rainbelt.

The Rainbelters did well from 1885 to 1887, despite the harsh winters. There was a punishing drought in eastern Kansas in the summer of 1886, but western Kansas received at least average rainfall. This followed the very wet years of 1883–85, and it must have seemed indeed as if the Rainbelt were moving west.[53]

A reporter for the *Denver Republican*, traveling through eastern Colorado in late 1887, concluded that "the condition of the people in these new sections is gratifying in the extreme." The settlers had come in the previous year with "limited means," and their experience had been a "rugged one." But they had raised enough food to see them through the winter, and even some to sell. The corn and other sod crops had "far exceeded the most sanguine anticipations of the veterans who have seen the development of Kansas and Nebraska." To them, the reporter continued, "the rain-belt section of Colorado is now what these states were six years ago."

A functional, though not yet aesthetically appealing, human landscape was sprouting on the Colorado plains, as described by the *Denver Republican* reporter:

The entire country along the Burlington Railroad in Colorado east of Denver is pretty generally settled. The most of the residents having gone in

during the past summer, their farms as yet have not assumed much beauty
as regards outward appearances, nor has much been done toward building
fences and pretentious structures; but the lands for from one to ten miles on
each side of the road are dotted here and there with newly erected cottages.
. . . Some are painted and lend thereby an appearance of thrift among the
people, while others yet retain the original color of the lumber with which
they are erected. The less costly "dug-out," is here and there a feature of the
surrounding country.[54]

In their interviews four decades later, the elderly settlers recalled the
early optimism and the fertile promise of the land. Thomas Jefferson
Huntzinger, who came as a young man with his parents to Kit Carson
County in 1888, and claimed to have "plowed the first furrow between
Akron and Hugo," thought eastern Colorado "the finest country in the
world." There, unlike in the Midwest, he did not have to "pick rock, pull
stumps or grub trees," but simply turn over the fertile earth. Many settlers
remembered that weeds were unknown, until shipped in with the grain
seeds, and, specifically, in the case of Russian thistles (tumbleweeds),
brought in by immigrating Russians. At least that's who got the blame.[55]

But the initial success proved to be an illusion. As reported in the *Colorado Farmer* in 1890, speculation was a systemic problem that counties
and genuine settlers had to pay for: "At an early date [settlers] have already
found the land near the railroads taken for speculation, and they had to
go further off, knowing that the immediate result of their work, if successful, would be to raise the value of speculation land which lies idle and
unimproved, while every farm improvement is taxed."[56]

Moreover, settlers soon found that the first year's bountiful sod crop,
nourished by centuries of accumulated humus, could not be sustained as
the soil was quickly drained of its stored moisture and nutrients. Extension agent Payne, on his rounds through eastern Colorado, captured this
vividly in contrasting photographs of adjacent fields of sorghum that had
been planted at the same time, one flourishing on virgin soil, the other
withered on "old ground" (fig. 17).[57]

But when the inevitable setbacks came, in 1887 and 1890, erratic rain-

SORGHUM ON OLD GROUND.

SORGHUM ON SOD.
(Same row, planted same day as preceding.)

17. Sorghum on old ground and on sod. Source: Payne, *Field Notes from Trips in Eastern Colorado*, 4.

fall was the main culprit (though in Huntzinger's case, it was hail, a single violent storm, that destroyed his crops and reduced him to bankruptcy). Rainfall records from the 1880s are few and far between. Measurements had been taken since the 1870s at Fort Larned and Fort Dodge in central Kansas, but their reliability is questionable. Then in 1886, the U.S. Signal Service sent trained observers to a number of states, including Kansas, Nebraska, and Colorado, with a plan to enlist at least one volunteer from each county to record temperature, rainfall, snow accumulation, and wind strength and direction.[58] The service provided volunteers with instruments and detailed instructions for their installation and use: thermometer on the north side of the house, out of the sun, and preferably under a porch; rain gauges on or near the ground, and no less than twenty feet from a building. Gradually, a reliable body of data was collected, though it remained skeletal until after 1890.[59]

According to the rainfall records, and the settlers' memories, the year 1887 started well. After the usual dry winter there was plenty of rain in spring and early summer and with it the promise of abundant crops. Then the rains stopped, and searing hot winds parched the crops to straw in the fields. The Kansas State Board of Agriculture reported that the drought was widespread in the "Western States," and "fell with much force on Kansas," making it one of the "most disastrous crop years in her history." In eastern Colorado, Eta Shannon's family gave up on farming and moved into Sterling. "If only we could have had rain at the proper season," Eta explained, "we might still be living in that section of the country." But as it was, she continued, "in the early spring we would plant our garden and corn and they would come up and do splendidly until about July, when the hot winds would come and in less than a fortnight they would be withered and gone."[60]

The impact of the 1887 drought is clearly expressed on the population graphs of western Kansas counties (figs. 6 and 7). In all cases, population peaked in 1887 or 1888, as settlers hung on for one more year after the drought, trying to recoup their losses. There was then a steep decline that was sustained through the next drought year of 1890 and into 1891.

It has been argued that 1887, which brought economic turmoil and a drying up of credit, as well as drought, was the beginning of a period of population decline that persisted through the 1890s, and some counties, such as Greeley and Stevens, do fit this profile.[61] But other western Kansas counties, and much of eastern Colorado, would see population gains in the wet years of the early 1890s, as settlers tried again to make a life in the Rainbelt.

These population graphs hide as much as they reveal. No doubt there were many failed farmers (and failed merchants who depended on their trade) because, like Eta Shannon and her family, they were poor people with no reserves. But the abrupt population decline may have also reflected the *success* of speculation and the transient nature of frontier settlement. Many homesteaders stayed just six months, commuted their claim, then mortgaged it or sold it at a profit, and moved on. As the Kansas State Board of Agriculture explained, "young men and others went there [the High Plains frontier] with no other purpose than to preempt a quarter section of land, and at the end of six months get a loan on it (generally about $500) and leave."[62]

The dry season of 1887 was followed by a year of generally adequate rainfall. Dodge City, for example, recorded twenty-three inches of precipitation, two inches above normal, and Lamar received its average amount of fifteen inches, with good distribution in the growing season. The Kansas State Board of Agriculture reported an "abundant harvest" throughout the state and claimed that the losses of the previous year had been "retrieved," though in western Kansas the population continued to plummet. In eastern Colorado, Elizabeth Richards, living with her husband on a claim forty miles south of Wray, remembered fine harvests of corn, rye, and wheat in 1888.[63]

The next year was even better. Holyoke, in Philips County, for example, received its average of about seventeen inches of precipitation, but nearly all of it fell during the growing season. Dodge City also received average precipitation with a fortuitous concentration in the growing season. The Kansas State Board of Agriculture described 1889 as a "thor-

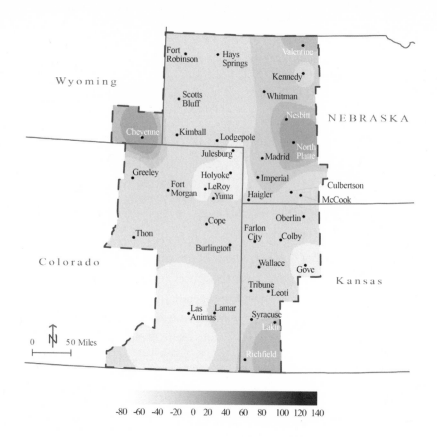

Wyoming

NEBRASKA

Fort
Robinson
Hays
Springs
Valentine
Kennedy
Scotts
Bluff
Whitman
Nesbitt
Cheyenne
Kimball
Lodgepole
Julesburg
Madrid
North
Platte
Greeley
Holyoke
Imperial
Culbertson
Fort
Morgan
LeRoy
Yuma
Haigler
McCook
Cope
Oberlin
Farlon
City
Colby
Thon
Burlington
Wallace
Gove
Colorado
Tribune
Leoti
Kansas
Las
Animas
Lamar
Syracuse
Lakin
0   50 Miles
Richfield

-80 -60 -40 -20 0 20 40 60 80 100 120 140

18. Percentage precipitation deviation from average for the year, 1890.

ough specimen of a Kansas year of plenty, with overflowing granaries."[64]

Any population recovery in the Rainbelt, however, was forestalled by the arid year of 1890, which (to continue the refrain of the Kansas State Board of Agriculture), was "a specimen of a Kansas year of scarcity, with lean granaries." The Board reported that it was "the driest and hottest season in twenty years, almost destroying the corn crop in many parts of the state and shortening it greatly elsewhere." The same story came from Nebraska, which, according to State Meteorologist Goodwin D. Swezey, experienced "the hottest and driest year on record." The timing of the drought, which began in June and intensified in July, with searing hot winds that "curled" the crops, compounded the settlers' distress.[65]

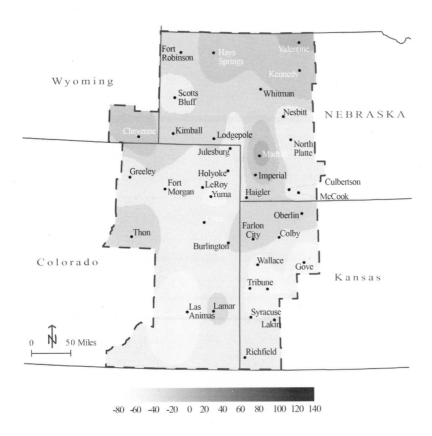

19. Percentage precipitation deviation from average for the growing season, 1890.

The 1890 drought was particularly severe in the Rainbelt, where for the first time there were sufficient stations reporting to allow the spatial variations to be mapped (figs. 18 and 19). The drought was deepest in eastern Colorado, both for the growing season months from May to September, and for the entire year. Holyoke, for example, recorded only 8.77 inches in 1890, barely half the average; less than 1 inch fell from June through September. In southeastern Colorado, Las Animas received 5.3 inches in 1890 (compared to an average of 12 inches), and barely an inch from June to December. Dry conditions prevailed throughout the Rainbelt.[66]

Settlers who had hung on through the drought of 1887, and perhaps had seen hopes revive in 1888 and 1889 (despite low crop prices), gave up in 1890. The Rainbelt's population kept dropping. In thirty-one counties in western Kansas there was a population loss of 34,660 in 1889–90, almost one-third of the total. On May 10, 1890, two days after the wind blew the roof off his sod house, George Washington Franklin rented his land to neighbors, packed his wagon, and left Perkins County for his sister's place in Iowa. Like many others who left in 1890, he would return.[67]

By this time, the settlers must have begun to realize that if there was a connection between plowing the soil, planting trees, and rainfall, then it was a fickle one. Even the optimistic experts at the Kansas State Board of Agriculture had to concede that while "persistent breaking of prairie" and "planting of trees" might yet "gradually improve the hot season" (by preserving scarce moisture in the soil and shading it against evaporation and scorching winds), the process was so gradual that "the present generation can scarcely hope to benefit from it." Sargent T. B. Jennings of the Signal Service, went as far as to admit that he was "unable as yet to discover any safe rule for the long-range predictions of weather," noting only that "there are without doubt dry and wet periods alternating, but with great irregularity."[68]

The population exodus and economic downturn brought railroad construction to an abrupt halt. Judge Humphrey's annual report on the railroads of Kansas veered from the heady optimism of 1887 to a tale of despair in 1889. The year ending June 30, 1889, he wrote, "was an exceptionally unprofitable one for the railroads." In the far-flung Union Pacific system, for example, only the main line from Omaha to Ogden was making money. Humphrey acknowledged that the railroads "had seen fit to build or purchase lines where there is not enough population at present to support them," with the result in Kansas being annual net earnings that amounted to less than 5 percent of their bonded indebtedness.[69] New railroad construction stopped and would not resume again until after 1896.

Then tantalizingly (and typically), the rains returned in abundance in 1891 and 1892. Settlers, with short memories and a willful optimism, were once again persuaded that the Rainbelt was moving west, and the lines on the population graphs again trended upward (figs. 6 and 7). But the new boom would be short lived and, as it would turn out, the disillusionments and failures of 1887 and 1890 were only dress rehearsals for the environmental and economic catastrophes that would follow in the mid-1890s. It is significant that the elderly residents of eastern Colorado who were interviewed in 1933–34 rarely mentioned the 1887 and 1890 setbacks, but the events of 1893–95 were still alive in their minds.

3

Life in the Rainbelt, circa 1890

———— ‧•‧ ————

Alvin Steinel, in his authoritative *History of Agriculture in Colorado* (1926), characterized the settlers who poured into the Rainbelt from 1886–89 as completely unprepared for life in the semi-arid, shortgrass country. He was right. But that's not what most Colorado papers said at the time. They frequently pointed out that the newcomers had previously lived in Nebraska and Kansas and were, therefore, pre-adapted to the Rainbelt. This ignores of course the steady decline of rainfall west across the Plains, and also the fact that stopovers in eastern Kansas and Nebraska had often been brief.[1]

No one had given the settlers sound advice on how to farm in an area that received less — often much less — than fifteen inches of rain a year. The federal government was interested only in settling people on the public domain; what happened after that was their own business. The state governments of Kansas, Nebraska, and Colorado just wanted their empty lands filled and wealth generated, and did not feel bound to offer balanced advice. And the agricultural colleges were just getting started and did not yet have effective extension divisions in place to educate the settlers (though, because of experts like the Cheyenne Wells agricultural extension agent J. E. Payne, this was building).

Most advice the settlers did receive was glossed, hopelessly optimistic. The gushing editorial that appeared in the *Elbert County Democrat* on April 15, 1887, describing an area that would become Kit Carson County

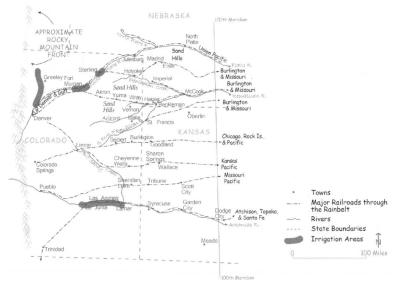

20. The Rainbelt, circa 1890.

two years later, is typical. Following an abundant rain of, it was claimed, six inches in twenty-four hours (half the annual total, which is not impossible, given the way rain is delivered in violent convectional storms on the Great Plains), the newspaper pronounced that "the question of moisture is no longer a speculation, but it is an assured fact. . . . All that is needed is to plow, plant and attend to the crops properly; the rains are abundant."[2] If the rainfall wasn't there yet, it was coming soon, thanks to the agency of the farmers.

The *Colorado Farmer* was more cautious, conceding that harvests had been good in 1886, but asking "will it last?" There was no hard evidence from the past, the paper argued, that farming could succeed in a country that had previously been seen as "only fit for grazing." "We will just have to wait and see," the editorial continued, "and hope there is no disappointment or disaster in store for the brave pioneers. . . ."[3]

As it was — these are Steinel's words — "land hungry people did not trouble to analyze or seek confirmation of exaggerated claims."[4] The Rainbelt was their last best option, and given their poverty and the high price of land to the east, the only place they had a chance to prosper, or at least get by (fig. 20).

Water

The settlers' immediate need upon arriving in the Rainbelt was water, a need not easily satisfied in such a dry place. Shelter could be improvised, and food was brought in, no matter how plain. But water, a bulky product, could not be imported in quantity, yet it was needed immediately and continuously by settlers and their stock. As Arthur James Pearce, a settler near Burlington in 1887, put it: "Water was a very precious thing in those days, and believe me, we did not waste a drop of it."[5]

A sequence of recycled use was developed. The water that was not drunk by settlers was used for cooking, then bathing, then for laundry and dishes, and finally to scrub the floor, if indeed there was the luxury of a wood floor. The cooking and dish water was also recycled to the cattle, hogs, and poultry, which needed large quantities in the hot days of summer. Wastewater was also used to irrigate the garden.[6]

The options for obtaining water were limited. Rain barrels, a common method of collecting water in the eastern Great Plains, where there were roofs of shingles and boards, were not useful in a country where sod houses, with their absorbent turf roofs, were everywhere. Settlers melted snow in winter, but this was a poor option in a dry season in a dry country.

The South Platte and Arkansas Rivers, fed by Rocky Mountain snowmelt and catchment basins, had water year-round, although already by 1890 inefficient ditch irrigation and lack of storage facilities were reducing the volume of their flow. In any case, their frontage was controlled by cattle ranchers and speculators, and irrigated land, selling at fifty to one hundred dollars an acre, was way beyond the means of the Rainbelters, who only had the uplands, and the false promise of increasing rainfall, in their sights.[7]

Other major rivers that headed on the Plains, like the Republican and Solomon, and which sometimes carried water year-round in their main courses, had also been appropriated by the cattlemen and the earliest homesteaders. Some Rainbelters, like Elizabeth Richards of eastern Arapahoe County, did have access to Republican River water, which she and her family hauled four miles each day in barrels in a wagon pulled by mules. But Mrs. Richards was reluctant to drink water where cattle had stood, and done much more.[8]

The tributaries of the major rivers, shown encouragingly as solid lines on the maps of the time, were actually dry, except when downpours briefly turned them into raging torrents. Frenchman Creek, for example, which forms the headwaters of the Republican in Logan and Phillips Counties in Colorado, was generally without water until it reached Nebraska, and Dry Creek in Kit Carson County, lived up to its name. But the beds of the creeks sometimes held pools of water in shallow depressions ("raises"), their stagnant surfaces covered with a layer of green algae and swarming with mosquito larvae. Settlers would commonly haul this water for their stock, or take their laundry there, boil it over a fire of buffalo "chips," then drape the washed clothes over the prairie to dry.[9]

Settlers with no alternatives were obliged to drink this scummy water, and similar stagnant water that accumulated temporarily in the innumerable shallow depressions (known at the time as "buffalo wallows" but more likely caused by subsidence at a depth) that pocked the surface of the High Plains (fig. 21). The algae and "pollywogs" did not faze Thomas Jefferson Huntzinger, who maintained that once the water was strained through cheesecloth, boiled, then strained again and cooled, it was "pretty good to drink."[10]

A better option, and one widely used, was to dig a hole in the dry bed of the creeks, then sink a barrel into the sand and gravel and wait for it to fill with cool, clear water. Alice Pantzer's family, who lived twenty miles southeast of Burlington, got their water this way from Dry Creek, and they also dug into the creek bed to make water holes for their cattle.[11]

It was good fortune indeed if there was a spring on the property, where the Ogallala Aquifer, moving over an impervious bed of rock or clay, ran or seeped out from a valley side. There were at least three major springs along Frenchman Creek in Phillips County, Colorado, and lines of springs

21. Typical "buffalo wallow." Source: Johnson, *The High Plains and Their Utilization*, 702.

along the Arikaree River and South Fork of the Republican in Yuma and Kit Carson Counties. Many of the earliest place names in eastern Colorado, such as Willow Spring, Cotton Spring, and Crystal Springs, celebrated this valuable water source, though other names — Alum Spring and Salt Spring — indicate that their waters could be bitter and saline. Most of the good springs had probably been taken by the cattlemen, as they made their transition into stockmen, before the nesters arrived. There were exceptions: Jennie Davis's family, living in a sod house sixteen miles north of Limon, was blessed with its own spring. Jeannie considered herself fortunate "not having to drink from water holes like many other pioneers."[12]

The subsurface water was just as hard to get at. The Ogallala Aquifer underlies almost all of southwestern Nebraska and western Kansas, as well as Sedgwick, Phillips, Yuma, Kit Carson, and Baca Counties, in their entirety, in eastern Colorado and parts of Logan, Cheyenne, Kiowa, and Prowers. Even at the time it was recognized that this underground reservoir was not a single level surface but was found at different depths. The distance to the water table — the top of the completely saturated ground — varies from more than two hundred feet below the surface of the uplands to just below the ground on the Platte and Arkansas floodplains. Locally, it was impossible to predict where the water table lay because of the variation in subsurface deposits. The main flows are in veins of sand and gravel, marking old stream courses, that hold the slowly moving water between their particles and grains. But these relic channels are mixed in with mortar beds, where calcium carbonate has cemented the sand and gravel into a solid mass, with strata of hard rock that have survived from earlier geological times, and with dense clay beds that have no appreciable interstices for the water to run through.[13]

Because of this complex, hidden, underground geography, one settler might have no luck at all in sinking a well to water, while another, nearby, might be successful in a single try. In 1890 wells on the uplands of Sedgwick County were 250 to 300 feet deep, tubed with two-inch pipe, and pumped by windmills. In Phillips and Washington Counties, which had no "living streams," the only source of water was from wells dug or drilled to 200 feet or more. In Akron, the town well was 900 feet deep and held only a small amount of water. At Kit Carson, a well was drilled to the depth of 1300 feet without any success. On the other hand, there was artesian water in Meade County, in southwestern Kansas, where underground water, compressed between a sinking surface and an impermeable layer of clay, rose to the surface of its own accord. But this beneficence was a rare circumstance on the High Plains.[14]

Every settler wanted a well, an independent supply of water. Once you had a well, you were, as Isaac Messinger expressed it, "the richest man in the county." Not in a monetary sense, because neighbors who flocked to the new wells were often given the water free, though they would be charged for watering their stock. But because it was a luxury not to have to haul it every day. Worley remembered that "during the first two or three years the men spent most of the time hauling water." The women did too: Nellie Buchanan, living with her husband and two babies fifteen miles south of Goodland, Kansas, drove her wagon ten miles to the Smoky Hill River every few days. She brought the water back in barrels covered by old carpet to prevent spillage.[15]

The first wells were sunk by the railroads, because trains were always in need of water. These water tanks became the nuclei of towns like Vona, Cheyenne Wells, Yuma, Hoyt, and Holyoke. Vona's railroad well, for example, drew settlers from a radius of fifteen miles, and the wagons stood in lines to collect the water. The railroad wells were supposed to be used only by company employees and their families, but in practice they were public property. Nellie Buchanan, whose husband eventually worked in the Burlington yards at Siebert, kept the key to the Hoyt well and gave it to anyone who needed the water.[16]

The early wells on the uplands were dug by hand, either by the homesteaders themselves, often working communally, or by men who hired out for the work at the going rate of about twenty cents a foot. The hole was opened up with a spade, then excavated with a pick and shovel. The dirt was lifted to the surface in buckets using a windlass and a rope, drawn either by hand or a mule or a horse. Periodic strata of sand and gravel had to be curbed with boards to prevent cave-ins. In Kit Carson County, Thomas Jefferson Huntzinger used a short-handled ax and a three-gallon syrup keg to dig down 125 feet to water. It took him four weeks. A neighbor helped out for three days in return for an acre of plowing. In Perkins County, George Washington Franklin spent two months digging a neighbor's well in the winter of 1886, on days when the temperature fell as low as 17 degrees Fahrenheit below zero. Franklin used a derrick and a ground pulley, drawn by his team of colts, to do the work. He cut through layers of clay and hard rock, a cross-section through Plains geology, and he hit water at about one hundred feet. It was hard and hazardous work: in Phillips County, Charlie McKee was buried deep inside the well he was digging, and that's where he stayed.[17]

Improvements by the 1890s included drilling with augers that were turned by horses or cranks (fig. 22) and pulling water to the surface by windmills and cylinder pumps. Even with these improved methods, the amount of water generated was small, enough at most for domestic use, a stock tank, and a patch of irrigated garden. This all cost money of course: as much as a dollar a foot for paying a professional driller to sink his auger; boards for the curbing of hand-dug wells often ran as high as forty

22. Deep-well making on the uplands. Source: Johnson, *The High Plains and Their Utilization*, 734.

dollars. But it paid off in the long run. Elizabeth Richards and her family went from hauling water in 1889, to drawing water from a 190-foot-deep hand-dug well by means of a mule and a bucket in 1890, to installing a windmill in 1891. The additional water allowed her to sustain ten cows, and the money she made from selling milk and butter helped defray the costs of the improvements.[18]

Soon there were professional well-diggers in every vicinity, and other entrepreneurs like Fred Borland, who sunk a well in the sandy bottom of Frenchman Creek and delivered water to "Holyoke housewives" at the price of twenty-five cents a gallon. There was money to be made out of water, a glass of which cost the same (five cents) as a glass of beer.[19]

The problem of obtaining water for domestic use was gradually solved, though because of the vagaries of the geology, some settlements, like Sheridan Lake in Kiowa County, remained dry. The quality of the supply was also variable: in 1887, the distribution of contaminated water to

23. First home of Mrs. Margaret Sneider, Seibert, Colorado. Source: Colorado Historical Society. CHS. X4735. Courtesy History Colorado (Original Photographs Collection, Scan 20004735).

Yuma residences caused a typhoid epidemic, which, according to John G. Abbot, carried off many of the town's "brightest and best."[20]

Shelter

Shelter was also needed from the first day on, but it was more readily available (in rudimentary forms) than water. Dug-outs and sod houses were ubiquitous early homes in the rural areas, and often in the towns too, though they weren't the first. Settlers like Chuck Morgan of rural Holyoke slept on boards covered by straw ticking under a wagon cover until a sod house was put up. Cynthia Boyles and her family lived out of the wagon box at first, on their homestead south of Burlington. Those who walked in from western Nebraska or Kansas, carrying everything they owned, simply slept under the firmament of stars, alongside an excavated fire pit.[21]

Life was just as basic in the towns: Lamar was entirely a tent city in 1886; the first building in Julesburg in 1886 was a dug-out saloon; and in Flagler in 1888 the grocery store was a tent, and the other businesses operated out of wagons.[22]

A dug-out, frequently referred to in the Colorado interviews as "three up and three down," or a cave hollowed out of a hillside, might serve as the next temporary home until a more substantial sod structure could be built. These sufficed in the short run, unless, like James Dawson of Sedgwick County, you built your dug-out in a low lying area, and watched it fill up with water when it rained. After the sod house was built, the dugout was relegated to use as a cellar, convenient for storing potatoes.[23]

The shortgrass country, with its thickly matted turf, was the true sod house frontier (fig. 23). Farther east, in the mixed and tallgrass prairie, sod houses were scarcer because the sod under bunch grasses like the bluestems didn't cohere as solidly as buffalo and grama grass sod (though they were sometimes used), and there was also more timber for construction. Moreover, the light grasshopper plow, which cut long uniform strips of sod much more effectively than a spade, did not come into general use until the 1880s, by which time much of the tallgrass and mixed grass prairie had already been turned over.[24]

There were various ways to build a sod house. S. S. Worley, who seemed to know just about everything about pioneering, gave a detailed account of how it was done in Phillips County. In 1886 every building in Phillips County was made of sod, either around a dug-out floor, or rising directly off the cleared surface of the earth. The sod houses faced east to catch the warmth and light of the sun, just like the Indians' earth lodges before them. Typically they were a single room, about twelve feet by fourteen feet in size, with a height of six feet at the eaves. There was no space for privacy; James Dawson recalled that there was nowhere to change out of work clothes if unexpected company arrived. Sometimes sheets were hung, closing off a corner, giving at least an illusion of privacy.[25]

The site for the sod had to be chosen carefully, ideally a moist surface depression where the grass was thick and the soil bound tightly in its wiry roots. Stiff clay soils were ideal, and loose, sandy soils did not work well. The grasshopper plow, which Worley said was "so light you could carry it with one hand," turned the sod over into three- or four-inch slabs that were then cut into bricks about two feet long. This "prairie marble" was

24. G. W. Franklin Farm. Source: Nebraska State Historical Society. RG3614. PH: 4–1.
Courtesy Nebraska State Historical Society.

laid grass-side down in a double wall. As the layers were added, the joints
were filled with soil and the surface pounded with a spade. Transverse
layers were interjected to stabilize the walls. Spaces were left for windows
and a door. The roof, preferably made of a foundation of two-by-fours,
two thicknesses of tar paper, and a layer of sod, grass-side down, was generally hipped, extending about a foot beyond the walls. It was not unusual
to see grass and cactus sprouting from the roof. Lumber was needed also
for the door and window frames, for the door itself, and, if economically
feasible, for the floor too. Stables, sheds, and corral walls were often built
of sod.[26]

Most settlers were new to this construction challenge, and sometimes
it took a few attempts to get it right. Luella Belle McKenzie, who settled
in Kit Carson County with her parents in 1889, remembered waking up
under a blanket of snow after the wind had stripped the tar paper from
the roof. George Washington Franklin spent his first months on the flats
of Perkins County building a sod house. He finished covering the roof
and installing the door and window frames (using willow he hauled from
Stinking Water Creek, ten miles away) just in time for winter. He was so

proud of his accomplishment that he took a photograph of it, standing lonely and forlorn on the flat, treeless prairie (fig. 24). But despite his best efforts, and the thermal benefits of thick sod walls, his house was "dripping and cold" throughout the long winter months.[27]

The settlers strained to make their rude sod houses livable. The landscape of the High Plains was soon speckled with lime pits, and the interior walls of the sod houses were whitewashed, camouflaging the reality that the settlers were living in the earth. They were thankful for such small embellishments. James Herbert Priest, a settler near Hoyt in 1887, thought that his sod house, with its lime walls and wooden floor, was a "pretty good place to live." Wallace Hoze Wilcok nostalgically recalled, "we never had prettier walls than those were, for when the lamp was lighted the walls sparkled as tho' there were specks of gold or silver in them." Sometimes the walls were covered with newspaper, which provided another thermal layer and which, other than the Bible, might be the only reading material on hand.[28]

In northeastern Colorado in the early days, the lumber for the roof, door, window frames, and floor had to be hauled from Haigler, Nebraska. This is how James Herbert Priest made his living. Given the expense involved, the boards for the floor of the sod house were often sacrificed. The Jacober family from Russia, for example, was too poor to cover the floor. So Mrs. Jacober mixed clay and straw and laid a "nice clean floor" that swept easily and hardened so thoroughly that "you couldn't break it with a hatchet." Like many others, Cynthia Boyles covered the dirt below with an old rag carpet.[29]

Inside, in addition to the essential stove, there might be a clock shelf that also held a looking glass, a dry goods box pegged to the wall that served as a cupboard, a homemade table with cracker boxes for stools, an improvised bed raised on two-by-four-inch boards, a couple of cheap comforters, and pillows made of flour sacks stuffed with feathers from the geese that passed through in spring and fall. Wallace Hoze Wilcok had enough money to buy six chairs in Haigler. His family, practicing enduring frugality, was still using them forty-seven years later.[30]

The first schools and churches were also built of sod. In Kit Carson County, a sod schoolhouse was communally built near Sandy Creek, with the money for a board roof, window and door frames, and door being raised by "popular subscription." The humble structure was soon filled with thirty-three students and a woman teacher and was also used for church services, Sunday school, the literary society, spelling bees, singing school, and plays.[31]

These sod structures were looked upon as temporary expedients, merely adequate until there were resources to build a frame house. Temporary could be a long time, however. Reuben Brammeier, who homesteaded six miles southwest of Burlington in 1887, lived in his sod house until 1926, when he finally replaced it with a frame building.[32]

Frame houses—lighter, cleaner, and more respectable, but not necessarily warmer—were often no bigger than the previous sod house. Harry Wells's family of six "lived comfortably," he claimed, in a twelve-by-fourteen-foot frame house near Wray. Some were considerably larger. James B. McCombs, who settled with his sister on adjacent claims near Siebert in 1888, built an elongated forty-five-by-fourteen-foot structure, part dugout and part frame, with three rooms. The house overlapped his sister's claim, presumably satisfying the residency requirements of the Homestead Act for both settlers with a single (but impressive) improvement.[33]

The new frame house dispensed with the dirt and stigma of the sod house, but it did not necessarily signify comfort. Mrs. Hans Christiansen, newly married and settled on a claim near Wray in 1892, described how her eleven-by-thirteen-foot frame home was set on a foundation of four rocks, and when a high wind blew (which was often in this, the windiest part of the country), it shifted around and had to be recentered.[34]

There was some variation in this landscape of meager homes. Log cabins were built along the Republican, where cottonwoods and willows grew in more abundance. Some settlers built homes from railroad ties taken from abandoned tracks; others built solid flagstone houses, using rocks picked up from stream beds and outcrops. Adobe structures of baked clay bricks were also represented, a Hispanic system of construction that long predated the American presence in the region. Oliver Graham of rural Wray was fortunate to inherit such an adobe house on his purchased relinquishment.[35]

Brick structures soon appeared in the towns. Both Yuma and Burlington, for example, established brickyards at local clay pits on the edge of town. Yuma had four substantial brick blocks by 1890, with three of the buildings two stories high. But the towns consisted mainly of small frame buildings, which baked as dry as bone in the heat of the summer and posed a real fire hazard. Nearly all of Yuma's buildings had "burned like candles" on August 9, 1887, forcing the town to begin anew.[36] Frame buildings could be erected quickly, in a matter of two or three days, but they could be destroyed instantaneously, as if to emphasize the tenuous hold of humanity on the formidable plains.

Subsistence

Settlers, limited in resources and, even if they came all the way by railroad, limited in the amount of possessions, water, and food they could carry, could only bring so much into the Rainbelt. But being "well set up" was important, because it would be at least nine months (if they came in the fall), or in times of drought much longer, before a harvest yielding food or income could be reaped.

Basic possessions that settlers brought into the Rainbelt were bedding, utensils, and clothes, and the bare essentials of food were cornmeal and flour. The Jacober family came into eastern Colorado with only three sacks of cornmeal. They lived on corn mush, without salt or milk, through the entire first winter of 1892–93. Angelina Fuller and her family, who came directly from Illinois to Kit Carson County in 1888, were only slightly better off. They brought in beans, as well as cornmeal, and subsisted for months on a spare diet of fried mush for breakfast and supper, with beans for the midday meal. Flora Ferris, who settled with her large extended family (they came west in a covered wagon) nine miles north of Vona in Kit Carson County in the fall of 1887, ran short of flour before the winter was over. She was obliged to ration the food: the children and the parents ate corn mush three times a day, while the flour was reserved to make biscuits for the grandparents.[37]

Many settlers also came in with dried meat. Charles Albert Yersin, who brought his wife and three children to what he described as "a most dreary and desolate wilderness," forty miles out of Cheyenne Wells in 1888, had butchered six hogs before he left Missouri, so they were able to start pioneering with a good store of a thousand pounds of salted pork. Similarly, Sarah Blakeman, traveling with her children in 1892 to join her husband (who typically had gone out the year before to get the claim established), brought with her the meat and lard from three butchered hogs. The cattlemen who were already in the Rainbelt were much better off in this regard, of course, because they had an immediate source of meat. They rarely ate their own cattle, however, but did not hesitate to kill "mavericks" that had strayed from other outfits. This was standard practice, according to John G. Abbot, and regarded as "turn about fair play."[38]

A person was very "well set up" indeed if, like Minnie Chase of Friend (a Quaker colony in Kit Carson County), she could afford to bring in "canned foodstuffs." These kept the Chase family going for four months. But canned food and coffee (which sold at the time for twenty-five cents for a two-pound bag) were generally regarded as luxuries that were only brought out when company arrived.[39]

Settlers were wise to bring poultry and cows with them, or else acquire them as soon as possible. Meat, butter, eggs, milk, and cream diversified and fortified the spare frontier diet. They were also a source of income. Eggs and butter sold in town at the going rate of six cents a dozen or pound. In dry years this might be the only income for the household, and because they were the wife's responsibility, she would be the main breadwinner for extended periods of time. More often, eggs and butter were themselves a medium of exchange, bartered for other foods, clothing, or services, like digging a well or breaking the prairie. In general, this was a barter economy: George McConley was only exaggerating a little when he said, "We had little use for money except to pay taxes."[40]

The importance of dairy products to frontier subsistence was highlighted by extension agent Payne in a bulletin entitled *Advice to Plains Settlers*. The first two items on Payne's essential list had to do with poultry and cows:

> First. If you have a milk cow give her the best care possible, and get as many as you can. Sell cream or make good butter or cheese. Sod cowhouses are within reach of all who can work.
>
> Second. Keep as many hens as you can take care of. Feed well and protect from coyotes and other beasts of prey.[41]

Some settlers seemed to have taken this advice to heart: the Census of Agriculture reported that 80,369 pounds of butter were produced in Yuma County (population 2,596) in 1890, and 83,033 pounds in Phillips County (population 2,642).[42] When hard times came in the 1890s, cows and chickens were often the difference between those who managed to stay in the Rainbelt and those who fled.

Once a successful harvest was in, settlers' diets were enhanced by fresh or parched corn, sorghum molasses (3,344 gallons were processed in Yuma County in 1890), potatoes (Yuma County produced 31,238 bushels in 1890), melons, and a wide variety of garden vegetables. Payne, for example, wrote that his family had "many meals consisting only of whipped cream and popcorn," which he regarded not as a deprivation but as a luxury. Income from selling corn, rye, oats, flax, hay, and spring and winter wheat might even be used for something special, such as dried fruits from a Montgomery Ward catalog or, after 1893, a Sears-Roebuck catalog.[43] But successful harvests were few and far between in the Rainbelt, and when the crops failed settlers fell back on living off the land.

The options for living off the land in 1890 were few. The bison herds, the resource that had sustained Plains Indians for millennia as well as settlers in the 1860s and 1870s, were gone by 1890, though the land was still white with their bones. These were collected and carted to railroad stations, where they brought anywhere from eight to sixteen dollars a ton (they were processed for use as fertilizer). Harry Wells remembered seeing a forty-foot-high mountain of bones at the Wray railroad station.[44] Bison were still providing subsistence long after the herds were gone.

There are many versions of the "last bison herd" in eastern Colorado. James Herbert Priest saw a herd of twenty-five near Hoyt in 1887. That same year, William Melvin Long just missed seeing "the last bison in Kit Carson County," which ran across his property only minutes after he had left to pick up supplies in Jacqua. His neighbors shot the bison, and everyone shared in the feast. Also in 1887, which really does seem to have been the last year of the bison in eastern Colorado, Auram McElfresh of eastern Arapahoe County was startled to see six bison run by his sod house. He and his neighbors hunted them down, and shot all but one, perhaps the lone survivor of the immense herds that only recently had thundered over this part of the Plains.[45]

Geese and ducks were shot as they migrated through in multitudes in spring and fall. Trout, according to W. C. Grigsby of Yuma County, were a "God-send" in dry years when all crops failed but there still were pools of water. Antelope were plentiful: in Sedgwick County, Charles Morgan reported that they were a "welcome change" to a bland diet, and when one was shot "all the bachelors" were invited to a meal. George Washington Franklin even invited his fellow bachelors to share a grouse with him, which he had clubbed to death after the unfortunate bird flew into his sod house. This communal sharing, a form of hospitality that was also pragmatic (a neighbor might have meat when you had none), was something the Plains Indians would have well understood. They would also have understood the settlers' gathering of sandcherries and chokecherries from the sand hills areas and of Indian tea herb (Greenthread), which was used as a poor substitute for coffee.[46]

Settlers found other ways to add meat to the standard diet of corn mush and potatoes. Franklin, for example, occasionally butchered a hog or sheep (he used the fat to waterproof his boots), and he sometimes received a share of beef for helping a neighbor butcher a cow. Settlers also obtained meat by rustling cattle that had strayed onto their property, a practice that seems to have been almost tolerated. Stealing someone's horse, on the other hand, was a capital offense. Horses were expensive (a good one might cost a hundred dollars) and essential in this land of great distances. A horse thief might end up hanging from a telegraph pole, one of the only vertical options in a country devoid of trees.[47]

The only meat that the poverty-stricken Jacober family saw came from rabbits that the children extracted from warrens using barbed wire. But as Mr. Jacober pointed out, "rabbits did not go far for a hungry bunch of children." Jacober told a story about going to town with two neighbors to get feed for the chickens. They put together twenty-five cents and bought a small amount. Mrs. Jacober mixed the feed with flour to make it go further. In the deprived fall of 1894, she got "real meat hungry," and killed two of the chickens. But as a result of the chickens' diluted diet, they were "too poor" even to cook. The hogs were so undernourished that Mrs. Jacober worried about the safety of the children.[48]

In the absence of trees, fuel was another subsistence challenge. Coal was available at railroad depots, but its cost was beyond the reach of most settlers. Reuben Brammeier and his brother procured coal in another way: in the dry fall of 1890, when their crops were "very short," they traveled for days along the Union Pacific tracks, collecting two wagons worth of coal that had dropped from the trains.[49]

Corn cobs, sagebrush, and soapweed were also burned in sod house stoves, but it was cattle dung (and aging bison dung), collected by the women and children, that was the mainstay fuel for cooking and heating. In the winter of 1889–90, according to James William Cody, buffalo chips were the "only fuel" in the entire eastern part of Arapahoe County. It was always evident when a woman was new in the country, Charles Morgan explained: at first she wore gloves to pick up the dung; after a while she dispensed with the gloves and washed her hands afterward; eventually she didn't bother to wash her hands.[50]

Because farming was so unreliable, either because of drought, low commodity prices, or both, settlers spread their subsistence base across the region and across the occupational spectrum. Men often returned to eastern Nebraska and Kansas to harvest crops, and it was common practice for entire families to go west to Greeley (which had been a center of irrigation agriculture ever since Horace Greeley established the Union Colony there in 1870) to pick potatoes in the fall and help harvest other crops. Harry Wells and his neighbor Glenn Bolander even took a steam-operated threshing machine to Greeley. They were doing well, making an amazing seventy-five dollars a day until someone, resenting the competition, blew up the machine.[51]

There was money to be made cultivating and planting timber claims for absentee owners, to comply with the law that stipulated that thousands of trees had to be cultivated on ten acres over eight years before title could be received. Digging wells, building and painting houses in town, collecting bounties on slain wolves and coyotes, and hauling crops, supplies, and water also brought in money. Eta Shannon recounted how her large Irish family managed to get by in diverse ways in Logan County: "By milking a few cows, hauling a few pounds of soft butter to Iliff, taking care of cattle on the shares [ranges], father and brother working on the railroad section for $1.25 per day, going to Ogallala and Kearney, Nebraska to shuck corn; to Greeley to dig potatoes in the fall; working in the mines of the Rockies; older sisters working in Sterling for $3.50 a week . . . by all these means, I say, we existed."[52]

Settlers who had a steady salary were in a much better position: "That's what made the difference from the poorer families," explained Martha Gilmore Lundy, whose husband worked for most of the year in Denver. Nellie Buchanan made the same point, that they were "better off than most," because they had a salary. Her husband was employed as a lineman on the Rock Island Railroad.[53]

There were various ways to earn a salary. An ordinary cowpuncher on a ranch made about twenty-five dollars a month, though top hands were paid as much as seventy-five dollars for a month's work. William Henry Yale's father ran the Yale Post Office from the family dugout and earned three hundred dollars a year for delivering mail from Jacqua, Kansas, to Friend, Colorado. "Having the mail contract," Yale said, "gave us money to live on, and we did not suffer the hardships that others did." Tom Jenkins's job with the Union Pacific brought in forty-five dollars a month, and William Arthur Richards was paid twenty-five dollars a month for teaching school in rural Kit Carson County. C. W. Hudgel, depot agent for the Burlington and Missouri, was reputedly the "highest paid man in Wray," with sixty-five dollars a month. Charles Albert Yersin gave up farming when his crops failed "year after year" and became a school teacher, and as the only ordained minister in Kit Carson County, he also earned money conducting weddings and funerals.[54]

Subsistence in the towns was based on providing goods and services to surrounding farmers and ranchers, as well as to railroaders and cattle-men who were working through the area. Starting in 1885, Peter Peter-son ran the dry goods store in Sterling, providing provisions on extended credit, because of the lack of money in the country. In summer the trail herds would come through, and he would be bought out. Peterson was paid "with checks written on brown wrapping paper," which he cashed in Ogallala "without any problem."[55]

Similarly, C. C. Huddleston, proprietor of the hardware store in La-mar, told how the trail outfits would spend two thousand dollars on clothes and supplies within a few hours. He also remembered the boom-ing business as settlers flocked in from 1886–89, when "goods seldom got out of the boxes and onto the shelves." Then, with the drought of 1890, "everything fell flat." The merchants, inextricably tied to the fortunes of the farmers and ranchers, were just as much at the mercy of drought.[56]

Elmer Harrison and his wife made their living by running the Mont-ezuma Hotel in Burlington. This was a two-story frame structure, com-plete with a dining room and twelve bedrooms upstairs, each with a wash bowl and a pitcher. Most rooms cost twenty-five cents a night, but a few, reserved for the "better-off travelling man," cost twice as much. Wheat and hay haulers slept in the hay loft above the horse stalls for a few cents a night.[57]

There was much switching and combining of occupations as settlers tried to make a living. George Washington Franklin, for example, did ev-erything right as a farmer, but still he failed. He used his team of horses to

25. Wallace v. Elsie baseball game, Elsie, Perkins County, Nebraska. Source: Nebraska State Historical Society. RG3614. PH: 4–3. Courtesy, Nebraska State Historical Society.

plow deeply, to allow the moisture to infiltrate and avoid evaporation; he cultivated only a few acres at a time, so he always had a sod crop; he diversified, raising pigs, sheep, and chickens, and planting an orchard of fruit trees and bushes; he grew corn, squash, melons, beans, and potatoes in his garden; and he tried apiculture, which was highly touted in the agricultural journals of the time. Franklin saw some success, as in 1889, when he harvested so much wheat, flax, millet, rye, oats, and potatoes that he had to store the bounty in his crowded sod house. But then came the drought of 1890, and he retreated to Iowa.

When he came back to the Rainbelt in 1892 it was as an aspiring photographer. He still did some farming, but much of his land was rented out to neighbors. He took out an advertisement in the *Elsie Journal* and opened a gallery on Elsie's main street, which he insured for $125, at a cost of $4. He started canvassing the surrounding county for customers and was paid to photograph the Elsie and Wallace baseball game, with the town of Elsie in the background (fig. 25). He placed this photograph in his shop window, hoping to entice customers. But his receipts did not cover his expenses, and within a month he had dismantled his studio, returned the construction lumber to the yard, and managed to retrieve $1.25 of his insurance payment.

Franklin continued taking photographs, using a tent next to his sod house as a makeshift studio (fig. 26). He recorded in his diary that he was getting "considerable photo work" during the winter of 1892–93. He took his tent to Madrid and Palisade, widening his trade area. He photographed schoolhouses, with their assembled teachers and students (fig. 27), baptisms, old settlers' reunions, "Peter Lingman's sod with 6 people," and "Ed Sanders' white rats" (which he couldn't get quite right, and besides, one of them "got sun struck" and died). But it was all to no avail. These frontier communities were overrun with photographers, and Franklin couldn't make a living. His total worth in 1893, after eight years of pioneering, was $96.[58]

The Rainbelt was a place and a past defined by austerity and poverty. There were some rich people, like Abner Baker, the "father of Fort Morgan," who made money by speculating on irrigation along the South Platte. But they were the exception. More typical was Wallace Hoze Wilcok, whose first taxes in Kit Carson County (assessed on the worth of his property) come to twenty-five cents. In total, the first tax assessment in Kit Carson County, in 1889, identified 1,904 horses, 217 mules, 2,239 cattle, 5 sheep, 584 swine, 57 musical instruments, 181 clocks and watches, and 742 "carriages of every description," not much in the way of possessions for 2,596 people.[59]

The very clothes the settlers wore expressed their poverty. The men, dressed in overalls made by a wife or mother, all looked the same. So did the women: "They were apt to look very much alike," Susan Tucker recalled, "because the storekeeper would get one bolt of gingham and they would all have dresses from it." A woman who wore a calico dress, with fashionable "leg o' mutton sleeves," was almost flamboyant.[60]

Children often went without shoes, which must have been painful in such a spiny country. Jennie Davis, living with her family on a remote homestead sixteen miles north of Limon, related "we never wore shoes

26. Residence and photo tent on farm of G. W. Franklin, five miles east of Elsie, Perkins County, Nebraska. Source: Nebraska State Historical Society. RG 3614. PH: 4–8. Courtesy Nebraska State Historical Society.

27. Schoolhouse at Elsie, Perkins County, Nebraska. Source: Nebraska State Historical Society. RG3614. PH: 4–02. Courtesy Nebraska State Historical Society.

when the weather was warm enough to save on them." In his interview in 1934, Elias Griffith Davis, whose father homesteaded on the upper Republican in Kit Carson County in 1885, still seemed mortified by the memory of being forced to wear his mother's button-up shoes to go to town, because he had none of his own.[61]

The Jacober family was probably representative of this pervasive regional poverty. They were so poor that Mrs. Jacober cut up the dresses she had brought west to make clothes for the children. She did laundry for a year without soap, because they could not afford it. And the children had to stay in bed while their meager trappings of barely washed clothes dried on the prairie.[62] But the Jacobers and many of their scattered neighbors managed to get by. After all, they had been poor all their lives.

Rhythms of Life

Settlers quickly established routines aimed at surviving, and hopefully prospering, in the Rainbelt. Much of the time early on was spent on the basics of hauling water, devising shelter, and breaking twenty or forty acres of prairie to plant corn, spring (and to a lesser extent, winter) wheat, rye, oats, and potatoes. The cycle of farming ran from March, when the land was plowed and harrowed in preparation for spring planting, to the harvest, beginning in July with winter wheat, and continuing through the fall. There was less to do in the winter, when the men tended to seek work elsewhere, but looking after children, hogs, and cows, as well as constant daily chores, kept the women busy. However, even dairy farming slacked off in winter, because range cows could only be milked for five or six months of the year (unless specifically trained to produce longer), and it made sense to concentrate the activity in summer when forage and milk were plentiful. Winter was also the slack time in the cattleman's year. The hands were paid off until spring, except for a skeleton crew.[63]

Gradually a social framework of organized counties, schools, and churches was established, but life remained attenuated, spread out over vast distances, and solitude was its defining characteristic. It was a full two years before the first visitors — "a lady and her small children" — stopped by Thomas Jefferson Huntzinger's sod house in Kit Carson County. They had seen "a little black spot" on the prairie and wondered who lived there. Beforehand, Huntzinger had only "rattlesnakes, coyotes, and a few grey wolves" for company.[64]

In general, the men had wider circulation patterns than the women. Often the men would take the cattle down to the Arkansas valley for the winter months, where there was cultivated forage. It was the men who went east to harvest corn, and who moved around the region digging wells, cultivating tree claims, or working on the railroad. It was also usually the men who went to town for mail and supplies. Every six weeks, for example, Huntzinger would walk the forty miles into Akron to pick up the necessities of life. Women didn't go to town much according to Minnie Chase, who added, "What was there to go there for?"[65]

In the early years, settlers were connected to towns, and to each other, by trails that angled across the largely unfenced prairie. As Worley put it, "We were not compelled to travel east or west, north or south. . . ." Similarly, from Judge Irving Barker: "It was more to the advantage of the settler if he would just make his own trail, cutting across the prairie to his own destinations." Later, counties would issue bonds, and go into debt, to hire men to burn and grade roads along section lines, squaring off circulation patterns into the grid.[66]

The problem was that it was easy to get lost on the winding trails, even in good weather, but especially in a blizzard, when there were no straight roads to follow home and no fence line to grope along to safety. On November 7, 1885, for example, George Washington Franklin, still new to the country, went to Elsie to pick up mail and "got lost on the way home, going via Grasslie's timber claim."[67]

The trails were well used, for hauling crops and supplies for sure, but also for "visiting," the practice of stopping by a neighbor's place to socialize. Visiting was a way of life, especially on Sundays, but really at any time. It was a way to mitigate the loneliness of isolated living, an expression of the need for human connection, as explained by Sarah Pantzer of Kit Carson County in her 1934 interview: "The children of today do not know the meaning of hardship, of loneliness. We had to be content with simple things. There was little reading matter; neighbors were few and far between; we really knew how to visit."[68]

The spare diary of George Washington Franklin reveals a life of such loneliness. Sometimes his entry for the day was no more than "washed and shaved," or "rinsed two socks," or "washed overalls, they were getting moldy." His first Christmas in Perkins County (1885) passed without mention, and New Year's Eve was acknowledged only by a deflated "Guess it's after 12 at night." He spent his solitary time on his claim planting, cultivating, and harvesting his crops, tending to his hogs, chickens, and cows, and in general "choring around." He also sewed, wrote letters, read widely, and cooked, though by his own admission he was poor at this last endeavor.

But Franklin's diary also reveals a man who was very much part of a community. Within a month of his arrival in Perkins County he had established a pattern of visiting, and receiving visitors, mainly fellow bachelors, but also families in the vicinity. They assisted each other in the fields, and together mended machinery, butchered hogs, and dug wells. The bachelors often stayed overnight, three or four of them at a time, sharing their plain food, cutting each other's hair, singing songs while sewing, playing cards, with the loser doing the dishes. It suggests a scene right out of a silent movie.

Franklin was also a good musician, and he'd take his fiddle, accordion, and mouth harp with him on his perambulations. Being able to play an instrument was a distinct social advantage on the frontier in general, a sure route to popularity. The one doctor in Kit Carson County in 1888, for example, Dr. C. A. Gillette, was known as much for his fiddle playing as for his medical skills, and he often played at dances until day break.

Franklin frequently walked or rode the five miles into Elsie, in 1888 an aspiring railroad town with a hundred people and seventeen services, from saloon to dressmaker. He would sell his crops and eggs there, pick up and send mail, and simply enjoy being around people. He was ecumenical in his church attendance, seeking company as much as religion. On a single Sunday in April 1890, he listened to sermons at three churches, Baptist, Congregational, and Methodist. He initially voted Republican, but as the clamor for agrarian reform grew in the late 1880s (a response to low commodity prices, inadequate credit, and exploitive transportation rates), he joined the Farmer's Alliance and frequently attended their meetings. In fact, together with two other settlers, he wrote the constitution for the local branch of the Alliance. Later, in the 1890s, he supported the People's Party (Populists) and voted for William Jennings Bryan in the 1896 presidential election. He participated in Sunday school and two literary societies. He might have been lonely, but he wasn't alone.[69]

Because of the frequent absences of husbands, women particularly spent a lot of time alone, or alone with the children. To a significant extent, this was a different place and a different experience for men and

women. Women's workload was heavy, and to such perennial concerns as
the kitchen, the garden, and the children (and much more) had to be added the job of farmer or rancher when the husband was gone. Nellie Buchanan, for example, stayed with her two babies on a homestead in Sherman County, Kansas, for about six months of the year, running the farm
while her husband was working as a lineman on the Rock Island Railroad. Anna Quinn operated the ranch (and looked after five children)
during the weekdays while her husband was employed as a section boss
in Flagler. Sometimes thousands of range cattle swarmed around the sod
house, sticking their horns in the walls, trampling the garden, and threat-
ening to overrun everything. Her sod house was infested with "prairie
fleas," and sometimes with rattlesnakes.[70]

Of course women were homesteaders in their own right, by virtue of
being single, widowed, divorced, or head of household. In-depth studies from various parts of the Great Plains have revealed that between 5
and 10 percent of homesteads were headed by women, with the proportion increasing as time went on. The Civil Works Administration interviews in eastern Colorado do not include examples of single women who
came west on their own to homestead. But they do include a good number of examples of women who came out with an extended family and
homesteaded in proximity to the others, and women who came out in-
tending to marry and took out a homestead next to their future husband's
homestead, prior to the event, so doubling the family land. Elizabeth Cutting Lengel had her own preemption and timber claims about two days'
journey from Burlington, but her father and brother had adjacent claims.
Whether they were the official homesteader or not, however, women often ended up running the claim.[71]

For some of the women, the hardest times were when there was nothing to do. The lack of reading material was a common lament in the settlers' interviews, and it was expressed especially by the women. Every little town had its own newspaper, but it was quickly read, and besides, it
cost money (or eggs). Women might be snowed in for days at a time with,
to quote Nellie Buchanan, "not a soul near us, not a house in sight." Even

in 1934, the abiding image in Elizabeth Cutting Lengel's memory was "how lonesome it was at nights, when the cold winds blew and the coyotes howled so mournfully." She kept the "lonesomeness" at bay by reading and sewing.[72]

For many of the settlers, the nearest doctor was more than forty miles away, so, as Jennie Davis said, "We did not dare to get sick." But dangers abounded. A simple injury could spiral out of control. George Washington Franklin, for example, had frequent "bowel complaints," and he had great difficulty getting over a finger injury in December of 1892. It remained "lame and swelled" for weeks, and he fretted over it until it was cured eventually by a salt and vinegar bandage. Death was commonplace: one bleak entry in Franklin's diary was a matter-of-fact, "neighbor's baby choked on a piece of plaster."[73]

The main threats were environmental: prairie fires, blizzards, dust storms, and rattlesnakes, all of which were commonplace. There were many sad stories, such as the one about the nine-year-old Christianson boy from Kit Carson County, who was engulfed by a dust storm and found suffocated in a canyon the next day. Or the Holyoke boy who was frostbitten and had his legs amputated below the knees. Many of the women recalled waiting anxiously at the sod house door, looking for their children to make it back from school before a blizzard blew in.[74]

Some of the original settlers spoke of murders and lynchings, though the fact that the same few stories were repeated suggests that such extremely violent events were not common. One story that seemed to have lodged in the settlers' memories was the hanging of L. R. Baker from the Cheyenne Wells water tower in 1888. Baker, known to be a "quick-tempered man," was arrested for shooting two settlers who had crossed his property on the trail from Haigler to Burlington. The sheriff put him in jail in Burlington, where an incensed mob threatened to lynch him. Under cover of night, the sheriff spirited Baker away to Cheyenne Wells, where they hoped to catch the Union Pacific train to Denver. But the train was delayed two hours, allowing the mob to catch up, and Baker was left hanging from the water tower. In 1933 James Callon Pearce, a settler near

Burlington, said the Baker hanging was the only exciting event he could remember.[75]

In general, however, the settlers did not even bother to lock their doors. Nellie Buchanan described her dispersed neighborhood as "one big family." Sarah Blakeman, also of Kit Carson County, was of the opinion that "We were happier then than folks are now, for we didn't need so much to make us contented and happy." The women, in particular perhaps, depended on each other's support: "The neighbors were kind," remembered Minnie Chase, "and a woman never hesitated to help another during sickness."[76]

Together, the women shaped many of the fundamental institutions and practices of social life, including schools and churches and how death was handled. Nellie Buchanan told a story about a neighboring family that lost its oldest child the same day another was born. The mother was distraught because she had nothing decent to bury the child in. The women in the area got together and sewed a dress. Someone built a casket, and they lined it with white cloth trimmed with lace. The "wee one" was then "all laid out," looking "like a sweet little doll." Nellie took the little casket into the bedroom where the mother had recently given birth. "I'll never forget," Nellie said, "how very grateful she was that her little darling was to be given a decent burial."[77]

At first, the dead were simply buried in the corner of a claim: "no minister, no cemetery, just a few verses, a hymn, a prayer, and the lonely prairie for a grave." But gradually the reserved sacred space of cemeteries appeared on the landscape. Martha Gilmore Lundy was responsible for creating the first cemetery in her part of Kit Carson County. She and a friend persuaded a homesteader to donate an acre of land, and they raised enough money to fence it with barbed wire, so that the coyotes and badgers wouldn't dig up the bodies.[78]

The schoolhouse was the center of social life in these far-flung communities. It also often served as a church and a community hall, hosting spelling school, literary societies, local talent plays — "Ten Nights in a Bar Room" was mentioned more than once — and dances.

There was a process to getting a school system started. Elsie Jane Hunt-zinger, for example, took it upon herself to organize the first school district in eastern Arapahoe County. She drew a map showing the distribution of homesteads in her area and sent it to the county superintendent in Denver. He selected the site for the school, which opened in a sod house for a four-month term in the summer of 1889. Typically, at first, the students would just sit on the floor, gathered around a schoolteacher with minimal training. The settlers supplied the books initially, but later they were procured by the teacher, or even sent down from school district headquarters in Denver with a prescribed curriculum. In time, schools were open for most of the year. In 1933, Luella Bell McKenzie could still, in her mind's eye, see her children setting off to walk the mile and a half to school in winter with gunny sacks wrapped around their feet for warmth. Eventually, substantial frame schoolhouses were built, such as the one at Elsie, photographed by George Washington Franklin in 1893 (fig. 27).[79]

Church services were irregular in eastern Colorado in 1890. As Nellie Buchanan explained, "People lived too far away to permit such meetings." Itinerant preachers would sweep through every now and then and deliver their fiery sermons at the schoolhouse or the railroad depot.[80]

The religious landscape emerged slowly. Even in 1892, Yuma County had no religious edifices. There were seven church organizations in the county, serving 139 members, but they must have held their meetings in the schoolhouse or rotated them around settlers' homes. Kit Carson County was a little more advanced in this regard, with two church buildings, though only four congregations with 89 members. Logan County, on the South Platte where the Burlington and Union Pacific lines converged, was less off the beaten track and home to seven church buildings and fourteen congregations with 662 members.[81] Perkins County, Nebraska, as suggested by Franklin's diary, had a denser religious geography, having been settled a little earlier.

Many of the old settlers interviewed in 1933–34, men and women alike, fondly recalled dances, invariably describing them as the "chief amusement" in their lives. According to Nellie Buchanan, it was not unusual to drive a wagon many miles, dance all night, and come back in the dawn. Like the church services, dances were held every few months in the schoolhouse or in the more substantial homes of settlers. They seemed to be most common and successful when there were cowboys around, young men who could often play the fiddle and who liked to dance. Two of the cowboys who worked for the Republican Cattle Company in the Republican valley of Kit Carson County were particularly popular fiddlers, and when they were in town, "crowds gathered for a good time." However, in Reuben Brammeier's part of the county there was "little if any dancing," because there "were no cowboys or large cattle ranches around."[82] Cowboys really did seem to have more fun.

Then there were special events, such as baseball games and croquet competitions, quite the rage at the time, that provided a good context for courting. Raising the Christmas tree in the county seat was another occasion for the community to come together. In Sedgwick County, the big event — the "Red-Letter Day" — was the Standard Sheep Company's "settlers' picnic." There were no trees for shade, so lumber was brought in from Venango, Kansas, to "build shade." Two or three hundred settlers would converge. An eight-piece band from Holyoke provided the music. People came by horse, mule, bike, wagon, and buggy. Children played Drop the Handkerchief, Blind Man's Bluff, and Ring Around the Rosy. Young people danced to such tunes as "Yankee Doodle Dandy" and "Darling Nellie Grey." Men "talked about how things should be done in this new country." Women prepared food. This was a conventional, and enduring, division of social activity on the High Plains.[83]

Another big event was the Rainbelt Farmers' Institute, the first of which was held in Yuma on January 15 and 16, 1890. Various papers advocating such matters as deep plowing and subsurface packing (to allow moisture to infiltrate the soil, but not too far), frequent stirring of the surface of the soil (to break up the capillary action that returned moisture to the atmosphere), stock breeding, and the value of fruit trees and fodder crops were solemnly presented. It was mostly men who gave the papers, although a Miss Mary L. Pratt impressed everyone by explaining how she had realized seven hundred dollars in a single year by making butter and cheese using a hand creamer that had cost two hundred dollars. Then, during the noon recess, the farmers' wives "uncovered richly filled lunch baskets, and soon the tables were covered with the products of the Rainbelt," a "crowning argument" in favor of its "fertility and prosperity."[84]

In the towns, the general store was the focal point of social convergence. In 1918, lawyer, amateur historian, and original settler John G. Abbot, wrote a nostalgic and evocative description of the old Sheedy general store in Yuma, which had been built in 1888. The occasion of the article was the demolition of this old frame building and its replacement by a two-story brick structure. Abbot saw this as community progress, but he lamented the passing of a landmark. In 1890, the store had been the main trading point for families within a forty-mile radius. Farmers and ranchers alike gathered there, men in their overalls, the women wearing the sunbonnets that were exclusively reserved for a visit to town.

Abbot described the cigars that were kept near the entrance of the store and gifted to settlers "who had paid a bill that had been months, perhaps years, accumulating." Nearby were candies, handed out to help mothers deal with fretful children. Behind the counter were shelves of sugar (twenty-two-pound bags for a dollar each), canned goods, and hanging strings of bologna sausage. Auger holes drilled in the floor held ropes of various quality, knotted to prevent them falling through to the basement, where the bulk of their length lay coiled. One aisle held men's clothes, mainly overalls, but also suits, selling at twelve to fifteen dollars each. The adjacent aisle and counters displayed calicos, percales (plain, closely woven cotton or linen fabric), ginghams, muslins, and an additional "thousand and one articles of attire and adornment." Women thronged these counters all Saturday long, chattering, laughing, and haggling with the clerks.

While their elders gossiped and bartered, elsewhere in the quieter confines of the store, young people engaged in "innocent flirtations." At noon precisely, the women opened their lunch baskets or, if they were feeling flush, spent a dime on crackers, cheese, and salami. By nightfall, only the men remained, sitting around the wood-burning stove on boxes and barrels, filling their pipes with gratis tobacco, "a loquacious group . . . settling all the questions of the day."

As he watched the old Sheedy store be demolished, and realizing that memories fade without a place to set them, Abbot quoted Charles Kingsley: "So fleet the works of men, back to the earth again, ancient and holy things fade like a dream."[85] In truth, this could stand as an epitaph for all the Rainbelters, who would soon see their dreams turn to dust in the drought and depression of the 1890s.

4

The Last Days of the Rainbelt, 1890–1896

Following the dry year of 1890, and the associated population exodus, a very wet year in 1891 and a year of sporadic but generally adequate rainfall in 1892 restored faith in the promise of the Rainbelt. In Julesburg, John G. Abbot remembered "two years of golden harvest" in 1891 and 1892, and similar recollections of halcyon days came from all around the region.[1]

Local newspapers trumpeted the success: the *Akron Pioneer*, for example, reporting on December 2, 1892, from "The Garden Spot of the Famous Rain Belt," claimed universally high soil fertility over all of Washington County and assured prospective settlers that abundant crops could be raised with "half the effort" needed to the east. The dry year of 1890 was declared an aberration.[2]

Resilient settlers came back to give it another try. George Washington Franklin, having spent two years getting by as a hired hand in western Iowa (but also learning his photography trade, as well as shorthand and telegraphy, and reading such books as *Everybody's Handbook of Electricity* — he was a tireless self-improver), harnessed up his mare, Nellie, and "started back to Nebraska." In Fort Morgan, newspaperman Lute Johnson, who had seen enough to believe that farming would only succeed with irrigation in Morgan County, was incredulous at the Rainbelters' renewable enthusiasm — at the way "they came, starved, moved out in legions, came again."[3]

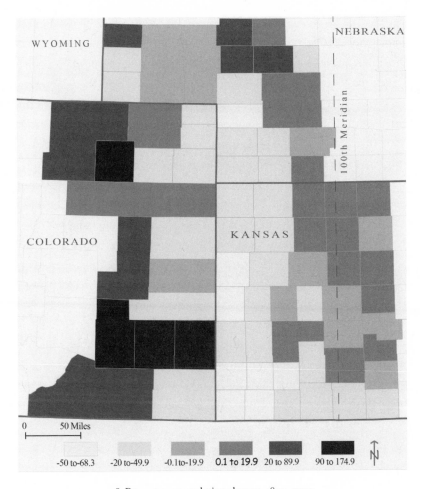

28. Percentage population change, 1890–1900.

A host of brand-new settlers also converged on the Rainbelt, filling the lands left by those who had given up for good after the 1890 drought. On New Year's Day 1892, for example, a special immigration train packed with aspiring settlers from Bloomington, Illinois, pulled into the Madrid station, not far from Franklin's place. The *Keith County News* reported approvingly that they were all "well-equipped for farming." In late February, the *Keith County News* again reported a "swelling tide of immigration interest." This was to be expected. The harvests had been so good that the generous citizens of Red Willow and Hitchcock Counties had been able to dispatch carloads of surplus corn to "the starving peasants of Russia."[4] The lines on the population graphs again trended upward (figs. 6 and 7).

But the 1890s would turn out to be a microcosm of the boom and bust syndrome that defined Great Plains settlement in the second half of the nineteenth century, and the biggest bust of all came in the dry years from 1893 through 1895. The arid climate of the southwestern United States migrated into the Rainbelt, and other equally exogenous forces pushed the region (and beyond, the nation and a good deal of the world) into deep economic depression. Settlers, still entranced by what John G. Abbot called "the lucinous memories of 1891 and 1892," tried to hang on, cultivating more land, mainly for wheat, hoping for a turnaround in weather and prices. The Colorado agricultural newspaper, *Field and Farm*, was not sanguine about their prospects, musing, "It is a strange hallucination that binds the rainbelt settlers to their chosen country."[5]

By the end of 1895, after three years of bone-dry weather, the hallucination of the Rainbelt had lost its shape and power. Settlers who could do so, left; those who couldn't afford to leave survived on charity, state aid, and their resourcefulness. By 1900, many counties in the Rainbelt had lost more than half their populations (fig. 28), and that's counting those who returned with the rains after 1896.[6]

Rain and Rainmakers

The rainfall maps for 1891, showing percentage departure from average for the growing season (when it was needed most) and for the year (figs. 29 and 30), indicate that the entire Rainbelt received ample moisture. From Julesburg (37 percent above normal for the year) to Lamar (58 percent above normal), and from Holyoke (24 percent above normal) to Madrid (58 percent above normal), abundant rains washed away the bad memories of 1890. The state meteorologist of Nebraska celebrated the "largest precipitation in 14 years of record."[7]

The next year, 1892 (figs. 31 and 32), followed suit but only after a slow start and a worrying dry period in the summer. On February 24, the *Keith County News* reported only "a fair rainfall year so far." But the rainfall

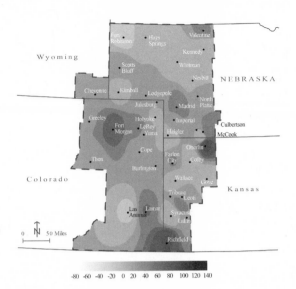

29. Percentage precipitation deviation from average for
the year, 1891.

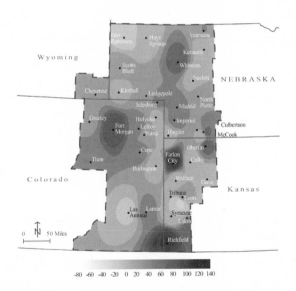

30. Percentage precipitation deviation from average for the
growing season, 1891.

picked up in the spring, especially in northeastern Colorado and south-western Nebraska. Holyoke received more than eight inches in April and May, Wray about the same, and Haigler only a little less. On June 3, the *Keith County News* ran an article with the headline, "Rain, Rain, Rain," which told how the winter wheat and rye were ripening in well-watered fields, and the spring wheat and corn were successfully planted and look-ing good.[8] It seemed like smooth sailing ahead.

Then the rain stopped. Holyoke received only 0.3 inch in June, Wray 0.4 inch, and Haigler a scant 0.2 inch. On July 17, the *McCook Times* of-fered that "a nice shower would be gladly accepted. The corn would be the better for it." By July 1, the *Keith County News* was forced to admit (lo-cal newspapers were always reluctant to broadcast bad tidings that could stifle growth) that "the last four weeks have seen no rain at all, and the fields of wheat are a total loss from the dry weather."[9] This is exactly what had happened in 1890 — a wet spring followed by a windswept, desiccat-ing summer and worthless crops. The entire region was thrown into a meteorological panic.

Despairing settlers, no longer persuaded that rainfall would increase through their own farming efforts, sought solace in a new delusion, that rainfall could be artificially produced by scientific ingenuity. In the ear-ly 1890s especially, rainmaking became a profitable enterprise for a wide array of pseudo-scientists and charlatans.

The rainmakers employed a variety of methods, from concussion to chemicals (fig. 33), and they promised moisture on demand for a price. Most famously, in 1891 and 1892 General Robert St. George Dryenforth, with congressional backing, applied his technique of detonating balloons hoisted by kites and filled with a volatile mixture of oxygen and hydro-gen in the skies over West Texas, promising that the explosions would "squeeze the water out of the air like a sponge." His initial, apparent (how could you tell if the rain fell naturally or not?) successes were widely her-alded in the press, which increased enthusiasm for rainmakers in the short run. But his eventual failures would leave him lampooned as "Gen-eral Dryhenceforth."[10]

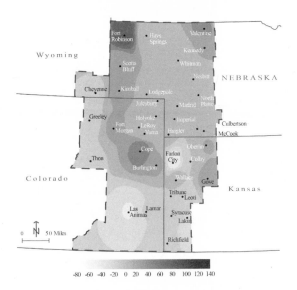

31. Percentage precipitation deviation from average for
the year, 1892.

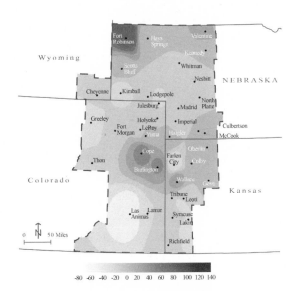

32. Percentage precipitation deviation from average for the
growing season, 1892.

THE RIVAL RAIN COMPELLERS.

FROM A BARN IN CHEYENNE.

ON THE STAKED PLAINS IN TEXAS.

"Uncle Sam" rends the heavens with his heavy artillery, while Melbourne—gentle as a dove—coaxes copious showers from his eyrie in a barn.

33. The rival rainmakers. Source: *Rocky Mountain News*, Sept. 6, 1891, 1. Denver Public Library Western History Collection.

Still, even skeptical communities worried that if rainmakers forced the moisture out of the atmosphere over neighboring towns and counties, then there would be none left for themselves. They felt they were competing for a scarce resource. So despite the lack of rain-making proof, it remained a seller's market in the early 1890s, and in Kansas especially, enterprises such as the Swisher Rain Company and the Goodland Artificial Rain Company grew to meet the demand. The most notorious of the Rainbelt "pluviculturalists" was a tall, gaunt, forty-seven-year-old Irishman called Frank Melbourne, popularly known as "Melbourne the Rain Wizard."[11]

Frank Melbourne blew through the Rainbelt like a fast-moving storm in the late summer of 1891. He claimed to have produced copious amounts of rain in arid Australia on twelve occasions and further claimed that his methods had also proven successful in New Zealand, and most recently in Canton, Ohio. He kept his procedure secret, but hinted that it involved chemicals of his own derivation that were pumped into the atmosphere by a machine small enough to be carried in a suitcase.

Melbourne landed in Cheyenne, Wyoming, on August 27, 1891, in the middle of the summer drought. He was sponsored by a local committee of leading farmers, cattlemen, businessmen, and politicians. He set up headquarters at the home of Frank Jones, a civil engineer who subsequently became his impresario, responsible for arranging contracts with communities throughout the western Plains. Melbourne's brother, Will, came along too, arranging bets on the outcome of the experiments, and thereby increasing potential profits. Melbourne was given until September 1 to produce at least one-half inch of rain for a payment of $150.

On August 31, the heaviest rainfall of the season fell in and around Cheyenne. The experiment was adjudged to have been an "unqualified success," and Melbourne was paid his money. A second performance, on September 7, also produced rain, and Melbourne's fame spread. Denver's *Rocky Mountain News* ran the headline "Melbourne Made the Sky Weep in Cheyenne" and depicted "Melburne" as Jupiter Pluvius, the reliever of droughts (fig. 34). A syndicate of local monied interests who constituted Denver's Chamber of Commerce offered the "Rain Wizard" $150 to come to town and "give proof of his power over the elements." They had a vested interest, because they were absentee owners of large tracts of land in eastern Arapahoe County. The newspaper commented: "Should Melbourne establish his claims as a rain producer he will find a dozen millionaires in Denver who will back him in reclaiming the arid wastes of eastern Arapahoe County."[12]

But Melbourne was too much in demand to take up the Denver offer, and he traveled instead to Kelton, Utah, where he earned $400 for a small amount of rain, then to Goodland, Kansas, where again he was deemed to have produced enough precipitation to be paid. He then dropped out

MELBURNE AS JUPITER PLUVIUS.

THE EARTH

CHEYENNE

He Made it Rain Yesterday in Cheyenne.

34. Melburne as Jupiter Pluvius. Source: *Rocky Mountain News*, Sept. 8, 1891, 1. Denver Public Library Western History Collection.

of sight (probably not coincidentally in the driest season of the year), only to reappear with the spring rains in 1892.

Melbourne's trajectory through the Rainbelt in 1892 — his rapid rise and fall — can be traced in the local newspapers. His name first cropped up in the *Keith County News* on December 18, 1891, in an article that discussed the "Frank Melbourne system of rainmaking." Apparently, Frank Jones was trying to set up a meeting in Cheyenne for representatives from all the Nebraska counties west of the 99th meridian. Melbourne's ambitions (and fees) were growing: he wanted ten cents an acre for his services, or two hundred thousand dollars, with no charge if he failed to make it rain. The *Keith County News* cautiously noted that there was much local interest in making the contract, but it worried that many rainmaking companies were "rackets" and insisted that Melbourne should be held to specific totals and dates, because it would make no sense to pay him for rain that would have fallen anyway.[13]

Nothing came of this grand scheme, probably because there was some precipitation in January and February of 1892 without Melbourne's help. He was said to be away working in Texas and New Mexico. But despite the "superabundance" of rain in the spring, communities were still interested in employing Melbourne as a hedge against any future drought. So when Frank Jones sent a letter to the *Keith County News* on March 18, hoping to set up a meeting in Ogallala with farmers and community leaders from southeastern Wyoming, northeastern Colorado, western Nebraska, and southwestern South Dakota, it attracted positive attention. "Now is the time to act," urged the *News*, adding, "%0s of Keith County people would pay liberally to ensure rain."[14]

Again, this plan for a major regional contract seems to have fallen through, and Melbourne reduced the scale of his ambitions. On June 15, two weeks after it had stopped raining, he contracted with Logan, Sedgwick, and Phillips Counties in the northeastern corner of Colorado to produce one to two inches of moisture, as measured in official government rain gauges at Sterling, Julesburg, and Holyoke.

Melbourne and Frank Jones came down on the Burlington from Cheyenne and set up operations in a tent at the Willard depot, sixteen miles west of Sterling. All spectators could see was a stovepipe extending out of the top of the tent, and all they could hear was a noise like "a hive of bees." Melbourne worked for forty-six hours straight at Willard, then moved his endeavor to Fleming, thirty miles west of Holyoke. Within three hours, clouds gathered and there was a single clap of thunder. It began to rain at Fleming at 5:00 p.m., and over the course of the evening, as the system moved east, there was rain at Holyoke and Julesburg, a "good shower" south of Ogallala, and a "splendid shower" at North Platte.

Because insufficient rain fell at Julesburg, Melbourne was not paid for his efforts there. The *Keith County News*, however, was persuaded, and wrote: "There can be no doubt in the minds of all reasonable thinking persons that Melbourne produced rain," and the newspaper advocated entering into a contract for his services.[15]

On June 18, 1892, a "large and enthusiastic crowd" assembled at the Keith County courthouse in Ogallala and sent Melbourne a telegram promising to pay him a thousand dollars for "rain at once." But Melbourne had already contracted with a group of eight counties — Washington, Logan, Phillips, Sedgwick, and Yuma in Colorado, and Perkins, Dundy, and Chase in Nebraska — to furnish a half inch of rain over 85 percent of their collective area within a week for a payment of two thousand dollars. It seems that Keith County had been explicitly excluded because Melbourne and Jones were upset that they were not to be paid for the rain that had fallen south of Ogallala the previous day.

"Ogallala has been lost in the shuffle," lamented the *Keith County News*, which nevertheless still held out hope that they could get Melbourne to produce a "small wetting" over their vicinity. So the county dispatched a representative, H. Carnahan, to the sand hills outside of Sterling where Melbourne and Jones were working in their tent. Carnahan was not allowed to approach the tent, but Melbourne and Jones came out to speak with him. Carnahan pleaded with them to include Keith County in their field of operations, saying that they were badly in need of rain, and that their crops would soon fail without it. But it was to no avail: Melbourne would not even consider it until his current contract was finished. Furthermore, Carnahan reported, "they seemed to want the earth for their services."[16]

By July 1, after a month without significant rain, and with the fields of wheat again "a total loss from the dry weather," the Keith County authorities were indeed willing to pay the earth for Melbourne's services. The Keith County Bank offered four thousand dollars cash for enough rainfall to ensure the success of the crops. But it was too late: Melbourne had already moved his operations east to Nuckolls County, Nebraska, the center of a block of five counties that had agreed to pay him twenty-five thousand dollars for rain. The *Keith County News* despairingly compared their present circumstance with the disaster of 1890, and also reported that S. M. Bradley, who ran the hardware store in Ogallala, had offered to detonate a hundred tons of dynamite, using the "Drysenfuith" [sic] method, if Melbourne didn't come through.[17]

Then, on July 8, 1892, there was a "good soaking rain"—almost six inches in twenty-four hours at Ogallala—and the "drought of 36 days and 12 hours" was broken. The wheat crop was saved, and the newspaper rejoiced that "people are smiling for the first time in a long while." Immediately, there was a new influx of settlers, as noted in the *Perkins County Sentinel* of Grant: "Scarcely a day passes but there are several parties arriving in search of land. If the procession continues, it will not be long before Perkins County will have a settler on nearly every quarter section."[18]

In October 1892, the *Perkins County Sentinel* expressed its skepticism concerning rainmakers, wittily writing, "They are always successful in wet weather, but when a drought was prevailing their chemicals didn't work, or the wind blew in the wrong direction, or their stove pipe wasn't tall enough." Melbourne had not produced the wet weather, and his services were no longer needed because of it. Moreover, someone discovered that Melbourne had been calibrating the timing of his experiments with the weather forecasts of the Reverend I. R. Hicks, who published the "monthly family and scientific paper," *Words and Works*, and was popularly known as the "Storm Prophet of St. Louis" (and who was surely a story in himself).[19]

One of the last mentions of Frank Melbourne in the Nebraska papers was in the *McCook Times* on September 2, 1892, where it was reported that he had failed to make it rain in Grand Island. Apparently, according to the newspaper account, during the entire contract period "the sky was as unclouded as the brow of a bride." The report humorously concluded: "It seems that if we want rain, then we will have to rely on old-fashioned means, such as arranging for picnics and holding outdoor religious services."[20] With Melbourne discredited, and with three years of drought in the offing, the heyday of the rainmakers was over.

Melbourne dropped out of sight. He briefly reappeared in the dry summer of 1893, when he failed to produce rain near Cheyenne, Wyoming, then he again disappeared from sight. In 1894 his decomposed body was found in a rundown Denver hotel. He was identifiable only by the letters "F. M." on the suitcase in which he had carried his rainmaking machine. His death was ruled a suicide.[21]

The next drought in the Rainbelt wasn't just a matter of a dry month or two, but was instead the wholesale occupation of the region by an aridity that lasted three years. The drought started in the fall of 1892 and intensified over the winter. This might be expected to a degree, because in winter cold, dry polar air masses can sit over the western Plains for weeks at a time, producing clear blue skies without the intrusion of a cloud. Still, on average, Holyoke should receive almost 7 inches of precipitation in the eight months from the beginning of September to the end of April, Madrid 6 inches, Las Animas also 6 inches, and Garden City more than 8. Instead, for those months in 1892–93, they received, respectively, 3.4 inches, 1.6 inches, 0.8 inch, and 0.9 inch. The lack of stored moisture going into the growing season was a handicap from the start.

Rainfall increased a little in the summer months of 1893 (again, as might be expected), but not sufficiently to prevent disastrously low totals for the year. The entire Rainbelt was dry, but the drought was most intense in southeastern Colorado and over the plains of western Kansas and Nebraska between Wallace and Haigler (figs. 35 and 36). On June 27, 1893, the *Rocky Mountain News* reported that "the first rain for twelve months of any consequence fell this afternoon," and farmers and cattlemen hoped it was the end of the drought. But instead it was only the beginning. Lamar and Las Animas each received only about six inches for

35. Percentage precipitation deviation from average
for the year, 1893.

36. Percentage precipitation deviation from average for the
growing season, 1893.

the year, Garden City and Wallace less than ten inches, and Haigler just a little more. All these totals were less than half the annual averages.

The drought persisted and deepened in 1894, which was the driest year on record (drier even than 1890) for many Rainbelt stations. The 1894 maps (figs. 37 and 38) show a deep canyon of aridity stretching the length of eastern Colorado from Las Animas to Julesburg. Las Animas received only 3.8 inches of precipitation in 1894, Haigler and Julesburg each 7.8 inches, Holyoke 6.5 inches, and Burlington 8.4 inches, all between one-third and one-half of what would be expected.

The rain that did fall was delivered in violent thunderstorms, and much of it ran off into the dry creek beds and away. The thunderstorms were often accompanied by hail — this is also the "Hail Belt," with more frequent events than any other part of the United States. Hail falls mainly from May to July, and so it was particularly damaging to the settlers' winter wheat, which would be maturing during those months. Corn could sometimes recover from a moderate hail storm, but wheat rarely came back after being damaged. Searing southern winds, as hot as a prairie fire, added to the environmental hazards, parching the crops and evaporating what little moisture did fall. The grass cover thinned, the midsized grasses disappearing first, until even the carpet of buffalo grass was threadbare. Prickly pear cactus and sagebrush colonized the exposed earth. The winds stirred up the soil, exposing the crop roots, and causing dust storms long before the 1930s made them famous.[22]

Some rainmakers sought to try their luck again. On September 1, 1894, a certain Henry Baker of Oregon wrote to Nebraska governor Lorenzo Crouse offering his services as a "rain producer." Baker guaranteed that for a payment of one thousand dollars he would "produce a watershed of fresh rain in quality and quantities to suit, and at any time of the year."[23] This quixotic offer was not pursued.

The year 1895 saw the drought relent, but not disappear. Its grip was loosened over southeastern Colorado and southwestern Kansas, but its hold remained tenacious in northeastern Colorado and southwestern Nebraska (figs. 39 and 40). By 1896, when average or above-average precipi-

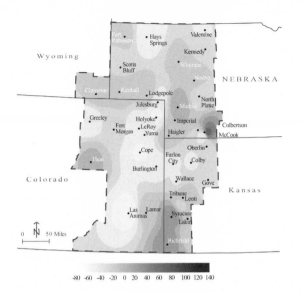

37. Percentage precipitation deviation from average for
the year, 1894.

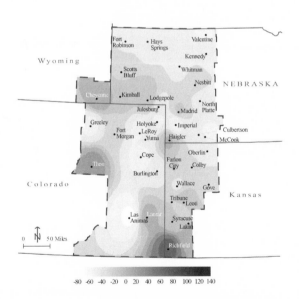

38. Percentage precipitation deviation from average for the
growing season, 1894.

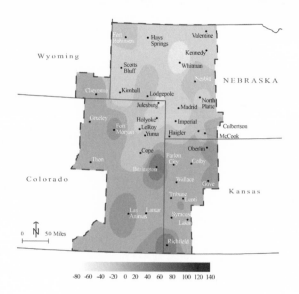

39. Percentage precipitation deviation from average for the
year, 1895.

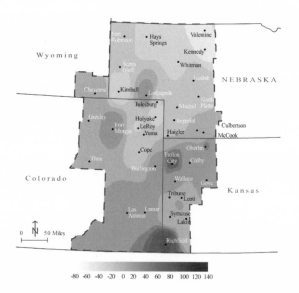

40. Percentage precipitation deviation from average for the
growing season, 1895.

tation returned, accumulated deficits amounted to nineteen inches in Las
Animas, twenty inches in Holyoke and Julesburg, and twenty-eight inches in Garden City: in each place, well over a year's worth of rain was lost
in a three-year period. Even in 1934 and 1935, in the middle of the Dust
Bowl, the area was not as dry as this, though the number of drought years
was greater during the thirties.[24]

The state agricultural boards of Kansas and Nebraska (Colorado did
not have an equivalent organization at the time) did their best to down-
play the calamity. The Kansas State Board of Agriculture euphemisti-
cally described the biennial period of 1893–94 as "one of less than usual prosperity," and stopped issuing the meteorological reports that had
been regularly featured since the 1870s. Nebraska's state meteorologist acknowledged that 1893 was a dry year, and a poor one for crops, but even
as the drought intensified in 1894 he equivocated, finding solace in imaginary long-term prospects: "To say that the 1894 crop results in Nebraska were disastrous without precedent does not mean to disparage or reflect upon ability to produce maxima in the opposite direction, and which
has been the case during our existence in a large majority of seasons." He
then reluctantly admitted that the next year, 1895, was also "one of deficient rainfall and rather high temperatures." But he must have felt vindi-
cated by the reassuring rains of 1896, when he was able to report that Nebraska had never seen such "remunerative crops." Local newspapers too,
if they didn't fail along with their communities, tended to avoid candid
discussion of the dessication.[25]

The settlers did not have the luxury of equivocation: the dry years of
1893–95 were seared into their minds, and the memories were still burning when they were interviewed forty years later. James Dawson of Sedgwick County, for example, recalled that the grass "didn't even start" in
the spring of 1893, and the winds were so hot that "one's clothes seemed
to burn the flesh."[26]

Similar descriptions came from all over the Rainbelt. In Vernon, Yuma
County, Timothy Burns told how the corn and wheat didn't even sprout
in 1893 and 1894, and he claimed that not a single bushel of either crop

was raised in the county those two years. In Logan County, according to Mary Ellen Bagley Wood, the wheat and corn seeds didn't even show above ground in 1894 and 1895. In Kit Carson County, Arthur James Pearce recalled that the grain "did not sprout until after the big rain of June 4, 1894," when it was too late, and Bob Hasart recollected that 1894 was so dry that the withered crops were not even worth harvesting for feed. Agricultural statistics, available only for Kansas on a year-by-year basis, confirm these memories: in Sherman County, for example, farmers got barely a bushel an acre for their winter wheat in 1893 and 1894, and not much more for their corn.[27]

It is possible that over time the severity of the drought had become magnified in the minds of the settlers, adding drama to what was already a dramatic event. W. C. Grigsby claimed that in Yuma County "less than one inch of rain" fell in 1894 and 1895 together. Charles Timberlake remembered eighteen months in 1893 and 1894 when there was no rain at all in Logan County. Likewise, Cary Mathias Jacober maintained that there "was not a drop of moisture" in Kit Carson County for eighteen months in 1893 and 1894. William Hastine, also from Kit Carson County, had a similar recollection that there was no rain at all for eighteen months in 1893 and 1894.[28]

The weather records, of course, as presented in the state meteorological reports of the time, show that these counties did get some rain, albeit deficient. But it is entirely possible that wide stretches of the Rainbelt were completely dry for long periods of time, because precipitation, falling in violent convectional storms, is localized on the western Plains, an event rather than a pattern.[29]

There were other environmental hazards in the dry years of 1893–95, as the experience of Timothy Burns attests. Burns, an Irishman who came to Yuma County with his wife in 1887, was initially a successful farmer. He accumulated three-quarters of a section through timber culture and preemption claims and the purchase of the mortgage of a failed settler. He was hit so badly by the drought in 1893 and 1894 that he brought in nothing from his fields, was forced to sell his cattle, and let his horses loose on the prairie to fend for themselves. Trying to start up again in 1895, Burns borrowed money to buy chickens, cattle, and hogs and planted a hundred acres of wheat and corn. He was experienced enough by this time to be prudent, so he took out hail insurance for the substantial sum of $123. Burns was completely "hailed out" before he could harvest his crops. Meanwhile, his insurance company had declared bankruptcy and suspended all payments. He lost everything.[30]

Then there were the grasshoppers, or Rocky Mountain locusts, which seemed to descend in every drought with a dreadful primordial vengeance. John G. Abbot left a particularly vivid description of the infestation in Yuma County in 1895. The grasshoppers appeared in spring as "small specks" on the ground that rose in a "cloud-like mist" when disturbed. Then they started crawling, until the earth itself looked as if it were moving. They ate the paint off buildings, the wooden handles off farm machinery, and everything that was growing above ground. They coated the railroad tracks, and when the trains ran over them, Abbot recounted, "a terrible burning smell permeated the air for miles around." Only the chickens and turkeys thrived on what was to them a bounty of food, but as a consequence their eggs and meat were unpalatable. Faced with drought, hail, grasshoppers, and much more, defeated settlers left on foot, by horseback and wagon, and, for the few who could still afford it, by rail.[31]

In the first decade of American settlement, following the land rush of 1886, there had been five seriously dry years when hardly any crops were gained. Forty years later, from a safe distance, Charles Timberlake was able to joke, "We lived in the country eight years and had a good crop every year but six." At the time it was no joke: bitter disillusioning experience, as well as increasingly authoritative weather records, were proof enough that the climate of the Rainbelt was not improving, but shifting, sometimes swerving, from year to year according to its own rules. New panaceas—irrigation, subsoiling, drought-resistant crops like kafir corn and sorghum—were now proposed by the agricultural experts as practical ways to make a living in a periodically dry place. These were sensible adjustments for sure, but they came too late for the tens of thousands of failed settlers who abandoned the Rainbelt in the 1890s.[32]

Depression and Debt

The drought by itself would have been sufficient to cause a mass exodus from the Rainbelt, but its effects were compounded by a lengthy, paralyzing economic depression that traumatized the entire nation. In the embryonic global economy of the late nineteenth century, the United States was jolted by the speculative bubble that burst in Britain (her main trading partner) in 1890–91, causing bank failures and commercial stagnation there. British and other European investment in the United States contracted, American exports to Europe declined because they were too expensive to buy, and Europeans, needing money, repatriated American securities, causing an outflow of gold. The diminishing American gold reserves made Europeans even more concerned about the viability of their investments in the United States, and more gold flowed out of the U.S. Treasury. Falling bank reserves and general economic anxiety led to a tightening of credit in the United States, curbing investment and stifling growth.[33]

At the same time, new grain-producing countries such as Argentina and Australia were increasing their exports, and this, combined with rising agricultural American productivity on ever-expanding croplands, glutted world markets and resulted in falling market prices and declining farm revenues. Wheat prices in the Rainbelt and elsewhere did not exceed a dollar a bushel for the entire decade of the 1890s and went as low as twenty cents a bushel in 1892. Corn prices were so low — often only ten to twenty cents a bushel — that it was hardly worth growing; in fact, the ears were sometimes burned in place of coal.[34]

However, many of the causes of the economic collapse of the nineties were homegrown in the United States. A key factor was the cessation of railroad construction in 1887. It would not pick up again for a decade. For years, expanding the rail network had been an engine of economic growth, accounting for as much as 20 percent of the capital expenditures of the nation. By 1887, after a frenzy of speculative building into unpopulated country, the railroads were overextended, operating at a loss, and deeply in debt. This came to a head in 1893, when the mighty Union Pacific and Santa Fe lines went into receivership. In all, 119 railroads failed that year. Associated industries like iron and steel (the railroads accounted for 90 percent of the country's rolled steel production) were carried down with them. Building construction also declined after 1893, reducing demand for a wide range of dependent products.[35]

The stock market plunged on May 5, 1893, and credit became even more difficult to obtain. Investors, distrustful of the banks, rushed to take out their cash. Small town banks quickly ran short of funds with which to pay their anxious depositors. They sent requests for reserves up the hierarchy to regional and national banks, but they too were strapped for funds. By the end of the year, nationwide 642 banks had failed, including half the banks in Denver.[36]

Economic distress in the cities (where unemployment rates reached 20 percent) and on the land led to social unrest and a popular demand for the printing of additional currency against a silver standard. One reason for this was that it would lead to inflation, making it easier to pay outstanding debts with cheaper money. The Farmers' Alliance and the Peoples' Party grew from the protest over low farm prices and in opposition to the large corporations, which increasingly dominated the economy. In this Gilded Age, there developed a yawning income gap between rich and poor that would not be matched again until the 1920s and then again in the first decade of the twenty-first century. While J. P. Morgan and other large financiers were rich enough to rescue the United States with a massive gold loan in 1895, multitudes of homeless "tramps" roamed the country and filled shelters.[37]

On May 11, 1894, workers in Pullman, a one-industry suburb of Chicago that built cars for the nation's railroads, went on strike to protest wage cuts. The American Railroad Union, 150,000 strong, came out in sympathy. Railroad traffic radiating from the hub of Chicago ground to a halt and did not resume until June, and then only after fourteen thousand state and federal troops put a bloody end to the strike.[38]

There was no hiding from the repercussions of the strike and the wholesale economic collapse even in the remote recesses of the Rainbelt. In the summer of 1894, Rainbelt towns were virtually without supplies. The settlers had little locally grown food because of the drought, so they had to buy what they needed to survive. But when the freight trains stopped running, there was no coal, sugar, coffee, soap, and many other essentials of life. Town merchants, in an effort to be self-reliant, started to pool their stocks, so if one store ran out of a particular product they could obtain it from another store (in much the same way that banks in trouble drew on other banks with surplus reserves). This refusal to import from the East until absolutely necessary only reduced the volume of rail freight further when train service resumed.[39]

It could be argued that most Rainbelt settlers were outside of the money economy. By dint of necessity they were subsistence farmers who exchanged products and services, such as eggs and labor, for goods such as flour and clothes. Moreover, in a perverse way, the drought of 1893–95, by almost eliminating crop production, made the falling wheat and corn prices irrelevant. The inescapable issue, however, was the farmers' indebtedness, and their inability to make payments on loans when there were no crops coming in, low prices for them in any case, and land that had lost all value. The towns, dependent on the farmers' trade, were deprived of their means of support, and they dwindled.

As had been the case since the 1860s, Great Plains farms and towns in the last decade of the century were heavily indebted to Eastern and European investors. The descent into indebtedness, at both the individual and county levels, deepened during the frantic boom of 1885–87 that initially populated the Rainbelt. The drought of 1887, and the hard winter that followed, ended what one contemporary writer called the "era of financial follies" and another described as a "wave of insanity sweeping over the land." There followed three or four years of perpetual property and bank failures. During the brief recovery in 1891 and 1892, a good number of delinquent mortgages were paid off, but new settlers — by this time the second or third wave — restarted the process of going into debt.

Then came the economic panic of 1893 and the drought of the mid-nineties, which ensured that the personal and regional indebtedness would continue.[40]

The 1890 federal census enumerated for each county the "percentage of encumbrance of value" for farms and towns. The data show that the highest degree of indebtedness on the Great Plains occurred in the most recently settled counties. For Kansas as a whole, mortgages amounted to 37.3 percent of the true value of farms and towns, but in the western Rainbelt counties the degree of debt to value exceeded 50 percent, and in the extreme case of Wichita County reached 73 percent. There was a similar pattern in Colorado, where the state "encumbrance of value" was 34.8 percent, but Kit Carson County, for example, was indebted to the amount of 66.4 percent of total value. And in Nebraska, where the state figure stood at 32.2 percent, indebtedness in the southwestern Rainbelt counties was more than 50 percent.[41]

The entire advance into the Rainbelt had been predicated upon going into debt. Farmers came with little or nothing and found that they couldn't make money quickly, so they took out at least one mortgage — typically for six hundred to a thousand dollars — as soon as they had acquired title by commuting their homesteads and preemptions after six months. There was a sense that they had to get established quickly, before schools and roads went in and taxes went up. Towns, dreaming of becoming commercial hubs, recklessly laid out additions in the corn fields, and "mushroom" loan companies, sprouting everywhere, rushed to issue mortgages on lots and properties. Towns also floated bonds to attract desirable businesses and to build splendid courthouses, one of which (in western Kansas) cost twenty thousand dollars and had a fireplace in every room, even though there was no wood at all in the county.[42]

Eastern and European investors, attracted by the 10 to 15 percent interest rates on the frontier (compared to 6 percent in Michigan and 8 percent in Iowa), fell over themselves trying to give the settlers money. Charles Moreau Harger, editor of the *Abilene Daily Relector* and director of the Abilene National Bank, described his desk being "piled every morning with hundreds of letters, each containing a draft asking to send a farm mortgage from Kansas and Nebraska."[43]

As more and more capital became needed, Harger explained, the local individual bankers who had previously negotiated loans (and who at least knew the real value of the land) gave way to large financial institutions, which hired agents from elsewhere to secure all the mortgages they could. The agents received a share of the 10 percent commission that accrued to the mortgage company in each transaction, so it was in their interest to issue as many mortgages as possible and to inflate the value of the land. Sometimes agents were bribed by settlers to overvalue their land and thereby increase the amount that they could borrow. The mortgage companies, as James Willis Gleed (a leading Kansas lawyer and intellectual) elaborated, "were ready to advance money upon mere acres, regardless of whether those acres were good ground or stony ground, swamp ground or sand hill," and they also backed "uncalled-for houses in premature and unpeopled townsites and additions to townsites."[44]

The farmers, willing victims, wanted to borrow as much as they could. That supposedly was the way to succeed: new machinery would increase the amount of land that could be cultivated and multiply the value of the crops that were harvested. The borrowers also contracted to pay the taxes, as well as the interest on the loan, and to keep the farm buildings insured. But in the dry, depression years of the mid-nineties they had no money, and their only remaining asset, their land, had lost all its cash value, retaining only a trading value. Farms and city properties were foreclosed and repossessed by the banks and mortgage companies, which "put them under the hammer," divesting them at a fraction of their previous value. Banks like the First National Bank and the Farmers and Merchants Bank in Grant, Perkins County, went into receivership because they couldn't pay the taxes on properties they had repossessed, and their assets were garnished by the county. According to Harger, writing in 1898, of the three hundred or so loan companies that were chartered in Kansas during the land boom of the mid-1880s, "only six stood the test of time and pulled through."[45]

The Geography of Desertion

Many of the Rainbelters did not "stand the test of time" and pull through. The region was skimmed of its population. The uplands of eastern Colorado, where the dryland farmers had thickly settled from 1887–89, were almost deserted and reverted to an open range for a scattering of cattlemen. Peter Peterson of Julesburg described how the tableland between the South Platte and Frenchmen Creek in Sedgwick and Phillips Counties, "which once boasted of having a settler on every quarter, was virtually depopulated." Even along the tracks of the Burlington and Missouri, a prime location that had been completely filed upon in the late 1880s, settlers were now eight or more miles apart.[46]

To the south, in Yuma and eastern Arapahoe Counties, the Vernon and Idalia Divides between the north and south forks of the Republican, once some of the most coveted lands, lost almost all their settlers, and many of their towns. Yuma, then the county seat of Yuma County, lost half of its population over the course of the decade, ending up in 1900 with only 139 residents. John G. Abbot described a town that was almost abandoned for periods of time in the late 1890s, its main street "a narrowing wagon truck . . . fighting back the encroachments of grass."[47]

South again, in Kit Carson County, which had been substantially settled in its eastern portions, there was a mass exodus in 1893, leaving surviving settlers like Harry Hoskin with no neighbors within eight miles. Stray horses, cattle, and hogs that had been set loose by departing settlers wandered aimlessly over the impoverished prairie, searching in vain for forage and water. Empty trains from elsewhere crossed the silent, vacant countryside, passing quickly through dusty, hollowed-out towns.[48]

Leila Shaw Walters of Kit Carson County captured the drama of this evacuation in two evocative letters she wrote to her Pennsylvania grandparents in August and October of 1894:

> A good many people have left the country, in fact nearly all that could get away, for there are so many mortgages that compel them to stay; a few families left in the night. One man who did our plastering went by moonlight,

but he left his cattle and farm machinery that were mortgaged on the prairie. His horses were so poor that they had to be helped up and one of them died in the morning; but one of our neighbors had a burro strayed in that direction, and they must have taken it and gone on and the burro has never been heard of since. A neighbor woman near here stole another woman's rocking chair. . . ."[49]

Leila's family was better off than most. Her parents had taken full advantage of the land laws in the late 1880s, acquiring 480 acres through the preemption, homestead, and timber culture acts, then selling the timber claim to incoming settlers for a good price. But even they were completely without food, because the railroads were again on strike, and all deliveries had stopped. "There isn't a sign of a vegetable here," Leila lamented, referring to Burlington. But they had learned that there was an "abundance of potatoes" in Colorado Springs and decided to take a wagon there. Remarkably, given the serious situation, they turned a trip of necessity into one of pleasure, a small five-week tour to Colorado Springs, Manitou Springs, Denver, and Greeley. As Leila wrote to her grandparents: "I think it will be nice to see the scenery."

The family packed into a covered wagon equipped with a small stove for cooking, and fell in with a procession of failed settlers heading west. "Sometimes we would get in with a train of five or ten wagons," Leila wrote, and she described the exodus as "so thick." At night, off into the distance toward the mountains, the trail was illuminated by flaring campfires.

Leila's family loaded up on potatoes at Payton, near Colorado Springs, paying the going rate of seventy-five cents for a hundred. Leila liked Colorado Springs, a "quiet town," a "spa city for the sick," a place wise enough, in her opinion, to have passed an ordinance prohibiting saloons. They drove up to Manitou Springs and were suitably impressed by the Garden of the Gods. They had intended to take the cog rail to the top of Pikes Peak, but decided against it, "the fare being too enormous in hard times." Instead, they rented horses and rode up the mountain, looking for the grave of Helen Hunt Jackson, the renowned author and activist who was buried in a private grave near the summit of Cheyenne Mountain. But "the thin air took a toll," and they turned back without finding the site. Clearly, Leila's family was more educated than most of their fellow Rainbelters.

They returned to Colorado Springs, then drove four days over hilly roads to Denver and camped in town for three days. Leila traded for a "nice new serge dress," her first new dress since she was married. They even went to the theater. Heading north again along the Rocky Mountain Front to Greeley, they drove for two days through a lush landscape of small irrigated fields of melons and tomatoes.

Then they turned east, leaving the prosperous country behind. They followed the Missouri Pacific tracks through "desolate country" to Fort Morgan, then the Burlington and Missouri tracks "through sandhills and almost a depopulated country" to Haigler, Nebraska. On their way, they encountered about thirty wagons heading to Greeley from southwestern Nebraska, western Kansas, and northeastern Colorado. "What they expect to do, I don't know," Leila wrote. "Spud picking only lasts for two weeks." But the disillusioned settlers had concluded that they "might as well starve there as here," and Leila got the impression that "they looked upon us with such disgust for coming back to this place."

Leila and her family kept moving toward home, against the tide of departing settlers. They traveled down through Cheyenne County, Kansas, and on to Lansing in eastern Arapahoe County, which, like many towns in the region, had emptied out. Then it was only forty miles back to their land near Burlington. Leila was relieved to be home, even in such hard times. The five weeks seemed to have been both "very long and very short."

Estimates of how many settlers left the Rainbelt in the 1890s vary considerably, depending on the source, and the extent of the country considered. The ecologist Frederic Clements believed that half a million people abandoned "the parched regions of the western Plains" over the course of the decade. This seems too many, given the relatively small population to begin with. Of course, his region is vaguely defined, and if central Nebraska and Kansas (which also lost population) are included, then his estimate seems more realistic. Harger claimed that 100,000 people left the western third of Kansas and Nebraska from 1887–97, which is more feasible. Census reports show more authoritatively that the counties settled in the 1886–89 land rush—essentially the two easternmost tiers in Colorado, six counties in the southwestern corner of Nebraska, and the two westernmost tiers in Kansas—lost 28,982 people from 1890 to 1900, or 38 percent of the 1890 population. The pattern in Kansas (where the 1895 state census provides an extra layer of data) was one of large losses in the first half of the decade, and slower declines from 1896 to 1900, as some of the failed settlers trickled back in. It was not unusual to see short notices in local newspapers, like the one in the *Elsie Leader* on March 5, 1896: "Frank Burns who left here one or two years ago returned last week and will farm in this country the coming season."[50]

The landscapes of abandonment were vividly captured in a series of bleak photographs taken by geologist Willard Johnson in the late 1890s (figs. 41 to 44). Perhaps Johnson had a particular affinity for these forlorn scenes. He suffered from persistent depression and ended up committing suicide in 1917. Johnson didn't say exactly where these photographs were taken, but given the focus of his hydrological research it is evident that their setting is western Kansas or eastern Colorado. Deserted towns, just recently "well-appointed" and full of hope and ambition, had been reduced, Johnson wrote, to "parallel rows of cellular excavations, with iron fire hydrants perhaps at street crossings, and occasional isolated public buildings of brick or stone from which all doors and windows and interior furnishings have been removed." The frame structures had been "carried off bodily to distant valleys for use as farm buildings." In the countryside, the ubiquitous sod farmhouses, with their roof beams removed, were quickly being reclaimed by the earth, leaving, finally, only a cistern to show that this had once been someone's home. Substantial brick schoolhouses, monuments to the failed investment in the future of a community, stood silent and alone on the deserted plain. Within the plowed

41. Abandoned town. Source: Johnson, *The High Plains and Their Utilization*, 688.

roadways of the grid, marking off square-mile sections, old cultivated fields, "amounting to millions of acres" were going back to prairie, and the leaning fence posts, dangling strands of barbed wire, were stark evidence of what Johnson described as the "utter failure" of the "agricultural experiment."[51]

It is difficult to know exactly where the departing Rainbelters went. The census does not report this, as opposed to where settlers came from, and then only at a general level of state or country. Wherever they went, they were damaged: Johnson described it as an "immigration into other regions of a class of citizens broken in spirit as well as fortune."[52]

It made some sense for ruined settlers, such as those encountered by Leila Shaw Walters, to keep heading west down the gradient of land prices and taxes, though just where the next agricultural frontier would be was not at all clear. A good number were probably absorbed into the prosperous irrigated areas along the Colorado Front Range that Leila's family had traversed. These areas, including Larimer and Weld Counties,

42. Sod house ruins. Source: Johnson, *The High Plains and Their Utilization*, 690.

substantially increased their populations in the 1890s. Certainly Denver, which added thirty thousand people from 1890 to 1900 and had a flourishing manufacturing base that employed more than sixteen thousand people by the latter date, was another likely destination. A similar western drift would also take place in eastern Montana when the initial settlement boom, prompted by the Enlarged Homestead Act of 1908 (which doubled the amount of land that could be obtained free), collapsed in the drought of 1916, and on the dried-up southern Plains in the 1930s, when the cardinal direction of long-distance migration was also to the west, this time channeled along Route 66 to California.[53] There was more to this than just economics: the West was always the setting for American dreams, an idealized country where you could be born anew.

But most settlers who quit the Rainbelt turned their wagons back to the east, seeking the support of extended families in Iowa, Missouri, and eastern Nebraska and Kansas (in contemporary parlance, "the wife's folks").

43. Cistern near sod house ruins. Source: Johnson, *The High Plains and Their Utilization*, 690.

From his heaped desk in Abilene, Charles Morgan Harger claimed that in one season alone (he doesn't say which, but in retrospect it could have been 1887–88, 1890, or any of the years from 1893–95), "eighteen thousand prairie schooners passed over the Missouri River bridge at Omaha, never to return."[54]

George Washington Franklin was one of these turnaround migrants. Franklin rented out all his Perkins County land in 1893, following the total failure of his winter wheat crop during what he called "the driest spring I ever saw." He retraced his footsteps to western Iowa, where his sister and parents lived. He toyed with the idea of heading south to Arkansas or Texas and investigated buying land on the Winnebago Reservation in northeastern Nebraska. He got by "helping out" and doing some railroad work, and in 1898 he was able to buy forty acres for nine hundred dollars in Monona County, Iowa.

44. Abandoned schoolhouse. Source: Johnson, *The High Plains and Their Utilization*, 688.

Franklin took the train back to Perkins County in the spring of 1899 and brought all his possessions — his wagon, harrow, breaking plow, stove, and trunk — back to Iowa. He cut his ties with Perkins County altogether in March, 1902, when he sold his preemption for $275, or $1.76 an acre, a profit of only $75 over the original cost, not much to show for seventeen years of hard work. Franklin eventually lived his life out as a bachelor farmer near Fort Scott, Kansas. He died there in 1935, in the middle of another drought, bitterly crying on his death bed, "I have wasted my life," a harsh self-declared epitaph for such an honest, hard-working man.[55]

Many other failed Rainbelters found work as tenant farmers in eastern Nebraska and Kansas. Willis Gleed remarked on this influx from the Rainbelt following the 1890 drought. He wrote that whereas Plains farms east of the 100th meridian were "begging for tenants" in 1890, the situation reversed in 1891, and tenants were "begging for farms."[56]

Newly opened lands in Indian Territory were another potential destination for penniless Rainbelters hoping to start over again. The opening of the "Unassigned Lands" on April 2, 1889, and of the Cherokee Strip on September 16, 1893, undoubtedly attracted settlers who had failed on the High Plains. Altogether, about seventy-five thousand settlers made the run (by wagon, horseback, bicycle, and on foot) into the Cherokee Strip from Caldwell and Arkansas City, Kansas, and Guthrie, Oklahoma. According to one newspaper account, these included thousands from western Kansas.[57]

In addition to long-distance emigration, there was also a drastic resortment of population *within* the Rainbelt. In many areas, there was movement into local towns. In about half of the Rainbelt counties that lost population, at least one incorporated place (usually the county seat) grew, suggesting that failed farmers sought the nearest opportunity to reinvent themselves. Again, this pattern of short-distance migration characterized the settlement readjustment in eastern Montana after 1916 and in the Dust Bowl on the southern Plains after 1930. So, for example, Sedgwick County, Colorado lost 322 people over the course of the decade of the nineties, but Julesburg added 169, and Sherman County, Kansas, lost 1,920 settlers from 1890 to 1900, while the county seat, Goodland, added 32. To give just a few examples from many, the Shannon family of Logan County were scorched off their land by drought and hot winds in 1892 and moved into Sterling, and Roscoe Yarnall of Kit Carson County gave up on farming in 1894 and moved into Burlington, where he and his mother ran the hotel.[58]

In counties that lost more than 40 percent of their total populations, however, even the county seats contracted, indicating a more complete, long-distance evacuation. For example, Washington County lost 46 percent of its population from 1890 to 1900, and the county seat, Akron, diminished by 47 percent. Also in northeastern Colorado, Phillips County saw its total population fall by 40 percent over the decade, and its county seat, Holyoke, declined by 31 percent. In general, the majority of counties in the heart of the Rainbelt fell into this category of wholesale population loss (fig. 28).[59]

The Rainbelt counties that gained population from 1890 to 1900 were those where irrigation was possible, mainly along the South Platte and Arkansas Rivers. Morgan and Logan Counties, for example, in northeastern Colorado, and Bent and Prowers, in southeastern Colorado, all added significant numbers of people, as did their county seats. Sedgwick County, however, also crossed by the South Platte, lost people, probably because so much water was taken out of the river above that none remained to irrigate fields there. Where irrigation acreage did increase over the decade, as in Morgan County (an increase of 125 percent) and Prowers County (2449 percent increase) there were also major gains in population. It is not that the Rainbelters would have had the money to buy irrigated lands, but they likely found laboring work, such as digging ditches or harvesting crops.[60]

It was mainly the poorest settlers who stayed in the Rainbelt. Isaac Messinger put it this way: "When a man had lost everything he had no way of leaving, so he just had to stay and make the most of it." Similarly, John G. Abbot explained that "those who stayed did so mainly because they could not afford to leave." J. E. Payne gave a fuller explanation, based on interviews with settlers in the late 1890s:

> When new settlers were constantly coming into the country times were good and poor men could live by working for those who had brought money with them. But when the hard years of 1893 and 1894 came, this source of revenue for the poor man was cut off. Most of the men who had extra riches left the country or stopped making improvements. . . . Many of the [poor] people had not enough property at that time to sell for enough money to pay their little store bills and pay their car fare to their old homes.[61]

A common response to drought and crop failure for farmers who stayed was to keep plowing even more land for wheat, in the hope that accumulating losses could be erased by one prolific harvest. Johnson tabulated this sequence in Sherman County, Kansas, for the twelve years from 1885–96. There was a steady increase in the cultivated area from 1885–89, as settlers slowly got established, then a tripling of crop acreage in 1889,

following the abundant harvests of the previous year that seemed to confirm that rainfall was increasing according to plan. The cultivated acreage was reduced by the drought of 1890, but then increased again rapidly
in the wet years of 1891 and 1892 to reach a maximum in 1893. That year
was described by Johnson as one of "desert dryness" and "complete loss,"
yet the cultivated area diminished only a little in 1894 and 1895, as settlers
tried to coax crops from the desiccated soil. In desperate straits, they even
found a use for Russian thistles, which were stacked up by the ton, sea-
soned with wheat, and used as winter feed. By 1896, however, after four
straight years of drought, planting was brought to a halt by "the exhaus-
tion of working capital."[62]

Part of the problem was that the settlers were so poor that they couldn't
afford the modern equipment — horse-drawn corn planters, disc har-
rows, listers, sub-surface cultivators — needed for progressive farming. At
best they could only scratch the ground, or even just broadcast their seeds
by hand on hard, unreceptive earth that was weed-covered or bare, hoping they would germinate following a good rain. Progressive farmers like
James McCombs of Kit Carson County were rare. "We always plowed the
ground deep," he related, "and thereby got a fairly good crop every year."
"Corn won't work," he explained, "unless you plow deep and let the moisture penetrate and be reserved for a dry spell." McCombs claimed he never failed to raise corn, whatever the year. He had the equipment, a horse-
drawn corn planter to get started, then a disc harrow to open up the soil
to air and moisture. But even McCombs could not make a living on crops
alone, so like many others who managed to "stick," he added cattle to
his operations, switched to feed crops, and succeeded by diversifying and
spreading his risks.[63]

The poorest people fell back on charity and state aid, much to the disgust of the editors at Colorado's *Field and Farm*: "On the verge of starvation from repeated failures at crop growing," the paper complained,
"they cannot be induced to leave, but ask for contributions of seed, that
they may try again the unhappy experiences of the past." *Field and Farm*
wanted to "furnish them with what might be required for their immedi-

ate and pressing wants and aid and encourage them to move elsewhere."
This was the first time (discounting the ethnic cleansing of the Indians
from their homelands), but not the last, that planned depopulation was
prescribed for the western Plains.[64]

After the drought of 1890 there was a deluge of letters and petitions
to governors, legislatures, and newspapers despairing of crop failure and
impoverishment, and pleading for aid. In early 1891 it was estimated that
fifty to one hundred families in each western Kansas county would not
be able to make it through the winter without support. From all over the
Rainbelt came heartfelt stories of deprivation and absolute starvation, of
children forced to go barefoot all winter, and women who wrapped their
feet in oil cloth or jute sack to keep them warm. There was distress in the
more settled portions of the central Plains too, but people there were better established and had more opportunities for subsistence, whereas the
settlers of the Rainbelt were no more rooted than a cottonwood.[65]

Initially the only relief came from charitable donations, which admirably flowed into the Rainbelt from all directions. Coal was donated from
the Pueblo mines, and clothes and food were delivered at no cost by the
railroads. Then in February and March of 1891, the state legislatures of
Nebraska, Kansas, and Colorado, putting aside their deep opposition to
government interference in private enterprise, appropriated funds for settler relief. In Nebraska, the legislature provided $100,000 through direct
appropriations and the sale of bonds to furnish food, clothes, fuel, and
seeds to destitute settlers, and the Kansas and Colorado legislatures followed suit with appropriations of $60,000 and $21,250, respectively. In the
debate in the Nebraska legislature, the case was convincingly made that
unless the money for aid was forthcoming, the western half of the state
would be depopulated.[66]

The state aid and the voluntary donations were administered by central relief commissions, which distributed the goods through local county
relief committees. The emphasis was on preventing starvation. The Reverend Luther B. Ludden ably headed the Nebraska Relief Commission,
supplying six to seven thousand families every four to six weeks each with

fifty pounds of flour, twenty-five pounds of corn meal, and small amounts of oatmeal, hominy, rice, and beans. Ludden would also have liked to provide the relative luxuries of tea and coffee to the elderly, but the pressing need was to relieve absolute hunger.[67]

Thanks to the relief efforts, and even more so the return of rain and good crops in 1891, the crisis was relieved. In fact, in 1892 surplus products from the relief efforts were collected by Ludden and shipped out, yet again, to the "starving peasants of Russia." Newspapers brimmed with good news — stories of government lands "going like hot cakes," towns with grand new buildings, sod houses being replaced by "ample farmhouses," cribs "bursting with corn." Then just as quickly, in the dry spring of 1893, desperate conditions returned, and with them the pleas for aid.[68]

The state relief commissions were reactivated, and the Kansas and Nebraska legislatures again raised money — one hundred thousand dollars and two hundred thousand dollars, respectively — for flour, livestock feed, coal, and fuel. The Colorado legislature also appropriated funds to buy seed for penniless farmers, but in this time of economic depression and austerity, the governor vetoed the action. Relief efforts in eastern Colorado devolved to the counties, which lacked the resources to respond. In her April 11, 1894, letter to her grandparents, Leila Shaw Walters wrote that twenty-five families in Kit Carson County were on local support, and the numbers of destitute were increasing so quickly that the county was facing bankruptcy. The county commissioners had pared the rations down to the bare necessities of flour, dried meat, potatoes, and beans. Leila finished her letter abruptly, saying that she did not want to give her grandparents "the blues."[69]

Counties continued to receive state aid in Nebraska and Kansas through 1895. Perkins County, for example, Franklin's former home, received five thousand dollars' worth of aid in 1895, mainly in the form of coal, clothing, flour, and other provisions. This was a typical profile. Charitable donations continued to flow in — shoes, clothes, cash gifts, some as small as a single cent, others substantial contributions, like the "splendid donation" of $5,525 sent to Nebraska by the *Christian Herald* of New York.[70]

There was some sentiment that the federal government should step in, the plausible argument being that settlers had been enticed into the Rainbelt through liberal land laws and subsidized railroad construction. This is how the *Nebraska State Journal* put it: "The federal government that opened up the semiarid region of western Nebraska to farmers and homesteaders has a duty to perform. . . . It should assist to prevent the suffering that has come upon so many people on account of their haste to take up lands that seem from experience hardly adapted to corn or small grains."[71]

But all that Nebraska received from Washington DC was a shipment of ninety-two thousand packets of garden seeds that were left over from the year before. Moreover, Nebraska was reminded that this was a one-time-only federal donation and not to expect it again. And, in a revealing statement concerning the complexities of states receiving federal aid, the authorities reassured Nebraska that this donation of seeds in no way reflected badly on the ability of Nebraskans to handle their own problems.[72] Federal aid for the Great Plains would not be forthcoming until the next climatic and economic disaster, in the 1930s, and then it came in large amounts and never really stopped.

The rains returned in 1896, the clouds of economic depression lifted, and the worst was over. When the dust of the dry years settled, the Rainbelt had a new geography. It was a much more sparsely populated region, with wide distances between homesteads and between towns. Throughout the western Plains, small-scale stock raising became the primary form of agriculture, with cattle grazing the opened-up range in the summer, then being brought in in winter to be sheltered and fed on Kaffir corn, sorghum, wheat, barley, hay, and, if necessary, Russian thistles. This was, in effect, a convergence of open-range cattlemen, who now recognized the benefits of growing supplementary forage crops, and wheat farmers, who had learned reluctantly that grain farming without livestock to fall back on was a risky business. There was also a new, surprisingly modern factor, promoting winter feeding: the Humane Society had dispatched agents throughout the Rainbelt looking for evidence of cruelty to cattle, such as leaving them to fend for themselves on snow-swept plains, and there were heavy fines when such cases were found.[73]

Willard Johnson was on hand to witness this rapidly changing geography:

> The great body of emigrants have either returned to the East, or have drifted further west. A small percentage has scattered along the bottom lands of the larger valleys. On the vast upland flats, however, an occasional settler remains, and he has become a stock farmer. His location is always first to be discovered by means of a windmill wheel turning above the horizon. A field of sorghum surrounds the house, and a "bunch" of cattle range within its rectangular fenced enclosure to a radius not too great for easy return to the pumping trough.[74]

Dry farming of spring and winter wheat persisted in a few small areas such as the Vernon and Idalia Divides, though yields averaged no more than eight bushels an acre. A major problem with wheat, in addition to the unreliable rainfall and hot winds, was the distance to market. The new attenuated geography meant that farmers had to haul their grain thirty or forty miles to market in Wray, Haigler, St. Francis, or Burlington, a four- or five-day round trip. Under the circumstances, Payne explained, it made good economic sense for farmers to raise crops that "could walk to market" in the form of beef cattle, or "could be condensed" by feeding dairy cattle and shipping out the low-bulk, high-value butter.

After 1896 the "mirage" of the Rainbelt, the belief that settlers could produce their own precipitation, was largely laid to rest. There was, at least temporarily, a more realistic, chastened, attitude toward farming on the western Plains. This was epitomized by the changing policy of the Kansas State Board of Agriculture, which announced in its 1896 report its intentions to become more "agricultural" and less about immigration. This amounted to an apology for its past excesses of boosterism.[75]

From that point on, the Kansas State Board of Agriculture, as well as the farm journals and experiment station experts like Payne, would advocate a more scientific farming. This involved drought-resistant crops like sorghum and Turkey Red Wheat, and new cultivation methods such as subsoil packing— to prevent moisture from penetrating too deeply, beyond the reach of roots—summer fallowing to rest the soil, stubble mulching to reduce evaporation, and fall and spring listing to allow moisture to infiltrate. These innovations would soon (1907) be codified in Hardy Webster Campbell's *Soil Culture Manual*, which became as common (and the focus of as much faith) as the Bible in settlers' homesteads. Campbell's confident argument that the problem on the western Plains was not a lack of rainfall, but an excess of evaporation, and that this could be prevented by his dry-farming methods, was also shown to be a false dream when periods of drought inevitably reoccurred. But as a human adaptation to a semiarid environment it was a major advance over the fantasies of the Rainbelt.[76]

By 1903 Payne was able to report that life in eastern Colorado was "improving rapidly." Some areas, such as the Vernon and Idalia Divides, had been fully repopulated. Payne saw that sod roofs were being replaced by shingles, and that it was rare for an old sod house to be replicated by a new one, as opposed to a frame house. Each year, he saw more people who had come to stay, and he noted that the landscape no longer had an "I want to sell out" appearance. Some farmers near Vernon and Wray were even connected by telephone. In fact, when Payne was staying overnight with one of them, "an orchestra was called up, and all on the line enjoyed a very entertaining concert."[77]

In time, and under different circumstances, the former Rainbelt would become the heart of one of the most successful grain-growing regions of the world. But the road to that success, especially early on, was strewn with the wreckage of human failure.

Epilogue

―◦◦◦―

After the Rainbelt

In many ways, life in the Rainbelt in the century or so following the settlement collapse of the 1890s has not changed much. This is still a sparsely populated land with great distances between settlements. Some areas, like the sand hills north of Wray and the dissected Arikaree valley in Yuma County have remained cattle country, and are so thinly settled that the signposts point to people, individual ranches, more often than to towns. On the flat uplands that the Rainbelters tried to settle, vast fields of winter wheat, showing bright green through the snows of spring, and golden in June before the harvest, stretch in strips to the far horizon.

In some of the heavily farmed areas, as around Idalia, farmsteads are spaced only a few miles apart, standing out as islands in a sea of grain. There is enough population here to support a K-12 school in Idalia, as well as a grain elevator, a fire station, a post office, and a few modest homes. Elsewhere there is often just wheat and not a farm to be seen. In these areas, the towns, with few people in their hinterlands, are little more than crossroads with a few ramshackle remains of buildings, no more substantial than when extension agent J. E. Payne passed through in the late 1890s.

Life in the former Rainbelt is still a significantly different experience for men and women. From 1991–96, geographer Cary W. de Wit conducted a series of interviews with women living on the High Plains of western Kansas and eastern Colorado, investigating their sense of place. He found that whereas men find the wide open spaces a liberating environment, with easy access to such outdoor activities as hunting and fishing, and enjoy the solitude and seclusion, women are commonly overwhelmed by the sheer exposure and incessant winds and stifled by restrictive roles and social isolation. Like their pioneer forebears, men continue to have more social interaction through their jobs (and more opportunities for jobs), while women, still often confined to the house, spoke of a pervasive sense of "numbing loneliness." Again, like their predecessors in the Rainbelt, women find solace and satisfaction in family and community relationships, while men tend to embrace the independence. De Wit concluded that "time has done little to change women's reactions to the Plains."[1]

The population of the Rainbelt is still poor, but it is no longer young. In Colorado as a whole, 9.3 percent of the population lives below the poverty level, but in the upland counties in the eastern part of the state the proportion who are poor ranges from 11 to 13 percent. Opportunities for jobs in the rural areas are few, and salaries for those who are employed are often low. Because of the out-migration of young adults, seeking economic and social opportunities elsewhere, the region now has a concentration of elderly. In Colorado in 2000, the average age of the population was 34.3 years, and 11.6 percent were above the age of 62. Corresponding figures for Phillips County were 39.8 years and 22 percent, and for Kiowa County, 37.9 and 20.5 percent. The average age of farmers in the counties of eastern Colorado ranges from 54 to 59 years: many young people lack the resources or the desire to follow in their parents' footsteps.[2]

Another thread in the fabric of life running from past to present is, of course, recurring drought, unpredictable yet guaranteed. There was the catastrophe of the 1930s, with 1934 the dry heart of a dry decade. Burlington received only 7.7 inches of precipitation that year, and most maps of the Dust Bowl place southwestern Kansas and southeastern Colorado (as well as the panhandles of Texas and Oklahoma) at the core of the disaster. Subsequent severe droughts occurred from 1952–57 (Burlington bottomed out at 6.18 inches of precipitation in 1954, its lowest total in more than a century of record), over much of the 1970s, and most recently from 2001–6. This last drought was so arid that no rain at all fell for more than a year in some parts of eastern Colorado, and dust storms once again blew over the land. Farmers in the Arkansas valley had to keep deepening their wells just to stay in contact with the falling water table. Across the state line in Syracuse, Kansas, desperate members of the community gathered in the high school gym to pray for rain, beseeching "Lord, we ask that you might again bless us with the beneficial rains that are so vital to our crops and our lives."[3] If the Lord answered these prayers, it was only slowly, because three more years of drought lay ahead.

There has also been a good deal of continuity in settlers' responses to the failures of the droughts and the successes of the years in between. The drought of 1893–96 had demolished the fantasy that farmers could produce their own ameliorated climate. Writing in 1908, climatologist L. G. Carpenter, in an article offering advice to yet another new generation of settlers on the Colorado Plains, admitted that "there is no method of cultivation which will manufacture moisture." Carpenter continued, "The most to be expected is to lessen the losses by evaporation." Subsequently, dry farming, augmented by increasingly sophisticated mechanization, became the new salvation.[4]

Worster, in his provocative study of the Dust Bowl, characterized the prevailing attitude of Plains' residents as "an optimism at heart fatalistic," a stubborn and naïve belief that next year would be better. Also involved was a refusal to learn from the past. High Plains farmers interviewed by Thomas Saarinen in the 1960s consistently underestimated the frequency and severity of former droughts and exaggerated the bounty of the good years. Other foundational "attitudes of mind" have also persisted over the years: that nature should be subdued and exploited in the name of progress; that short-term profit rather than long-term sustainability is the appropriate goal; and that agricultural production need not be associated with the making of homes and meaningful places.[5]

In this last regard, absentee farming has been a defining characteristic of settlement on the High Plains from the 1880s to the present. There were the absentee, mainly British, cattle kings in the 1880s, and the wealthy men in Denver who owned much of eastern Colorado in the 1890s. But it was technological innovations in agricultural mechanization and geographic mobility in the early twentieth century that allowed farmers, especially wheat farmers, to operate from a distance. In the 1930s, according to a definitive study by Leslie Hewes, about one-third of all farm operators in western Kansas were absentee, living more than a county away from their property. Most were based in central Kansas, although one, inexplicably, lived in China. By the 1950s, this "suitcase farming frontier" had moved on into eastern Colorado, where again about one-third of the farmers lived elsewhere, mainly in western Kansas. Hewes concluded that suitcase farming had become a "regional characteristic." He was right. By 2007, in Kit Carson and Kiowa Counties in eastern Colorado, and in most counties of western Kansas, about 45 percent of farmers did not live on the land they cultivated.

These absentee owners involve a new phenomenon, which was not a factor in the 1950s: corporations now account for between 5 and 15 percent of all the operators (and a larger percentage of all land farmed) in eastern Colorado and Kansas.[6] One manifestation of this is the huge hog farms, which now have a presence in every county of eastern Colorado. They can't be missed by the traveler, who will drive by mile after mile of large metal production units that together house hundreds of thousands of sows, all virtually immobilized as they are fattened for the packing plant. The metal sheds can even be seen, glinting in the sun, from thirty thousand feet on flights heading east out of Denver.

Farmers on the western High Plains, past and present, have always gambled on wheat as the best chance to make money. This was recognized in 1926 by Alvin Steinel, who was heralding the inroads that dryland farmers had made into the grazing lands of eastern Colorado ("productive capacity has been enhanced a hundred-fold"), while pointing out the risk:

Even yet, with all the progress that has been made in the development of drought-resistant crops and in methods of soil culture, there are seasons when rainfall is so scant that farmers do not get yields that pay for the labor of planting and harvesting. To offset these abnormally dry seasons, there are other years when, under normal rainfall, or better than normal, a wheat crop might sell for more than the original cost of the land. This speculative feature has its attraction in drawing settlement.[7]

So the boom and busts that had characterized nineteenth-century Plains settlement persisted into the twentieth and twenty-first centuries. They continued to be calibrated to the swings of climate, as well as to equally uncontrollable fluctuations in crop prices, which are connected ever more tightly to the success or failure of harvests in other grain-producing parts of the world, such as Australia, Argentina, China, and the Soviet Union (after 1990, Russia and the Ukraine).

The first boom after the demise of the Rainbelt came in 1907–8, following two exceedingly wet years in 1905 and 1906. For a decade, the region had remained cattle country, resting on what Payne described as "the three legs of stock, winter forage, and summer pasture." That was the way Payne wanted it to stay, a mixed-forage crop and cattle-raising economy, with additional diversification from dairy cows, poultry, and garden produce. Payne was suspicious of what he called the "exploiters of Scientific Soil Culture," believing that even with drought-resistant crops, thorough seedbed preparation, deep plowing, and subsurface packing, this was a marginal area for crops, and best left to cattle.[8]

But this was not to be. Writing in a special edition of the Colorado Agricultural Experiment Station Bulletin in 1908, Payne observed that "many settlers have taken up residence in the Plains region during the last few months who have merely enough capital to put up houses, break a few acres of sod, and live during the first six months." Other contributors to the bulletin, devoted to preparing new farmers for life on the Plains, made similar statements: "Thousands of families are coming to Colorado this spring to locate on farms. Many of them are locating in the dry land sections of the state, often on land on which a furrow has never been turned"; and "Many hundred farmers, unfamiliar with the soil and climate condi-

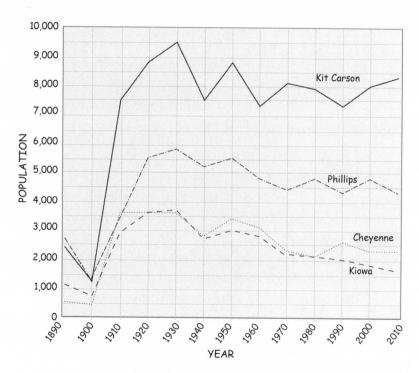

45. Population change, 1890–2010.

tions of our eastern Plains, are this year coming to make homes in eastern
Colorado, in regions where crops have not generally been grown. Many of
these settlers have but a limited amount of money and they cannot afford
a crop failure."[9] It was the boom of the late 1880s replayed: poor people,
with no reserves and no experience of farming in a periodically arid area,
banking on a chance wet year and a good wheat crop to get them started.

In subsequent years many of these settlers failed, although the steep
inclines on the population graph (fig. 45) from 1900 (or more accurately,
from 1907–8) to 1920 or 1930 indicate that a lot more people came than
left. The rural areas once again filled with farms, and towns like Yuma
and Wray awoke from their dormancy (each added more than a thousand
inhabitants from 1900 to 1920). Most upland Rainbelt counties reached
their maximum populations in the census years of 1920 or 1930. These
numbers have declined ever since.

Meanwhile, the number of farms in these counties has about halved since their peak census year of 1920, and the size of the farms has increased many times over since the settlers first took out their 160-acre homesteads and preemptions. Kit Carson County is typical: in 1920, there were 1,480 farms, with an average size of 500 acres; in 2007, there were 786 farms averaging 1,721 acres. In each upland county, one town, generally the county seat, has steadily grown in population, gathering former rural settlers who were no longer needed on farms that were increasingly mechanized.[10]

This is what happened to nearly all the old Rainbelters who were interviewed in 1933–34: they moved into nearby towns because they failed (or succeeded) on the land, and sold out; or because they wanted to be nearer a school for their children; or to seek other economic opportunities; or to retire. They invariably looked back on their Rainbelt experiences fondly, proud of the sacrifices they had made, and the hardships they had endured, in their roles as pioneer settlers.[11]

The early twentieth-century boom was sustained during World War I, when grain prices soared, and it was profitable as well as patriotic to grow wheat. Even when crop prices fell in the 1920s, farmers kept turning over the sod for wheat, and going into debt to buy their brand new Ford trucks, bright green John Deere tractors, and labor-saving combine harvesters. By 1926 there were no government homesteads left to claim in eastern Colorado.[12]

Then came the big bust of the 1930s. County populations fell for the first time since the 1890s (fig. 45). As in the 1890s, however, many of the towns, including Wray, Yuma, and Cheyenne Wells, actually added people during the 1930s, as failed settlers looked for alternative local opportunities. Again, as in the 1890s drought, farmers continued to plant wheat in the swirling dust. The Great Plains Committee, a panel of experts appointed to investigate the causes of the Dust Bowl and give recommendations for the future, were astonished to learn that 1936, one of the two peak years for dust storms, was also the maximum year to that date of planted wheat acreage.

Whatever their misgivings, the committee understood the incentive, realizing that "one-crop farming," while risky, was the farmer's best chance for immediate success:

> Undependable as is wheat in the drier portions of [the Great Plains], he has a better chance of producing a salable product from it than almost any other crop. It is, furthermore, a very economical crop to produce; it is better adapted than any other crop to machine methods and can be planted and harvested on greater acreages by one operator. But when there is a failure of wheat, which is all too frequent, the Plains farmer is left with no income whatsoever, while his fixed costs remain essentially the same.[13]

So, despite the hard lessons of the 1930s, when the rains returned in 1941 and 1942 (which were exceedingly wet years, as was 1944), and with the renewed stimulus of high wartime grain prices, the land was fully put back into wheat. The increase of land in crops, mainly wheat, in Kit Carson County from 1939–54, for example, was an extraordinary 328 percent.[14] This cycle of drought and crop failure, followed by rains and the expansion of wheat acreage, has continued right through to the present.

But after the bust of the 1930s, there were two very important differences in the human geography of the Rainbelt. First, the region became one of the most important concentrations of irrigated farming in the United States. And second, it became heavily dependent on federal payments to keep land out of agricultural production and to compensate for adverse environmental and economic conditions. From the 1930s on, then, while the booms were just as high, the busts were cushioned.

A national map of irrigated acreage in 1950 would show very little development on the High Plains. There was relatively small-scale ditch and canal irrigation along the Arkansas and South Platte Rivers, linking up with the more fully developed zone of irrigated farming along the Rocky Mountain Front from Colorado Springs to Greeley. Because of the stabilizing advantages of irrigation (but also because they are transportation corridors), valley counties like Logan in the north and Prowers in the south have shown almost uninterrupted gains in population since 1890.

A contemporary national map of irrigated acreage, or even one in 1980, would show a very different picture. From the Platte valley in the north, through the Rainbelt counties of eastern Colorado and western Kansas, and down through the Panhandle of Oklahoma to West Texas lies an area of intensive irrigation where, typically, between 10 and 40 percent of the farmland is artificially watered via tens of thousands of wells sunk down into the subterranean depths of the Ogallala Aquifer.[15]

For half a century or more, this development had not been considered feasible. In 1901–2 Willard Johnson concluded that irrigation on the uplands of the High Plains was "impossible," beyond the few acres that could be watered from a windmill. In 1936 the Great Plains Committee came to much the same conclusion and confidently predicted that "irrigation at best can cause only minor changes in the economic life of the Great Plains," because, it claimed, the underground waters were too "shallow" to serve more than domestic uses.[16]

The committee was quickly proven wrong. By 1940 the innovation of turbine pumps allowed water to be economically extracted from depths of three hundred feet or more. The subsequent innovation of center pivots in the 1970s increased the scale of extraction to a rate of a thousand gallons a minute over a quarter-mile radius. A new geometry of circles and semi-circles of cropland was added to the agricultural landscape of the Rainbelt.

Irrigated acreage on the Great Plains soared from 2.1 million acres in 1949 to 13.7 million acres in 1980. Parts of the Rainbelt, such as southwestern Nebraska, northeastern Colorado, and, especially, southwestern Kansas, became outliers of the midwestern Cornbelt, with industrial farming that starts with irrigated corn and soybeans, moves through sprawling feed lots, and ends in the slaughterhouses as packaged beef and pork. It seemed as if the problem of inadequate rainfall had been solved with this "climate-free farming." Because of the irrigation boom, a solid block of counties in southwestern Kansas reached their peak populations in the census year of either 2000 or 2010.

Despite dire warnings of the impending depletion of the Ogallala Aquifer, its overall capacity declined by only 6 percent from 1940 to 2000. In some areas, such as the Platte valley, the saturated thickness of the aquifer has actually increased, as irrigation waters filter back in. But it is the geographic variation in depletion that is significant. Depletion is proceeding in a south to north direction, reflecting the time that has passed since the onset of irrigation (which accounts for 95 percent of the aquifer's use). It also reflects thinness of the original saturated layer in the southern reaches of the aquifer. In the Texas Panhandle and southwestern Kansas the top of the water table has fallen by 150 feet, and the saturated thickness of the aquifer has been reduced by more than 50 percent to less than fifty feet. A saturated thickness of thirty feet is needed to successfully operate a high-capacity well, and the deeper the well the higher the energy costs to raise the water to the surface. So irrigation in much of the High Plains has a limited future. John Opie, in a recent comprehensive study, concluded that "pumping the Ogallala is still a one-time experiment, unrepeatable and irreversible." Moreover, he found that all the farmers he interviewed understood this, and acknowledged that the era of widespread irrigation was coming to an end.[17] The era of "climate free farming" may turn out to be only a spectacular interlude over much of the High Plains, and, if the past is any guide, wheat is the most likely candidate to fill the dried-up spaces.

The second transformation of life on the High Plains commenced in the 1930s with the massive amount of federal aid that flowed into the drought-stricken area. No other part of the country received as much federal aid per capita, quite an irony considering the congenital opposition to "big government" that prevails in the region. Moreover, this reliance on the support of Washington DC has not abated: the Great Plains still receives more money back per capita from the federal government than any other broad American region, while sending less back to Washington in per capita taxes, because incomes are well below the national average.[18]

Much of the federal aid comes in payments to farmers to hold land out of production, and thereby preserve high crop prices, as well as marginal farmland. This started with the Agricultural Adjustment Act in 1933, which paid farmers to reduce production of seven crops, including wheat and corn. The government also came to the aid of farmers then by purchasing millions of cattle that had been starving on land that had lost more than 75 percent of its grass cover. Federal involvement continued with the Soil Bank (1956), which again attempted to protect farm income by paying farmers to "set-aside" land that would normally have been put in wheat, corn, or sorghums. The farmers received an annual payment (averaging twelve dollars an acre) to maintain the land in grass.

A similar program, providing an income without much labor, while conserving soil and water and enhancing wildlife habitat, was introduced in 1985 and has remained popular ever since. Under the Conservation Reserve Program (CRP), farmers enter into long-term contracts to retire erodible land from production and keep it under a cover of grass, trees, or legumes. During the 1990s, average CRP payments were forty-three dollars an acre. The Great Plains became known as the "CRP Belt," sometimes entire farms were put into the program. From 1995 to 2009, CRP payments amounted to $63.1 million in Cheyenne County, Colorado, $49.4 million in Yuma County, $97.5 million in Kiowa County, and $103 million in Kit Carson County. Average payments in those counties in 2007 ranged from $20,000 to $23,000 a farm. These subsidies include "direct payments," which provide a "price floor," a guaranteed income, for farmers, whether crops are grown or not. Additional support—assistance for crop or livestock losses, as well as emergency farm loans—is also available when counties become eligible for federal disaster relief, which was the case throughout the Rainbelt for years at a time during the drought years of the early twenty-first century. In such hard times, federal payments might account for almost all of a farmer's income.[19] The Rainbelters, who received no federal aid at all (beyond packages of last year's seeds), would have been astounded at, and envious of, such government largess.

The government safety net is welcomed by Plains farmers, even though it goes against the grain and despite the fact that large operators, including corporations, collect the lion's share. The environment and the hunting industry have also greatly benefited from the retirement of marginal land from crop production. But as soon as the drought relaxes its grip and grain prices revive, the safety net becomes irrelevant. In 2010 and 2011, with grain prices at record highs (wheat was bringing more than ten dollars a bushel and corn, with a new market of ethanol, more than seven dollars a bushel), farmers began taking their land out of the Conservation Reserve Program and putting it back under the plow. It was a new boom. In the first year of high prices many farmers paid off their debts; in the next year they bought new machinery, and in towns throughout the former Rainbelt businesses hummed with new energy.

Meanwhile, as always on the Great Plains, drought waits in the wings, poised for a reappearance. By 2011 an intense drought had developed over the entire state of Texas and had spread its tentacles north into the southern half of the Rainbelt. Southeastern Colorado and southwestern Kansas were experiencing a D4 drought, the highest category, described as "Exceptional," and all of eastern Colorado and western Kansas south of the I-70 corridor was in a D3 drought, being merely "Extreme." The USDA declared the Colorado counties of Baca, Cheyenne, Kiowa, and Kit Carson, along with contiguous counties in western Kansas, a federal disaster area and provided cash payments to livestock producers who had suffered losses. As far as the Rainbelt goes, the desert, as Walter Prescott Webb put it in 1957, is "the guest who came to dinner, never to go away."[20]

There is one other factor at play now on the High Plains, and in fact throughout in the world, that would have been unimaginable in the late nineteenth century. This is the reality of global climate change. Humans everywhere are changing the climate of the Rainbelt, but not in the locally controllable ways that Melbourne and the other rainmakers promised. Because of increasing concentrations of carbon dioxide in the atmosphere, and the resulting greenhouse effect, temperatures rose 2 degrees Fahrenheit and precipitation decreased by 10 percent over the central Great Plains in the twentieth century. Climatic models, though not always in agreement, predict a continuation of these trends on the western Plains.[21] Occupying the High Plains has always been a tenuous endeavor, and the prospect of more frequent droughts, greater extremes of weather, increased competition for water, and new advantages for invasive species in a warmer place, suggest that in the future it will be even more so.

Notes

Introduction

1. Payne, *Field Notes*.

2. For example, Aughey and Wilbur, *Agriculture Beyond the 100th Meridian*. See also, Emmons, *Garden in the Grasslands*.

3. *Field and Farm*, May 29, 1886; Emmons, *Gardens in the Grasslands*, 128–61.

4. U.S. Bureau of the Census, *Twelfth Census of the United States Taken in the Year 1900, Statistical Atlas*.

5. Payne, *Field Notes*, 5–6.

6. Johnson, *High Plains and Their Utilization*, (1901) 681–90; Darton, *Report on the Geology and Natural Resources of Nebraska*, 719–85. Johnson, an important source of information, including photographs, for this book, learned his trade under the distinguished geologist, G. K. Gilbert. He was a master of topographical surveying and cartography. He was also an "impoverished, lonely, and sensitive man" whose life revolved around his scientific work. See "Willard Drake Johnson," *Complete Dictionary of Scientific Biography* (2008), at http://www.encyclopedia.com/doc/1G2-2830902208.html.

7. Turner, *Frontier in American History*, 147; Barrows, *Lectures*, 231.

8. U.S. Bureau of the Census, *Compendium of the Eleventh Census, 1890*, xlviii; Wrobel, *End of American Exceptionalism*; and Turner," *Frontier in American History*, 1–38.

9. For federal aid during the Dust Bowl years, see Worster, *Dust Bowl*.

10. Among the secondary sources that pay attention to this period and place are Fite, *The Farmer's Frontier*, 113–36; Miner, *West of Wichita*, and Miner, *Next Year Country*; Cunfer, *On the Great Plains*; Smith, " Advance and Recession of the Agricultural Frontier in Kansas"; Steinel, *History of Agriculture in Colorado;*, and Dunbar, "Agricultural Adjustments in Eastern Colorado," 41–92. I was influenced by all these works, and many more, but this book is primarily the result of engagement with the primary sources, the surviving documents of the time.

11. CWA, interviews conducted during 1933–34, pamphlets no. 341 and 350–52. The originals are at the State Historical Society in Denver, but the information is

also available on microfilm. Some of the interviews have recently been published in
Schweninger, *The First We Can Remember.* The CWA operated from November 1933
until March 31, 1934. Its primary mandate was to fund temporary construction jobs for
the unemployed. The program was deemed too costly and quickly abandoned.

12. Ricoeur, *Memory, History, Forgetting,* 1–132; and Lowenthal, *The Past is a Foreign Country.*

1. The Approach from the East, 1854–1885

1. Turner, *Frontier in American History.* For an example of Indian frontiers, see
White, "Winning of the West, 319–43.

2. Cronon, Miles, and Gitlan, *Under a Western Sky,* 6; Turner, *Frontier in American
History,* 1.

3. There are some problems with this population density measurement, not least
that some western counties, including a few in eastern Colorado, never reached two
persons per square mile, even while becoming modern. There are also more definitive methods for identifying a frontier condition at local scales. See, for example, Shortridge, "Post Office Frontier in Kansas"; Lehr and McGregor, "Using Schools to Map
the Frontier"; and McIntosh, "Use and Abuse of the Timber Culture Act."

4. Sauer, "Plant and Animal Destruction," 767; Walker, *Annual Report of the Commissioner of Indian Affairs,* 9.

5. Cohen, "Original Indian Title."

6. For a study of Plains Indian dispossession, see Wishart, *An Unspeakable Sadness.* It
should be noted that federal Indian policy, articulated in the assimilation program, was
explicitly a policy of *cultural* genocide, designed to make the Indians disappear.

7. Details of the various treaties are given in Kappler, *Indian Affairs,* especially vol. 2,
Treaties (1904); and magnificent maps of each Indian cession by state are in Royce, *Indi-
an Land Cessions in the United States.* Examples of speculation on Indian lands include
Egbert, "The Resettlement of Nance County" and Overton, "Eastern Remnant of the
Otoe-Missouria Reservation on the Big Blue River."

8. The figure on Comanche horses is from Hämäläinen, *The Comanche Empire,* 315.

9. Paul, "Frontier Forts," 827–28; Mann, "Sand Creek Massacre," 835; and Preece,
"Ethnic Cleansing," 2:163–67.

10. Select Committee on the Removal of the Northern Cheyennes, xvii.

11. *Fifth Biennial Report of the Kansas State Board of Agriculture for the Years 1885–86*
(Topeka: Kansas Publishing House, 1887), 12–13. Chinese had been barred from entry
into the United States in 1882, the first foreign group to be targeted in this way.

12. Webb, *The Great Plains,* 8; Kraenzel, *Great Plains in Transition,* 125.

13. The annual (after 1877, biennial) reports of the Kansas State Board of Agriculture provide the most definitive statistics on population density. For Nebraska and Colorado, which lack such a useful single source, decennial federal census counts, state
census reports, and county histories were used to estimate county population densities.

14. Fite, *Farmers' Frontier*, 117.

15. U.S. Bureau of the Census, *Population of the United States in 1860*, 166–67, 560; Shortridge, *Peopling the Plains*; Hudson, "Who Was Forest Man?," 69–83.

16. U.S. Bureau of the Census, *Population of the United States in 1860*, 166, 560. See also U.S. Bureau of the Census, *Statistics of the Population, 1870*, 325–29 for national maps of German and Irish settlement, which highlight the Omaha and Kansas City concentrations.

17. *The Nebraskan* (Omaha), May 26, 1856. Also Richardson, "Early Settlement of Eastern Nebraska Territory."

18. U.S. Bureau of the Census, *Population of the United States in 1860*, 140, 142, 187, 190, 197.

19. U.S. Bureau of the Census, *Statistics of the Population, 1870*, 190, 197.

20. Snoddy et al., *Their Man in Omaha*; Donaldson, *The Public Domain*, 232–34.

21. Snoddy et al., *Their Man in Omaha*, 88, 97, 463.

22. Snoddy et al., *Their Man in Omaha*, 86, 106.

23. Snoddy et al., *Their Man in Omaha*, 135; Silag, "Citizens and Strangers."

24. Richardson, "Early Settlement of Nebraska Territory," 68–98.

25. Charles Robinson, "Letters to the Editor," *Lawrence Herald of Freedom* (May 7, 1859); Malin, *History and Ecology*, 11.

26. Weaver, *Prairie Plants and Their Environment*, and *Native Vegetation of Nebraska*. In *Prairie Plants*, Weaver wrote that as many as two hundred species coexisted in a typical square mile of tallgrass prairie (51).

27. See the map of sawmills and other industries in Richardson, "Early Settlement of Nebraska Territory," 52.

28. Information on the various land laws is taken from Donaldson, *The Public Domain*, 215–16, 1023–28, 1220–21.

29. See the pie graph detailing land laws and speculation in Sheldon, *Land Systems*, 160–61. Sheldon, Nebraska's preeminent early historian, admitted to being a speculator himself.

30. Snoddy et al., *Their Man in Omaha*, 308. Barker noted that Nebraska's available agricultural college scrip was just about exhausted.

31. Jenkins, *The Northern Tier*, 14–19, 23, 32–34, 67.

32. Glacken, "Changing Ideas of the Habitable World," 70–92.

33. Snoddy et al., *Their Man in Omaha*, 104, 128.

34. Vollan, "Hell on Wheels," 15–18; Webb, "Air Towns and Their Inhabitants," 828–35.

35. Snoddy et al., *Their Man in Omaha*, 333, 512–18.

36. See the map of railroad land grants in Donaldson, *The Public Domain*, following page 948.

37. Gates, "The Railroad Land Grant Legend," 143–46. Before 1879, only Civil War veterans could homestead on the full 160 acres inside the land grants; after 1879, any-

one who fulfilled the conditions and stipulations of the Homestead Act could. See also, Bellovich, "A Geographic Appraisal."

38. Emmons, *Garden in the Grassland*, 128–61.

39. *Annual Report of the Commissioner of the General Land Office, 1868* , 143, 173–98. The early climate records are given in the *Fifth Biennial Report of the Kansas State Board of Agriculture, for the Years 1885–86*, 180. See also, Mock, "Drought and Precipitation Fluctuations," 26–57.

40. Aughey, "The Geology of Nebraska," 83–84; Emmons, *Garden in the Grasslands*, 151–52.

41. Elliott, *Industrial Resources*, 22–26; Elliott, "The Plains," 253–58; Emmons, *Garden in the Grasslands*, 146.

42. See, for example, Bowden, "Great American Desert," 389.

43. Elliott, "The Plains," 253.

44. "West and East," 225–28; Malin, *History and Ecology*, 199–202.

45. See, for example, Isenberg, *Destruction of the Bison*. The account of bison hunting by settlers appeared in the *New York Tribune* (Dec. 2, 1874), and was reprinted in the *Third Annual Report of the Kansas State Board of Agriculture, for the Year 1874* (Topeka: State Printing Works, 1874), 54–55.

46. *First Biennial Report of the Kansas State Board of Agriculture for the Years 1877–78* (Topeka: State Board of Agriculture, 1879), 341–44.

47. Nimmo, *Report In Regard to the Range and Ranch Cattle Business*.

48. See *First Biennial Report of the Kansas State Board of Agriculture, 1877–78*, 8, 343; and Kollmorgen, "The Woodsman's Assault," 215–39.

49. McIntosh, "Use and Abuse of the Timber Culture Act"; Donaldson, *The Public Domain*, 360–62.

50. Malin, *History and Ecology*, 209–14. Malin published his works from the 1930s to the 1960s.

51. Jenkins, *The Northern Tier*, 133–63.

52. McCartney, *Crisis of 1873*. Also, Sheldon, *Land Systems and Land Policies in Nebraska*, 105–7.

53. The State Board of Agriculture sent a survey to all Kansas counties requesting details of the grasshopper invasion and the degree of destitution. The results were presented in the *Third Annual Report of the Kansas State Board of Agriculture, 1874*, 12–54. It should be noted that chinch bugs, though less spectacular than swarms of grasshoppers, did just as much damage to wheat, corn, oats, and sorghum crops.

54. The last living specimen of the Rocky Mountain locust was collected in 1902. Their extinction was probably caused by agricultural development of the shortgrass prairies. See Lockwood, "Insect Lore," 305–6; and Joern, "Insects," 632–33. For what was known, or thought, at the time about the grasshoppers, see C. V. Riley, "The Future of the Hateful Locusts," in *Third Annual Report of the Kansas State Board of Agriculture, 1874*, 33–35.

55. *Fourth Annual Report of the Kansas State Board of Agriculture, 1875* (Topeka: State Publishing Works, 1875), 21.

56. Fenneman, *Physiography of Western United States*, 5; Thornbury, *Regional Geomorphology*, 287–321; and McGuire et al., *Water in Storage*.

57. *Fifth Biennial Report of the Kansas State Board of Agriculture for the Years 1885– 1886*, 10, 174. The Kansas State Board of Agriculture repudiated its immigration role in 1896.

58. *Fifth Annual Report of the Kansas State Board of Agriculture, 1876*, 59; *First Biennial Report of the Kansas State Board of Agriculture, 1877–78*, 11, which printed the report on the Kansas display from the Philadelphia *Times*.

59. Malin, *History and Ecology*, 144–64; Andreas, *History of the State of Kansas*, 1295– 99; Andreas, *History of the State of Nebraska*, 2:967–68. The monumental Andreas histories have been used only sparingly in this account, and only when corroborated, because they are not always reliable (despite their wealth of contemporary information). They were "vanity histories," published by Alfred Theodore Andreas, but edited—and to a great extent written—by William G. Cutler, his wife Mary Cutler, and his son, H. G. Cutler. William Cutler hired assistants to research and write the county histories, and the quality varied. See Malin, "Notes on the Writing of General Histories of Kansas," 598–639.

60. Malin, *History and Ecology*, 144–64; Andreas, *History of the State of Kansas*, 1608; Andreas, *History of the State of Nebraska*, 2:1097–98.

61. Andreas, *History of the State of Nebraska*, 2:1097–98. See also, Bare and McDonald, *An Illustrated History of Lincoln County, Nebraska*, 1:57–58, 1:182–83, 1:243.

62. Andreas, *History of the State of Nebraska*, 1:878–80, 930. Also, see the almost empty map for Frontier and Gosper Counties in *Official State Atlas of Nebraska*, 204.

63. *Annual Report of the Commissioner of the General Land Office for the Year 1887*, 69. Also, Brooks, "Land Alienation Patterns in the Nebraska Sand Hills South of the Platte River"; and Farmer, "Landboom of Southwestern Nebraska."

64. Hudson, "Towns of the Western Railroads," 46; Andreas, *History of the State of Nebraska*, 1:881–89.

65. Hudson, "Towns of the Western Railroads," 41–54; and Hudson, "The Plains Country Town," 99–118. Also, *Official State Atlas of Nebraska*, 32, 108, 117, 204; and *Nebraska State Gazetteer and Business Directory for 1882–83*, 161.

66. *Fifth Biennial Report of the Kansas State Board of Agriculture, 1885–86*, 16–27; Shortridge, *Peopling the Plains*, 72–141.

67. *Fifth Biennial Report of the Kansas State Board of Agriculture, 1885–86*, 16–27; Shortridge, *Peopling the Plains*, 72–141; Malin, *Winter Wheat in the Golden Belt of Kansas*, 133; McQuillan, *Prevailing Over Time*, 102–8, 196–97.

68. Malin, *History and Ecology*, 196–99. E. Gale, an early dendrochronologist, made a comprehensive study of tree rings in 1878 that revealed that rainfall in Kansas had not changed significantly over two hundred years. See also, Emmons, *Garden in the Grassland*, 128–61.

69. Aughey, *Sketches of the Physical Geography*, 44, 46, 47; Aughey and Wilbur, *Agriculture Beyond the 100th Meridian*, 5–6.

70. *Nebraska State Gazetteer and Business Directory for 1882–1883*, 1.

71. *Fifth Biennial Report of the Kansas State Board of Agriculture, 1885–86*, 176–80.

72. Johnson, *High Plains and Their Utilization*, (1901) 682–87.

2. Into the Rainbelt, 1886–1890

1. Newell, "The Reclaimation of the West," 22; *Colorado Farmer and Livestock Journal* (Jan. 23, 1890), 1, and (May 29, 1890), 8; *Fifth Biennial Report of the Kansas State Board of Agriculture for the Years 1885–1886* (backpocket map).

2. Johnson, *High Plains and Their Utilization*, (1901) 681.

3. Newell, *Report on Agriculture*, 90–135, quotes from p.120.

4. Steinel, *History of Agriculture in Colorado*, 136–37; Interviews, Mrs. Hans Christensen, Yuma Co., Doc. 8; Payne, *Cattle Raising on the Plains*, 6.

5. Interviews, Irving L. Barker, Yuma Co., Doc. 23; Steinel, *History of Agriculture in Colorado*, 145–50.

6. Interviews, M. L. Cromwell, Prowers Co., Doc. 11; Nimmo, *Range and Ranch Cattle Business*.

7. Steinel, *History of Agriculture in Colorado*, 132–35.

8. Steinel, *History of Agriculture in Colorado*, 159–61.

9. Nimmo, *Range and Ranch Cattle Business*, 111; Interviews, Harry Strangway, Yuma Co., Doc. 29.

10. Steinel, *History of Agriculture in Colorado*, 133–37; Interviews, Harry Strangway, Yuma Co., Doc. 29.

11. Interviews, Irving L. Barker, Yuma Co., Doc. 23; Steinel, *History of Agriculture in Colorado*, 132–33; Interviews, "14 Years in the Arkansas Valley," Prowers County, Doc. 17; Harry Strangway, Yuma Co., Doc. 29.

12. Interviews, Harry Strangway, Yuma Co., Doc. 29; Steinel, *History of Agriculture in Colorado*, 134; *Annual Report of the Commissioner of the General Land Office for the Year 1888* (Washington DC: GPO, 1888), 365.

13. Nimmo, *Range and Ranch Cattle Business*, 11–12, 43, 45, 48.

14. Johnson, *High Plains and Their Utilization*, (1901) 681–82.

15. Interviews, Mrs. Artie Richards, Morgan Co., Doc. 22; Lute H. Johnson, Morgan Co., Doc. 11.

16. Interviews, Craig Bolander, Yuma Co., Doc. 20; W. C. Grigsby, Yuma Co., Doc. 4; Fred D. Johnson, Yuma Co., Doc. 6; Ed Russell, Prowers Co., Doc. 7.

17. Nimmo, *Range and Ranch Cattle Business*, 37; Interviews, Mrs. Artie Richards, Morgan Co., Doc. 22.

18. *Omaha Daily Bee*, April 27, 1886; Johnson, *High Plains and Their Utilization*, (1901) 682–83. Note: these specific counties were chosen for the graphs because of the

continuation of their boundaries from 1880–1900 and because the Kansas State Board of Agriculture provided county population numbers every two years.

19. *Fifth Biennial Report of the Kansas State Board of Agriculture for the Years 1885–86*, 12–13. Sherman County, for example, was 72.6 percent male in 1885. Also, see the map entitled "The Predominating Sex," in Department of Interior, *Population of the United States at the Eleventh Census, 1890* (Washington DC: GPO, 1890), 1:ixxiv–ixxv.

20. Schedules of the Nebraska State Census, 1885. Nebraska State Historical Society. RG513, microfilm SG255, Rolls 18, 26, 35. Note how in small populations like these, an idiosyncratic unbalance in children's cohorts, as in Hayes County, can have a significant effect on the overall demographic profile.

21. Interviews, S. S. Worley, Logan Co., Doc. 27. See also the county descriptions in Newell, *Report on Agriculture By Irrigation*, 102–33.

22. Goodyknoontz, "The Settlement of Colorado," 2:465; and Colorado County Formation Maps, http://www.familyhistory101.com/maps/co_cf.html. Also, *Annual Report of the Commissioner of the General Land Office* (Washington DC: GPO., 1895), 142–43.

23. Interviews, S. S. Worley, Logan Co., Doc. 27.

24. Interviews, Elva Sisson, Yuma Co., Doc. 9.

25. Franklin, Diaries; Interviews, Thomas Jefferson Huntzinger, Kit Carson Co., Doc. 45.

26. Interviews, Wallace Hoze Wilcok, Kit Carson Co., Doc. 18.

27. Interviews, Oliver J. Graham, Yuma Co., Doc. 3. The 1890 federal census did not itemize state of origin at the county level, although it did so by country for foreign-born population.

28. Interviews, Bob Hasart, Yuma Co., Doc. 11; Cary Mathias Jacober, Yuma Co., Doc. 12; U.S. Bureau of the Census, *Report on the Population of the United States at the Eleventh Census, 1890*, 1:491–92.

29. *Keith County News*, Dec. 18, 1891; Interviews, Martha Gilmore Lundy, Kit Carson Co., Doc. 13; Angelina Fuller, Kit Carson Co., Doc. 38.

30. Interviews, Nellie Buchanan, Kit Carson Co., Doc. 4.

31. *Wray Republican*, July 12, 1889; Interviews, Lute H. Johnson, Morgan Co., Doc. 11.

32. Interviews, James William Cody, Kit Carson Co., Doc. 49.

33. Interviews, Reuben Brammeier, Kit Carson Co., Doc. 34.

34. Interviews, S. S. Worley, Yuma Co., Doc. 27.

35. *Fifth Biennial Report of the Kansas State Board of Agriculture, 1885–86*, 128–29; *Sixth Biennial Report of the Kansas State Board of Agriculture, 1887–88* (Topeka: Kansas Publishing House, 1889), 114, 152–53.

36. Brooks, "Land Alienation Patterns in the Nebraska Sand Hills South of the Platte River," 66, 81–82; Payne, *Unirrigated Lands of Eastern Colorado*, 8, 12–13.

37. Payne, *Unirrigated Lands of Eastern Colorado*, 8, 12–13; Newell, *Report on Agriculture By Irrigation*, 102.

38. Interviews, "Reminiscences of the Early Days," Yuma Co., Doc. 2; Goody-koontz, "The Settlement of Colorado," 2:465.

39. Interviews, Bob Hasart, Kit Carson Co., Doc. 11; for the disadvantages of an "in-land" location, see Hudson, "The Plains Country Town," 114–15.

40. Interviews, James Herbert Priest, Kit Carson Co., Doc. 6; Wallace Hoze Wilcok, Kit Carson Co., Doc. 18; and Reuben Brammeier, Kit Carson Co., Doc. 34.

41. Interviews, "Paper Read By S. S. Worley, June 12, 1908," Logan Co., Doc. 27.

42. Interviews, Glen Colander, Yuma Co., Doc. 20; *Nebraska State Gazetteer and Business Directory for 1884–85*, 182; and *Nebraska State Gazetteer and Business Directory for 1890–91*, 200, 210.

43. Interviews, C. C. Huddleston, Prowers Co., Doc. 3; *Lamar Register*, April 18, 1896, Prowers Co., Doc. 9; *Lamar Daily News*, May 25, 1933, Prowers Co., Doc. 8; Harry Boyles, Yuma Co., Doc. 7.

44. Statistics for the graphs are taken from the *Annual Report of the Commissioner of the General Land Office* for the years 1880 to 1890. Because of the lack of consistency in recording other land laws, but also because of their importance (together they account-ed for more than 75 percent of all entries) only homestead and timber culture entries are shown. Some land offices — North Platte, for example — are not included because their regions of jurisdiction changed during the course of the decade.

45. *Report of the Commissioner of the General Land Office For the Year 1885*, 55–56, 79, 267–70, 318–20.

46. *Report of the Commissioner of the General Land Office For the Year 1884*, 108–12.

47. U.S. General Land Office, *Land Tract Books*. Township 10N, Range 35, W, 46:9.

48. Interviews, S. S. Worley, Logan County, Doc. 27; McIntosh, "Use and Abuse of the Timber Culture Act"; Donaldson, *The Public Domain*, 360–62. In 1878, the plant-ing requirement was reduced to ten acres of trees for eight years.

49. *Annual Report of the Commissioner of the General Land Office For the Year 1888*, 52–82.

50. Spearman, "The Great American Desert," 232–45. For the debtor status of the West, see also "West and East," and, almost thirty years later, Gleed, "Western Land and Mortgages," 468–71.

51. Interviews, Glenn Bolander, Yuma Co. Doc. 20.

52. U.S. Bureau of the Census, *Compendium of the Eleventh Census, 1890*, xlviii.

53. *Fifth Biennial Report of the Kansas State Board of Agriculture, 1885–86*, 166.

54. *Denver Republican*, Jan. 1, 1888, quoted in Goodykoontz, "The Settlement of Colorado," 464–65.

55. Interviews, Thomas Jefferson Huntzinger, Kit Carson County, Doc. 45; Mrs. Hans Christensen, Yuma Co., Doc. 8.

56. *Colorado Farmer*, May 29, 1890.

57. Payne, *Field Notes*, 4.

58. Goodwin D. Swezey, "Meteorological Report for the Year 1891," in *Annual Re-*

port of the Nebraska State Board of Agriculture for the Year 1891 (Lincoln: State Journal Co., 1892), 189–95.

59. Climate records were published each year in the annual reports of the Nebraska State Board of Agriculture and the biennial reports of the Kansas State Board of Agriculture. The most convenient source of data, however, is the later publication by the U.S. Department of Agriculture entitled *Summaries of Climatological Data by Sections* (Washington DC: Weather Bureau, 1926), Vol. 2, sections 7, 8, 37, 38, and 39.

60. *Sixth Biennial Report of the Kansas State Board of Agriculture, 1887–88,* 6; Interviews, Eta Shannon, Logan Co., Doc. 23.

61. Miner, *West of Wichita,* 212–22.

62. *Seventh Biennial Report of the Kansas State Board of Agriculture, For the Years 1889–90* (Topeka: Kansas Publishing House, 1891), vii.

63. *Summaries of Climatological Data by Sections,* Section 38, 8 and Section 7, 5; *Seventh Biennial Report of the Kansas State Board of Agriculture, For the Years 1889–90,* vi; Interviews, Elizabeth Richards, Kit Carson Co., Doc. 26.

64. *Summaries of Climatological Data by Sections,* Section 7, 7 and Section 8,5; *Seventh Biennial Report of the Kansas State Board of Agriculture, For the Years 1889–90,* vi.

65. *Seventh Biennial Report of the Kansas State Board of Agriculture, For the Years 1889–90,* vi; *Annual Report of the Nebraska State Board of Agriculture For the Year 1890,* 70.

66. *Summaries of Climatological Data by Sections,* Section 7, 6, and Section 8, 7. The maps were constructed by Molly Boeka Cannon from point data using Arc GIS 10 and the Spatial Analyst Tool.

67. *Seventh Biennial Report of the Kansas State Board of Agriculture, For the Years 1889–90,* vii, 113; Franklin, Diaries, May 10, 1890.

68. *Sixth Biennial Report of the Kansas State Board of Agriculture, 1887–88,* 113–14; *Seventh Biennial Report of the Kansas State Board of Agriculture, For the Years 1889–90,* 230.

69. *Seventh Biennial Report of the Kansas State Board of Agriculture, For the Years 1889–90,* 192–93.

3. Life in the Rainbelt, circa 1890

1. Steinel, *History of Agriculture in Colorado,* 251–55.

2. As quoted in Steinel, *History of Agriculture in Colorado,* 253. Steinel noted that this newspaper was owned and operated by the Lincoln Land Company, which had a special interest in enticing settlers to the Rainbelt.

3. *Colorado Farmer,* Oct. 7, 1886, quoted in Steinel, *History of Agriculture in Colorado,* 254–55.

4. Steinel, *History of Agriculture in Colorado,* 253.

5. Interviews, Arthur James Pearce, Logan Co., Doc.27.

6. Dick, "Water, A Frontier Problem," 235.

172

Notes to pages 78–86

7. *Lamar Register*, April 18, 1896; Johnson, *High Plains and Their Utilization*, (1901) 692–96.

8. Interviews, Elizabeth Richards, Kit Carson County, Doc. 26.

9. Interviews, S. S. Worley, Logan Co., Doc. 27.

10. Interviews, Anna Quinn, Kit Carson Co., Doc. 10; Nellie Buchanan, Kit Carson Co., Doc. 17; Elizabeth Richards, Kit Carson Co., Doc. 26; and Thomas Jefferson Huntzinger, Kit Carson Co., Doc. 45. For the origins of the depressions, see Johnson, *High Plains and Their Utilization*, (1901) 702–5, and Thornbury, *Regional Geomorphology of the United States*, 304–6

11. Interviews, Alice Pantzer, Kit Carson County, Doc. 20.

12. Interviews, Jennie Davis, Kit Carson County, Doc. 9; Johnson, *High Plains and Their Utilization*, (1901) 629, 681; Wedel, "The High Plains and Their Utilization," 1–16. See p. 6 of Wedel for a map of High Plains springs. For some of the early place names of eastern Colorado, see "Postal Map of Kansas," in *Fifth Annual Report of the Kansas State Board of Agriculture, 1876*, frontispiece.

13. McGuire et al., *Water in Storage*, especially fig. 12 (p. 21), and 26–27; Johnson, *High Plains and Their Utilization*, (1901) 633–53.

14. Newell, *Report on Agriculture By Irrigation*, 99, 131–32; Johnson, *High Plains and Their Utilization*, (1901) 712–32.

15. Interviews, Isaac Messinger, Kit Carson Co., Doc. 35; S. S. Worley, Logan, Doc. 27; Nellie Buchanan, Kit Carson Co., Doc. 17.

16. Interviews, Mary Belle Kiser Haynes, Kit Carson Co., Doc. 63; Nellie Buchanan, Kit Carson Co., Doc. 17.

17. Interviews, Thomas Jefferson Huntzinger, Kit Carson Co., Doc. 45; S. S. Worley, Logan Co., Doc. 27; George Washington Franklin, Diaries, entries from Jan. 4 to Mar. 3, 1886; and Dick, "Water, A Frontier Problem," *passim*.

18. Dick, "Water, A Frontier Problem," 236; Interviews, Elizabeth Richards, Kit Carson Co., Doc. 26.

19. Interviews, S. S. Worley, Logan Co., Doc. 27

20. Interviews, John G. Abbot, Yuma Co., Doc. 2.

21. Interviews, Charles Morgan, Sedgwick Co., Doc. 3; Cynthia Boyles, Kit Carson Co., Doc. 55.

22. Interviews, "Town of Flagler," Kit Carson Co., Doc. 27; S. S. Worley, Logan Co., Doc. 27; M. L. Cromwell, Prowers Co., Doc. 11.

23. Interviews, James Dawson, Sedgwick Co., Doc. 2.

24. David Murphy, "Sod-Wall Construction," in Wishart, *Encyclopedia of the Great Plains*, 94–95.

25. Interviews, S. S. Worley, Logan Co., Doc. 27; James Dawson, Sedgwick Co., Doc. 2.

26. Interviews, S. S. Worley, Logan Co., Doc. 27; Murphy, "Sod-Wall Construction," 94–95; Steinel, *History of Agriculture in Colorado*, 257–59.

27. Interviews, Luella Belle McKenzie, Kit Carson Co., Doc. 1; George Washington Franklin, Diaries, Oct. 1, 1885 to Dec. 8, 1885.

28. Interviews, James Herbert Priest, Kit Carson Co., Doc. 6; Wallace Hoze Wilcok, Kit Carson Co., Doc. 18.

29. Interviews, James Herbert Priest, Kit Carson Co., Doc. 6; Cary Mathias Jacober, Kit Carson Co., Doc. 12; Cynthia Boyles, Kit Carson Co., Doc. 55.

30. Interviews, S. S. Worley, Logan Co., Doc. 27; Wallace Hoze Wilcok, Kit Carson Co., Doc. 18.

31. Interviews, Reuben Brammeier, Kit Carson Co., Doc. 34.

32. Interviews, Reuben Brammeier, Kit Carson Co., Doc. 34.

33. Interviews, Harry Wells, Yuma Co., Doc. 5; James B. McCombs, Kit Carson Co., Doc. 51.

34. Interviews, Mrs. Hans Christiansen, Yuma Co., Doc. 8.

35. Interviews, Jonathan L. Lengel, Kit Carson Co., Doc. 5; James Pearce, Kit Carson Co., Doc. 33; Oliver Graham, Yuma Co., Doc. 3; Murphy, "Clay Construction," 71–72.

36. Interviews, "Reminiscences of the Early Days," Yuma Co., Doc. 2; John G. Abbot, Yuma Co., Doc. 11. A single man, Dr. Raimond Von Horrom Schram, a "nervous bearded German of noble lineage," was personally responsible for erecting Yuma's brick buildings.

37. Interviews, Angelina Fuller, Kit Carson Co., Doc. 38; Cary Mathias Jacober, Kit Carson Co., Doc. 12; Flora Ferris, Kit Carson Co., Doc. 64.

38. Interviews, Charles Albert Yersin, Kit Carson Co., Doc. 30; Sarah Blakeman, Kit Carson Co., Doc. 37; John G. Abbot, Yuma Co., Doc. 11; W. D. McGinnis, Yuma Co., Doc. 31.

39. Interviews, Minnie Chase, Kit Carson Co., Doc. 22; James William Cody, Kit Carson Co., Doc. 49.

40. Interviews, Jennie Davis, Kit Carson Co., Doc. 9; Elizabeth Richards, Kit Carson Co., Doc. 26; James Dawson, Sedgwick Co., Doc. 2; George E. McConley, Logan Co., Doc. 11. For example, in 1889, George Washington Franklin traded five bushels of corn for a subscription to the *Elsie Journal*. Diaries, Dec. 14, 1889.

41. Payne, *Advice to Plains Settlers*, 4–5.

42. U.S. Bureau of the Census, *Report on the Statistics of Agriculture in the United States, Eleventh Census, 1890*, 10.

43. U.S. Bureau of the Census, *Report on the Statistics of Agriculture in the United States, Eleventh Census, 1890*, 46–63; Payne, *Advice to Plains Settlers*, 5; Interviews, Glenn Bolander, Yuma Co., Doc. 20.

44. Interviews, Jonathan L. Langel, Kit Carson Co., Doc. 5; Harry Wells, Yuma Co., Doc. 5.

45. Interviews, James Herbert Priest, Kit Carson Co., Doc. 6; William Melvin Long, Kit Carson Co., Doc. 16; Auram McElfresh, Kit Carson Co., Doc. 50.

46. Interviews, Charles Morgan, Sedgwick Co., Doc. 3; James Dawson, Sedgwick Co., Doc. 2; W. C. Grigsby, Yuma Co., Doc. 4; Franklin, Diaries, Nov. 14 and 15, 1885.

47. Franklin, Diaries, Dec. 11, 1885, Dec. 30, 1885; Dec. 12, 1889; John G. Abbot, Yuma Co., Doc. 11; Irving L. Barker, Yuma Co., Doc. 23.

48. Interviews, Cary Mathias Jacober, Kit Carson Co., Doc. 12.

49. Interviews, Reuben Brammeier, Kit Carson Co., Doc. 34.

50. Interviews, James William Cody, Kit Carson Co., Doc. 49; Charles L. Morgan, Sedgwick Co., Doc. 3.

51. Interviews, Harry Wells, Yuma Co., Doc. 5; Glenn Bolander, Yuma Co., Doc. 20. For more information on the Union Colony, see Ralph H. Brown, *Historical Geography of the United States* (New York: Harcourt, Brace and World, Inc., 1948), 458–59.

52. Interviews, Eta Shannon, Logan Co., Doc. 23. Also, George McConley, Logan Co., Doc. 11; Minnie Chase, Kit Carson Co., Doc. 22; Isaac Messinger, Kit Carson Co., Doc. 35., Peter Peterson, Sedgwick Co., Doc. 7; William Heindel, Yuma Co., Doc. 24.

53. Interviews, Martha Gilmore Lundy, Kit Carson Co., Doc. 13; Nellie Buchanan, Kit Carson Co., Doc. 4.

54. Interviews, William Henry Yale, Kit Carson Co., Doc. 14; Tom Jenkins, Sedgwick Co., Doc. 4; William Arthur Richards, Kit Carson Co., Doc. 39; Charles Albert Yersin, Kit Carson Co., Doc. 30; Amos Carl, Yuma Co., Doc. 28.

55. Interviews, Peter Peterson, Sedgwick Co., Doc. 7.

56. Interviews, C. C. Huddleston, Prowers Co., Doc. 3.

57. Interviews, Elmer Ellsworth Harrison, Kit Carson Co., Doc. 54.

58. Franklin, Diaries, May 16, 1890 to March 11, 1893, *passim.*

59. Interviews, Lute H. Johnson, Morgan Co., Doc. 11; "Notes on Burlington," Kit Carson Co., Doc. 24; Wallace Hoze Wilcox, Kit Carson Co., Doc. 18.

60. Interviews, Oliver J. Graham, Yuma Co., Doc. 3; James Dawson, Sedgwick Co., Doc. 2; Susan Tucker, Prowers Co., Doc.1.

61. Interviews, Jennie Davis, Kit Carson Co., Doc. 9; Elias Griffith Davis, Kit Carson Co., Doc. 43.

62. Interviews, Cary Mathias Jacober, Kit Carson Co., Doc. 12.

63. U.S. Bureau of the Census, *Report on the Statistics of Agriculture in the United States, Eleventh Census, 1890*, 279, 320–21, 358–59, 407, 462–63; Payne, *Dairying on the Plains*, 19–24; Interviews, Harry Strangway, Yuma Co., Doc. 29.

64. Interviews, Thomas Jefferson Huntzinger, Kit Carson Co., Doc. 49.

65. Interviews, Thomas Jefferson Huntzinger, Kit Carson Co., Doc. 49; Minnie Chase, Kit Carson Co., Doc. 22.

66. Interviews, S. S. Worley, Yuma Co., Doc. 27; Irving L. Barker, Kit Carson Co., Doc. 23.

67. Franklin, Diaries, Nov. 7, 1885.

68. Interviews, Sarah Pantzer, Kit Carson Co., Doc. 62; Charles K. Morgan, Sedgwick Co., Doc. 3.

69. Franklin, Diaries, Nov. 1, 1885; Nov. 4, 1885; Nov. 8, 1885; Dec. 31, 1885; Mar. 27, 1886; Sept. 9, 1889; Dec. 8, 1889; Feb. 3, 1890; Mar. 3, 1890; and *passim*; Interviews, C. A. Gillette, Kit Carson Co., Doc. 21.

70. Interviews, Nellie Buchanan, Kit Carson Co., Doc. 4; Anna Quinn, Kit Carson Co., Doc. 10.

71. Interviews, Elizabeth Cutting Lengel, Kit Carson Co., Doc. 3. For studies of Plains and midwestern women homesteaders, see, for example, Lindgren, *Land in Her Own Name*; Paterson-Black, "Women Homesteaders on the Great Plains Frontier," 67–88; and Sundberg, "'Picturing the Past,'" 203–20.

72. Interviews, Nellie Buchanan, Kit Carson Co., Doc. 4; Elizabeth Cutting Lengel, Kit Carson Co., Doc. 3; Franklin, Diaries, Aug. 18, 1889.

73. Franklin, Diaries, Jan. 5, 1890; Dec. 12, 1892; Dec. 15, 1892.

74. Interviews, Jennie Davis, Kit Carson Co., Doc. 9; Reuben Brammeier, Kit Carson Co., Doc. 34; S. S. Worley, Logan Co., Doc. 27.

75. Interviews, Charles Albert Yersin, Kit Carson Co., Doc. 29; James Callon Pearce, Kit Carson Co., Doc. 33; Ann Holm, Kit Carson Co., Doc. 2; "The Hatch Murder," Kit Carson Co., Doc. 32 (an interview given by a witness to the event who did not want to reveal his or her name).

76. Interviews, Nellie Buchanan, Kit Carson Co., Doc. 4, Sarah Blakeman, Kit Carson Co., Doc. 37; Minnie Chase, Kit Carson Co., Doc. 22.

77. Interviews, Nellie Buchanan, Kit Carson Co., Doc. 4.

78. Interviews, Martha Gilmore Lundy, Kit Carson Co., Doc. 13; Mary Ellen Bagley Wood, Logan Co., Doc. 48.

79. Interviews, Elsie Jane Huntzinger, Kit Carson Co., Doc. 46; Luella Bell McKenzie, Kit Carson Co., Doc. 1.

80. Interviews, Nellie Buchanan, Kit Carson Co., Doc. 4.

81. *Miscellaneous Documents of the House of Representatives, 1891–2*, 55.

82. Interviews, Nellie Buchanan, Kit Carson Co., Doc. 4; Burt Ragan, Kit Carson Co., Doc. 23; Reuben Brammeier, Kit Carson Co., Doc. 34.

83. Interviews, Bruno Kaiser, Kit Carson Co., Doc. 28; B. D. Palmer, Sedgwick Co., Doc. 1.

84. "The Rainbelt Institute," *Colorado Farmer and Livestock Journal*, Jan. 23, 1890.

85. Interviews, John G. Abbot, Logan Co., Doc. 2.

4. The Last Days of the Rainbelt, 1890–1896

1. Interviews, John G. Abbot, Yuma Co., Doc. 2; Charles Timberlake, Logan Co., Doc. 25; Bob Hasart, Kit Carson Co., Doc. 11.

2. *Akron Pioneer*, Dec. 2, 1892.

3. Franklin, Diaries, Mar. 23, 1892, and *passim*; Interviews, Lute H. Johnson, Morgan Co., Doc. 11.

4. *Keith County News*, Jan. 1, 1892; Feb. 26, 1892.

5. Interviews, John G. Abbot, Yuma Co., Doc. 2; *Field and Farm*, Feb. 14, 1891, quoted in Steinel, *History of Agriculture in Colorado*, 260.

6. Population data for the map are from U.S. Bureau of the Census, *Twelfth Census of the United States*, 1:80–88, 1:162–74, 1:252–63.

7. Rainfall data for the maps and the text are drawn from U.S. Department of Agricultural, Weather Bureau, *Summaries of Climatological Data By Sections* (Washington DC: Weather Bureau, 1926), Section 7, Southeastern Colorado; Section 8, Northeastern Colorado; Section 37, Southern Nebraska; and Sections 38 and 39, Kansas. Also, *Annual Report of the Nebraska State Board of Agriculture for the Year 1891* (Lincoln: State Journal Co., 1892), 189.

8. U.S. Department of Agriculture, Weather Bureau, *Summaries of Climatological Data by Sections*, Section 8, Northeastern Colorado, 7–8, and Section 37, Southern Nebraska, 5. Southeastern Colorado had different regime in 1892, with lower than average totals for both the growing season and the year. Also, *Keith County News*, Feb. 24 and June 3.

9. U.S. Department of Agriculture, Weather Bureau, *Summaries of Climatological Data by Sections*, Section 7, Northeastern Colorado, 7–8, 10, and Section 37, Southern Nebraska, 5. Also, *McCook Times*, June 17, 1892, and *Keith County News*, July 1, 1892.

10. Spence, *The Rainmakers*, 22–51.

11. The exploits of Melbourne, especially in Wyoming and Kansas, are covered in Spence, *The Rainmakers*, 52–78, and in Spring, "Rainmakers of the Nineties," 289–98. His activities in Nebraska are given brief attention in Pound, "Nebraska Rain Lore and Rain Making," 129–42. The account here is mainly based on local newspapers.

12. *Rocky Mountain News*, Sept. 5, 1891; Sept. 6, 1891; Sept. 7, 1891.

13. *Keith County News*, Dec. 18, 1891; Jan. 8, 1892.

14. *Keith County News*, March 18, 1892; June 3, 1892; June 17, 1892; *McCook Times*, July 15, 1892.

15. *Keith County News*, June 17, 1892.

16. *Keith County News*, June 24, 1892; also *Perkins County Sentinel*, June 22, 1892.

17. *Keith County News*, July 1, 1892.

18. *Keith County News*, July 8, 1892; *Perkins County Sentinel*, Oct. 20, 1892.

19. *Perkins County Sentinel*, Oct. 20, 1892; Steinel, *History of Agriculture in Colorado*, 261.

20. *McCook Times*, Sept. 2, 1892.

21. Steinel, *History of Agriculture in Colorado*, 261; *Rocky Mountain News*, June 28, 1893.

22. U.S. Bureau of Agriculture, Weather Bureau, *Summaries of Climatological Data By Sections*, Sections 7, 8, 37, 38, and 39; *Rocky Mountain News*, June 27, 1893. Flora, *Hailstorms of the United States*, 24, 78, 100, 117; Clements, "Climatic Cycles and Human Populations in the Great Plains," 193–210; and Malin, "Dust Storms, Part Three, 1881–1890," 391–413.

23. Governors' Records, Lorenzo Crouse, Box 5, Sept. 1, 1894.

24. High Plains Regional Climate Center, Historical Climate Data Studies. http://www.hpricc.edu/data/historical.

25. *Ninth Biennial Report of the Kansas State Board of Agriculture For the Years 1893 and 1894* (Topeka: Hamilton Printing Co., 1895), 5; *Annual Report of the Nebraska State Board of Agriculture For the Year 1893* (Lincoln: State Journal Co., 1894), 132; *Annual Report of the Nebraska State Board of Agriculture For the Year 1894* (Lincoln: State Journal Co., 1895), 31; *Annual Report of the Nebraska State Board of Agriculture For the Year 1895* (Lincoln: State Journal Co., 1896), 350; and *Annual Report of the Nebraska State Board of Agriculture For the Year 1896* (Lincoln: State Journal Co., 1897), 14–15.

26. Interviews, James Dawson, Sedgwick Co., Doc. 2.

27. Interviews, Timothy Burns, Yuma Co., Doc. 10; Mary Ellen Bagley Wood, Logan Co., Doc. 48; Arthur James Pearce, Kit Carson Co., Doc. 40; and Bob Hasart, Kit Carson Co., Doc. 11. Also, *Ninth Biennial Report of the Kansas State Board of Agriculture For the Years 1893 and 1894*, 241–43.

28. Interviews, W. C. Grigsby, Yuma Co., Doc. 4; Charles Timberlake, Logan Co., Doc. 25; Cary Mathias Jacober, Kit Carson Co., Doc. 12; William Hastine, Kit Carson Co., Doc. 11.

29. By comparison, in 2002, in the middle of another serious drought, Lamar, Colorado, received only one-half inch of rain in an eight-month period. This was reported in Timothy Egan, "Dry High Plains Blowing Away, Again," *New York Times*, May 3, 2002, A1, A14.

30. Interviews, Timothy Burns, Yuma Co., Doc. 10. The western High Plains still have the highest hail insurance rates in the United States. See Flora, *Hailstorms in the United States*, 78.

31. Interviews, John G. Abbot, Yuma Co., Doc. 2.

32. Interviews, Charles Timberlake, Logan Co., Doc. 25.

33. Steeples and Whitten, *Democracy in Desperation*, 1–65; Rezneck, "Unemployment, Unrest, and Relief," 324–45.

34. Steeples and Whitten, *Democracy in Desperation*, 52–53; Laughlin, "Causes of Agricultural Unrest," 577–85. About one-third of the American wheat crop was exported to foreign markets, but only 4 percent of the corn crop, so wheat farmers were much more affected by world events.

35. Steeples and Whitten, *Democracy in Desperation*, 26–41; Rezneck, "Unemployment, Unrest, and Relief," 334–36.

36. Steeples and Whitten, *Democracy in Desperation*, 14–41; Rezneck, "Unemployment, Unrest, and Relief," 324–36. Across the nation, newspapers were filled with sensational stories of bank failures and depositors' panic. See, for example, the daily reports in the *Rocky Mountain News* throughout the year 1893.

37. For the concentration of wealth in the hands of the few in the 1890s and comparisons with other eras, see Louis Uchitelle, "The Richest of the Rich, Proud of a New Gilded Age," *New York Times*, July 15, 2007, 1, 18–19.

38. Steeples and Whitten, *Democracy in Desperation*, 94–96; Rezneck, "Unemployment, Unrest, and Relief," 328–29, 335–36.

39. Interviews, Letter, Leila Shaw Walters to Cyrus and Lydia Shaw, Aug. 11, 1894, Kit Carson Co., Doc. 44. Also, see the editorial in the *Nation* (Aug. 24, 1893), 131–32.

40. Gleed, "Western Lands and Mortgages," 468–71; Ingalls, "Kansas, 1541–1891," 697–713; and Harger, "New Era in the Middle West," 276–82.

41. U.S. Bureau of the Census, *Report on Farms and Homes*, 385, 393–94, 403, 433.

42. Harger, "New Era in the Middle West," 276, 279; Spearman, "The Great American Desert," 232–45.

43. Harger, "New Era in the Middle West," 277.

44. Gleed, "Western Lands and Mortgages," 470. Also, Gleed, "The Wealth and Business Relations of the West," 631–43; and "Western Mortgages," 93–105.

45. Harger, "New Era in the Middle West," 277; Gleed, "The Wealth and Business Relations of the West," 97–98; Perkins County Nebraska County Board, Book 1, June 18, 1895, March 31, 1897.

46. Interviews, Peter Peterson, Sedgwick Co., Doc. 7; Payne, *Unirrigated Lands of Eastern Colorado*, 12–13.

47. Interviews, John G. Abbot, Yuma Co., Doc. 2; U.S. Census Bureau, *Twelfth Census of the United States, Population*, 1:88.

48. Interviews, Harry Hoskin, Kit Carson Co., Doc. 41; Payne, *Unirrigated Lands of Eastern Colorado*, 12–13.

49. Interviews, Letters, Leila Shaw Walters to Cyrus and Lydia Shaw, April 11, 1894 and Oct. 21, 1894, Kit Carson Co., Doc. 44.

50. Clements, "Climate Cycles," 4; Harger "New Era in the Middle West," 277; *Elsie Reader*, March 5, 1896; U.S. Bureau of the Census, *Twelfth Census of the United States, Population*, 1:80–88, 1:161–75, 1:252–63; and "Decennial Census," in *Tenth Biennial Report of the Kansas State Board of Agriculture for the Years 1895 and 1896* (Topeka: Kansas State Printing Co., 1896), 502–04. Note that elongated Arapahoe County, which reached all the way to Denver, and Prowers County, which was redistricted between 1890 and 1900, are not included in the Colorado population figures.

51. Johnson, *High Plains and Their Utilization*, (1901) 682, 690; *Complete Dictionary of Scientific Biography*, "Willard Drake Johnson."

52. Johnson, *High Plains and Their Utilization*, (1901) 681.

53. *Twelfth Census of the United States, Population*, 1:80, 1:88; U.S. Bureau of the Census, *Abstract of the Twelfth Census of the United States, 1900*, 124–25. For comparisons, see Raban, *Bad Land*; and Donald Worster, *Dust Bowl*.

54. Harger, "New Era in the Middle West," 277. See also Interviews, Sarah Elizabeth Pantzer, Kit Carson Co., Doc. 62.

55. Franklin, Diaries, June 4, 1893, June 9, 1893, May 25, 1899, May 27, 1899, May 31, 1899, and June 24, 1899. For the deathbed declaration, see Koch, "Farm Building on the Nebraska High Plains," 37–40.

56. Gleed, "Western Lands and Mortgages," 470.

57. *(Lincoln) Nebraska State Journal*, Sept. 13, 1893 and Sept. 17, 1893.

58. U.S. Bureau of the Census, *Twelfth Census of the United States, Population*, 1:88, 1:173. Interviews, Eta Shannon, Logan Co., Doc. 23; Roscoe Conklin Yarnell, Kit Carson Co., Doc. 53.

59. U.S. Bureau of the Census, *Twelfth Census of the United States, Population*, 1:88, 1:173.

60. U.S. Bureau of the Census, *Twelfth Census of the United States, 1900, Agriculture*, 2:831–36, 2:868–70.

61. Interviews, Isaac Messinger, Kit Carson Co., Doc. 35; John G. Abbot, Logan Co., Doc. 2; Payne, *Dairying on the Plains*, 19–20.

62. Johnson, *High Plains and Their Utilization*, (1901) 686–87.

63. Interviews, James McCombs, Kit Carson Co., Doc. 51.

64. *Field and Farm*, Feb. 14, 1891, and Feb. 21, 1891. See Worster, *Dust Bowl*, 44–63, for resettlement plans during the 1930s, and Raban, *Bad Land*, 300–58.

65. Ludden, *Report to the Honorable House of Representatives*, 1559–62; Ludden, *Report of the Nebraska State Relief Commission* (1892).

66. Fite, *Farmers' Frontier*, 129–31; Ludden, *Report to the Honorable House of Representatives*, 1560–61.

67. Ludden, *Report to the Honorable House of Representatives*, 1560–61.

68. *The Dundy County Pioneer* (Benkleman), Feb. 26, 1892; *(Lincoln) Nebraska State Journal*, March 10, 1892, April 6, 1892, and May 1, 1893.

69. Ludden, *Report of the Nebraska State Relief Commission*, 137, 177; Fite, *Farmers' Frontier*, 130; Interviews, Letter, Leila Shaw Waters to Cyrus and Lydia Shaw, April 11, 1894, Kit Carson County, Doc. 44; Dunbar, "Agricultural Adjustments," 48–50.

70. Ludden, *Report of the Nebraska State Relief Commission* (1895), 7.

71. *Nebraska State Journal*, March 2, 1895.

72. Ludden, *Report of the Nebraska State Relief Commission* (1895), 8.

73. Payne, *Unirrigated Lands of Eastern Colorado*, 8; Payne, *Cattle Raising on the Plains*, 13–14.

74. Johnson, *High Plains and Their Utilization*, (1901), 690.

75. *Tenth Biennial Report of the Kansas State Board of Agriculture for the Years 1895 and 1896*, vii.

76. Campbell, *Soil Culture Manual*; Fite, *Farmers' Frontier*, 131. Campbell drew many of his examples from eastern Colorado, and promised farmers there that if they used his methods, they would raise crops as abundantly as farmers in Illinois.

77. Payne, *Unirrigated Lands of Eastern Colorado*, 14–17.

Epilogue

1. de Wit, "Women's Sense of Place on the American High Plains," 35, 42. For a related study, see Gilbreath, "'A Little Place Getting Smaller,'" 25–41.

2. U.S. Census Bureau, *2000 Census of Population and Housing Colorado,* 108–17, table 15.

3. High Plains Regional Climate Center, Historical Climate Data Studies; Baird, "Drought Keeps Well Driller Digging for Water," *La Junta Tribune Democrat,* May 7, 2004, 1; Egan, "Dry High Plains Are Blowing Away Again"; also, see map of the Dust Bowl in Worster, *Dust Bowl,* 30.

4. Carpenter, *Rainfall Upon the Plains,* 21.

5. Worster, *Dust Bowl,* 26, 28; Saarinen, *Perception of the Drought Hazard on the Great Plains.* Great Plains Committee, *The Future of the Great Plains,* 63–67.

6. Hewes, *The Suitcase Farming Frontier,* 178, and 195, fig. 7; 197, fig. 9; 204, fig. 16; 205, fig. 17; usda, National Agricultural Statistics Service, Percentage of Farms Operated By Family or Individual, 2007; Percentage of Farms Operated By Corporation, 2007; and Percentage of Principal Farm Operators Not Residing on Farm Operated, 2007, at http://www.nass.usda.gov/Charts_and_Maps/index.asp.

7. Steinel, *History of Agriculture in Colorado,* 275.

8. Payne, *Advice to Plains Settlers,* 4–5.

9. Payne, *Advice to Plains Settlers,* 4; Cottrell, *Dairy Work for Plains Settlers,* 8; and Olin, *Summer Culture to Preserve Moisture,* 10.

10. For population numbers, see, most conveniently, Colorado State Demography Office, Historical Census Population, at http:dola.Coloradogov/demog_webapps/hsp_parameters.jsf. The statistics on the size and numbers of farms are from federal census data, beginning with U.S. Bureau of the Census, *Thirteenth Census of the United States Taken in the Year 1910.* Vol. 6, Agriculture (Washington dc: gpo, 1913), and ending with the 2007 Census of Agriculture, at http://www.agcensus.usda.gov/ Publications/2007/index.asp. See also Lavin, Shelley, and Archer, *Atlas of the Great Plains,* 111, fig. 3–19, for maximum census year of population.

11. For example, Interviews, Elizabeth Cutting Lengel, Kit Carson Co., Doc. 3; and Sarah Blakeman, Kit Carson Co., Doc. 37.

12. Steinel, *History of Agriculture in Colorado,* 275–76.

13. Great Plains Committee, *Future of the Great Plains,* 45.

14. Hewes, *The Suitcase Farming Frontier,* 204, fig. 16.

15. See the maps of irrigated farmland in Lavin, Shelley, and Archer, *Atlas of the Great Plains,* 134, fig. 4–3. Also, McGuire et al., *Water in Storage,* 19–21, figs. 11–13.

16. Johnson, *High Plains and Their Utilization,* (1902) 652–53; Great Plains Committee, *Future of the Great Plains,* 76.

17. McGuire et al., *Water in Storage and,* especially 6, fig. 4; 21, fig. 12; and 24, fig. 14; Opie, *Ogallala,* 286, 296.

18. See the map of federal aid per capita by county in the Great Plains Committee, *Future of the Great Plains,* 57.

19. Martin, "Agricultural Adjustment Administration," 32–33; Diebert, "Soil Bank," 39; Diebert, "Conservation Reserve Program," 50–51. Also Dan Morgan,

Gilbert M. Gaul, and Sarah Cohen, "Farm Program Pays $1.3 Billion to People Who Don't Farm," *Washington Post*, July 2, 2006. Statistics are from 2007 Census of Agricultural and Farm Subsidy Data Base at http://farm.ewg.org/progdetail.php ?fips=08/238progcode =total_er. It should be noted that in 2011, with the national debt soaring, federal agricultural support seemed likely to be cut.

20. U.S. Drought Monitor; Webb, "The American West," 25.

21. National Assessment Synthesis Team, *Climate Change Impacts on the United States*, 191–217.

Bibliography

Archival Sources

Civil Works Administration, Interviews Conducted During 1933–34 by the State Historical Society of Colorado. Pam. 341, 350, 351, 352. Colorado Historical Society, Denver.

Franklin, George Washington. Diaries. MS3614. Nebraska State Historical Society, Lincoln.

Governors' Records. Lorenzo Crouse. RG1 SG16. Nebraska State Historical Society, Lincoln.

Perkins County Nebraska County Board. Proceedings. RG222. Nebraska State Historical Society, Lincoln.

Schedules of the Nebraska State Census, 1885. RG513. Microfilm SG255. Rolls 18, 26, 35. Nebraska State Historical Society, Lincoln.

U.S. General Land Office. *Land Tract Books*. Nebraska State Historical Society, Lincoln.

Published Sources

Aistrup, Gerald K. "An Investigation of the Relationship between Climatic Conditions and Population Changes in Western Kansas, 1885–1900." Master's thesis. Fort Hayes Kansas State College, 1956.

Andreas, A. T. *History of the State of Nebraska*. Chicago: The Western Historical Company, 1882.

————. *History of the State of Kansas*. Chicago: The Western Historical Company, 1883.

Annual Report of the Commissioner of the General Land Office, 1868–1900. Washington DC: GPO, 1868–1900.

Annual Report of the Commissioner of Indian Affairs for the Year 1872. Washington DC: GPO, 1872.

Annual Report of the Kansas State Board of Agriculture, 1873–76. Topeka: Various Publishers, 1873–76.

Annual Report of the Nebraska State Board of Agriculture, 1874–95. Lincoln: State Journal Co., 1874–95.

Aughey, Samuel. "The Geology of Nebraska: A Lecture Delivered in 1873," in *Fourth Annual Report of the Board of Agriculture of Nebraska.* Lincoln: Journal Co., 1874, 67–85.

———. *Sketches of the Physical Geography and Geology of Nebraska.* Omaha: Daily Republican and Job Office, 1880.

———, and Charles D. Wilbur. *Agriculture Beyond the 100th Meridian: A Review of the Public Land Commission.* Lincoln: Journal Co., 1880.

Baker, James H., and LeRoy R. Hafen, eds. *History of Colorado.* 5 vols. Denver: Linderman Co., Inc., 1927.

Bare, Ira L., and William H. McDonald. *An Illustrated History of Lincoln County, Nebraska.* Chicago and New York: The American Historical Society, 1920.

Barrows, Harlan, H. *Lectures on the Historical Geography of the United States as given in 1933.* William A. Koelsch, ed. University of Chicago Department of Geography Research Paper No. 77. Chicago: University of Chicago, 1962.

Bellovich, Steven J. "A Geographic Appraisal of Settlement Within the Union Pacific Land Grant in Eastern Nebraska, 1869–1890." PhD diss. University of Nebraska, 1974.

Biennial Reports of the Kansas State Board of Agriculture, 1877–1900. Topeka: Various Publishers, 1877–1900.

Blouet, Brian W., and Frederick C. Luebke, eds. *The Great Plains: Environment and Culture.* Lincoln: University of Nebraska Press, 1977.

Bowden, Martyn J. "Great American Desert." In Wishart, *Encyclopedia of the Great Plains,* 389.

Brooks, Helen. "Land Alienation in the Nebraska Sand Hills South of the Platte River: A Geographic Analysis of Public Land Disposal, 1870–1894." Thesis. University of Nebraska–Lincoln, 1986.

Campbell, Hardy Webster. *Soil Culture Manual.* Lincoln: H. W. Campbell, 1907.

Carpenter, L. G. *Rainfall Upon the Plains.* The Agriculture Experiment Station of the Colorado Agricultural College. Bulletin 123. Fort Collins: Agricultural Station, 1908, 21–31.

Census of Agriculture. http://www.agcensus.usda.gov/Publications /2007/index/asp.

Colorado County Formation Maps. http://www.familyhistory101.com/ maps/co_cf.html.

Colorado State Demography Office, Historical Census, Population. http://dola .Coloradogov/demog_webapps/hsp_parameters.jsf.

Clements, F. E. "Climate Cycles and Human Populations in the Great Plains." *The Scientific Monthly* 47 (September 1938): 193–210.

Cohen, Felix S. "Original Indian Title," *Minnesota Law Review* 32 (December 1947): 28–59.

Complete Dictionary of Scientific Biography. Charles Scribner's Sons, 2008. http://www
.encyclopedia.com/doc/1g2-2830902208.html.

Cottrell, H. M. *Dairy Work for Plains Settlers.* The Agricultural Experiment Station of
the Colorado Agricultural College, Bulletin 123. Fort Collins: Experiment Station,
1908.

Cronon, William, George Miles, and Jay Gitlan. *Under a Western Sky: Rethinking
America's Western Past.* New York: W. W. Norton and Co., 1992.

Cunfer, Geoff. *On the Great Plains: Agriculture and Environment.* College Station: Texas
A&M University Press, 2005.

Darton, Nelson Horatio. *Preliminary Report on the Geology and Natural Resources of
Nebraska West of the One Hundred and Third Meridian.* Nineteenth Annual Report
of the United States Geological Survey, 1897–98. Part 4. Washington DC: GPO, 1899,
719–85.

de Wit, Cary W. "Women's Sense of Place on the American High Plains." *Great Plains
Quarterly* 21 (2001): 29–44.

Dick, Everett. "Water, A Frontier Problem." *Nebraska History* 49 (September 1968):
215–45.

Diebert, Edward J. "Soil Bank." In Wishart, *Encyclopedia of the Great Plains,* 50–51.

———. "Conservation Reserve Program." In Wishart, *Encyclopedia of the Great
Plains,* 39.

Donaldson, Thomas. *The Public Domain: Its History, With Statistics.* 47th Congress,
2nd Session, House of Representatives Misc. Doc 45, Part 4. Washington DC: GPO,
1884.

Dunbar, Robert C. "Agricultural Adjustments in Eastern Colorado in the Eighteen-
Nineties," *Agricultural History* 18 (January 1944): 41–92.

Egbert, Stephen L. "The Resettlement of Nance County: Land Alienation Patterns,
1878–1913." Master's thesis. University of Nebraska–Lincoln, 1983.

Elliott, Richard S. *Industrial Resources of Western Kansas and Eastern Colorado.* St. Louis: Levison and Blythe, 1871.

———. "The Plains," in *Report of the State Board of Agriculture for the Year 1873.* Topeka: State Printing Works, 1874, 253–58.

Emmons, David M. *Garden in the Grassland: Boomer Literature of the Central Great
Plains.* Lincoln: University of Nebraska Press, 1971.

Farm Subsidy Data Base. http://farm.ewg.org/progdetail.php? fips=08/238procode
=total_er.

Farmer, Floyd M. "Landboom of Southwestern Nebraska, 1880–90." Thesis. University of Nebraska, 1936.

Fenneman, Nevin M. *Physiography of the Western United States.* New York: McGraw
Hill Book Co., 1931.

Fite, Gilbert C. *The Farmers' Frontier, 1865–1900.* New York: Holt, Rinehart and Win-
ston, 1966.

Flora, Snowdon D. *Hailstorms of the United States*. Norman: University of Oklahoma Press, 1956.

Forsythe, David P. ed. *Encyclopedia of Human Rights*. Oxford: Oxford University Press, 2009.

Gates, Paul W. "The Railroad Land Grant Legend," *The Journal of Economic History* 14 (Spring 1954): 143–46.

Gilbreath, Aaron. "'A Little Place Getting Smaller': Perceptions of Place and the Depopulation of Gove County, Kansas," *Great Plains Quarterly* 32 (Winter 2012): 25–42.

Glacken, Clarence L. "Changing Ideas of the Habitable World." In *Man's Role in Changing the Face of the Earth*, edited by William L. Thomas, 70–92. Chicago: University of Chicago Press, 1956: 70–92.

Gleed, J. Willis. "The Wealth and Business Relations of the West," *Forum* 14 (1892–93): 631–43.

———. "Western Lands and Mortgages," *Forum* 11 (1891): 468–71.

———. "Western Mortgages," *Forum* 9 (1890): 93–105.

Goodyknoontz, Colin B. "The Settlement of Colorado." In Baker and Hafen, *History of Colorado*, 2:429–74.

Great Plains Committee. *The Future of the Great Plains*. Washington DC: GPO, 1936.

Hämäläinen, Pekka. *The Comanche Empire*. New Haven: Yale University Press, 2008.

Harger, Charles Moreau. "New Era in the Middle West," *Harper's New Monthly Magazine* 97 (1898): 276–82.

Hewes, Leslie. *The Suitcase Farming Frontier: A Study in the Historical Geography of the Central Great Plains*. Lincoln: University of Nebraska Press, 1973.

Hudson, John C. "The Plains Country Town." In Blouet and Luebke, *The Great Plains*, 99–118.

———. "Towns of the Western Railroads," *Great Plains Quarterly*, 2 (Winter 1982): 41–54.

———. "Who Was Forest Man? Sources of Migration to the Plains," *Great Plains Quarterly* 6 (Spring 1986): 69–83.

Ingalls, John James. "Kansas, 1541–1891," *Harper's New Monthly Magazine* 86 (1892–93), 697–713.

Isenberg, Andrew C. *The Destruction of the Bison: An Environmental History, 1750–1920*. Cambridge: Cambridge University Press, 2000.

Jenkins, Even Jefferson. *The Northern Tier: Or, Life Among the Homestead Settlers*. Topeka: G. W. Martin, 1880.

Joern, Anthony. "Insects." In Wishart, *Encyclopedia of the Great Plains*, 632–33.

Johnson, Willard D. *The High Plains and Their Utilization*. Twenty-First Annual Report of the United States Geological Survey, 1899–1900, Part 4. Hydrology. Washington DC: GPO, 1901, 609–732; continued in Twenty-Second Annual Report of the United States Geological Survey, 1900–1901, Part 4. Washington DC: GPO, 1902, 637–69.

Kappler, Charles J. *Indian Affairs: Laws and Treaties*. Washington DC: GPO, 1903–38.

Koch, William E. "Farm Building on the Nebraska High Plains: The Diary of George Washington Franklin." *Journal of the West* 16 (January 1977): 36–39.

Kollmorgan, Walter M. "The Woodsman's Assault on the Domain of the Cattleman." *Annals of the Association of American Geographers* 59 (1969): 215–38.

Kraenzel, Carl F. *The Great Plains in Transition*. Norman: University of Oklahoma Press, 1955.

Laughlin, J. Lawrence. "Causes of Agricultural Unrest," *The Atlantic Monthly*, 369 (1896): 577–85.

Lavin, Stephen J., Fred M. Shelley, and Clark Archer. *Atlas of the Great Plains*. Lincoln: University of Nebraska Press, 2011.

Lehr, John C., and Brian McGregor. "Using Schools to Map the Frontier of Settlement in the Canadian Prairies," *Great Plains Research* 18 (Spring 2008): 53–66.

Lindgren, Elaine H. *Land in Her Own Name: Women as Homesteaders in North Dakota*. Norman: University of Oklahoma Press, 1996.

Lockwood, Jeffrey R. "Insect Lore." In Wishart, *Encyclopedia of the Great Plains*, 305–6.

Lowenthal, David. *The Past is a Foreign Country*. New York: Cambridge University Press, 1985.

Ludden, Luther P. *Report to the Honorable House of Representatives of the Twenty-Second Session, Nebraska Legislature, March 19, 1891*. Omaha: Festner Printing Co., 1891.

———. *Report of the Nebraska State Relief Commission*. Lincoln: State Journal Co., 1892.

———. *Report of the Nebraska State Relief Commission*. Lincoln: Jacob North and Co., 1895.

Miner, Craig H. *West of Wichita: Settling the High Plains of Kansas, 1865–1890*. Lawrence: University of Kansas Press. 1986.

———. *Next Year Country: Dust to Dust in Western Kansas 1890–1940*. Lawrence: University of Kansas Press, 2006.

Malin, James C. *Winter Wheat in the Golden Belt of Kansas*. Lawrence: University of Kansas, 1944.

———. "Dust Storms, Part Three, 1881–1890." *Kansas Historical Quarterly* 14 (1946): 391–413.

———. "Notes on the Writing of General Histories of Kansas. Part 5: The Vanity Histories." *Kansas Historical Quarterly* 21 (1955): 589–639.

———. *History and Ecology: Studies of the Grassland*. Robert P. Swierenga ed. Lincoln: University of Nebraska Press, 1984.

Mann, Henrietta. "Sand Creek Massacre." In Wishart, *Encyclopedia of the Great Plains*, 835.

Martin, James. "Agricultural Adjustment Administration." In Wishart, *Encyclopedia of the Great Plains*, 32–33.

McCarthy, Earnest Ray. *Crisis of 1873*. Minneapolis: Burgess Publishing Co., 1935.

McIntosh, C. Barron. "Use and Abuse of the Timber Culture Act," *Annals of the Association of American Geographers* 65 (September 1975): 347–62.

McGuire, V. L., M. R. Johnson, R. L. Schieffer, J. S. Stanton, S. K. Sebree, and I. M. Verstraeten. *Water in Storage and Approaches to Groundwater Management, High Plains Aquifer, 2000*. U.S. Department of the Interior Circular 1243. Reston VA: U.S. Geological Survey, 2003.

McQuillan, D. Aidan. *Prevailing Over Time: Ethnic Adjustment on the Kansas Prairies, 1875–1925*. Lincoln: University of Nebraska Press, 1990.

Miscellaneous Documents of the House of Representatives, 1891–92. Vol. 50, Part 7. Washington DC: GPO, 1895.

Mock, Cary J. "Drought and Precipitation Fluctuations in the Great Plains During the Nineteenth Century." *Great Plains Research* 1 (February 1991): 26–57.

Murphy, David. "Clay Construction." In Wishart, *Encyclopedia of the Great Plains*, 71–72.

———. "Sod-Wall Construction." In Wishart, *Encyclopedia of the Great Plains*, 94–95.

National Agricultural Statistical Service. http://www.nass.usda.gov/charts_and_Maps.

National Assessment Synthesis Team. *Climate Change Impacts in the United States*. Cambridge: Cambridge University Press, 2001.

Nebraska State Gazetteer and Business Directory for 1882–83. Omaha: Herald Book Printing, 1883.

Nebraska State Gazetteer and Business Directory for 1884–85. Omaha: Herald Printing, Electrotyping, and Binding Establishment, 1884.

Nebraska State Gazetteer and Business Directory for 1890–91. Lincoln: J. M. Wolfe, 1890.

Newell, F. H. "The Reclamation of the West," *The National Geographic Magazine*, 15 (1904): 15–29.

———. *Report on Agriculture by Irrigation in the Western Part of the United States at the Eleventh Census: 1890*. Washington DC: GPO, 1894.

Nimmo, Joseph, Jr. *Report in Regard to the Range and Cattle Business of the United States*. Washington DC: GPO, 1885.

The Official State Atlas of Nebraska. Philadelphia: Everts and Kirk, 1885.

Olin, W. H. *The Thorough Tillage System for the Plains of Colorado*. The Agricultural Experiment Station of the Colorado Agricultural College. Bulletin 103. Fort Collins: Experiment Station, 1905, 2–31.

———. *Summer Culture to Preserve Moisture*. The Agricultural Experiment Station of the Colorado Agricultural College. Bulletin 123. Fort Collins: Agricultural Experiment Station, 1908, 10–12.

Opie, John. *Ogallala: Water for a Dry Land*. Lincoln: University of Nebraska Press, 2000.

Overton, Daniel Warren. "A Historical Geography of the Eastern Remnant of the Otoe-Missouria Reservation on the Big Blue River." Thesis. University of Nebraska–Lincoln, 1991.

Paterson-Black, Sheryll. "Women Homesteaders on the Great Plains Frontier," *Frontiers: A Journal of Woman Studies* 1 (Spring 1976): 67–88.

Paul, R. Eli. "Frontier Forts." In Wishart, *Encyclopedia of the Great Plains*, 827–28.

Payne, J. E. *Advice to Plains Settlers.* The Agricultural Experiment Station of the Colorado Agricultural College. Bulletin 123. Fort Collins: Experiment Station, 1908, 4–5.

———. *Cattle Raising on the Plains.* The Agricultural Experiment Station of the Colorado Agricultural College. Bulletin 87. Fort Collins: Experiment Station, 1904, 7–17.

———. *Crops for Irrigated Land.* The Agricultural Experiment Station of the Colorado Agricultural College. Bulletin 123. Fort Collins: Experiment Station, 1908, 6–7.

———. *Dairying on the Plains.* The Agricultural Experiment Station of the Colorado Agricultural College. Bulletin 88. Fort Collins: Experiment Station, 1904, 19–24.

———. *Field Notes from Trips in Eastern Colorado.* The Agricultural Experiment Station of the Agricultural College of Colorado. Bulletin 59. Fort Collins: Experiment Station, 1900, 5–16.

———. *Unirrigated Alfalfa on Uplands.* The Agricultural Experiment Station of the Colorado Agricultural College. Bulletin 90. Fort Collins: Experiment Station, 1904, 31–36.

———. *Unirrigated Lands of Eastern Colorado.* The Agricultural Experiment Station of the Colorado Agricultural College. Bulletin 77. Fort Collins: Experiment Station, 1903, 5–16.

———. *Wheat Raising on the Plains.* The Agricultural Experiment Station of the Colorado Agricultural College. Bulletin 89. Fort Collins: Experiment Station, 1904, 25–30.

Pound, Louise. "Nebraska Rain Lore and Rain Making," *California Folklore Quarterly* 5 (1946): 129–42.

Preece, Jennifer Jackson. "Ethnic Cleansing." In Forsythe, *Encyclopedia of Human Rights*, 2:163–67.

Raban, Jonathan. *Bad Land: An American Romance.* New York: Vintage Books, 1996.

Rezneck, Samuel," Unemployment, Unrest, and Relief During the Depression of 1893–97." *The Journal of Political Economy* 61 (August 1953): 324–45.

Richardson, Charles H. "Early Settlement of Eastern Nebraska Territory: A Geographical Study Based on the Original Land Survey." Diss. University of Nebraska, 1968.

Ricoeur, Paul. *Memory, History, Forgetting.* Chicago and London: University of Chicago Press, 2004.

Royce, Charles C. *Indian Land Cessions in the United States.* Eighteenth Annual Report of the Bureau of American Ethnology, 1896–97. Washington DC: GPO, 1899.

Saarinen, Thomas Frederick. *Perception of Drought Hazard on the Great Plains.* Department of Geography Research Paper No. 106. Chicago: University of Chicago, 1966.

Sauer, Carl O. "Theme of Plant and Animal Destruction in Economic History." *Journal of Farm Economics* 20 (November 1938): 765–75.

Schabas, William A. "Genocide." In Forsythe, *Encyclopedia of Human Rights*, 2:294–304.

Schweninger, Lee. *The First We Can Remember: Colorado Pioneer Women Tell Their Stories*. Lincoln: University of Nebraska Press, 2011.

Select Committee on the Removal of the Northern Cheyennes. Senate Report No. 708. 46th Congress, Second Session. June 8, 1880, i–xxvi.

Sheldon, Addison E. *Land Systems and Land Policies in Nebraska*. Publications of the Nebraska State Historical Society, Vol. 22. Lincoln: The Society, 1936.

Sherow, James Earl. *Watering the Valley: Development Along the High Plains Arkansas River, 1870–1950*. Lawrence: University of Kansas Press, 1990.

Shortridge, James R. "The Post Office Frontier in Kansas," *Journal of the West* 13 (July 1974): 83–97.

――――. *Peopling the Plains: Who Settled Where in Frontier Kansas*. Lawrence: University of Kansas Press, 1994.

Silag, William. "Citizens and Strangers: Geographic Mobility in the Sioux City Region, 1860–1890," *Great Plains Quarterly* 2 (Summer 1982), 168–83.

Smith, Hilda. "The Advance and Recession of the Agricultural Frontier in Kansas, 1865–1890." Thesis. University of Minnesota, 1931.

Snoddy, Don, Barry Combs, Bob Marks, and Dale Weber, eds. *Their Man in Omaha: The Barker Letters 1860–1868*. Omaha: Douglas County Historical Society, 2004.

Spearman, Frank. "The Great American Desert," *Harper's New Monthly Magazine* 77 (1888): 232–45.

Spence, Clark C. *The Rainmakers: American 'Pluviculture' to World War Two*. Lincoln: University of Nebraska Press, 1980.

Spring, Agnes Wright. "Rainmakers of the Nineties." *Colorado Magazine* 32 (1955): 289–98.

Steeples, Douglas, and David O. Whitten. *Democracy in Desperation: The Depression of 1893*. Wesport CT: Greenwood Press, 1998.

Steinel, Alvin T. *History of Agriculture in Colorado, 1858–1926*. Fort Collins: State Board of Agriculture, 1926.

Sundberg, Sara Brooks. "'Picturing the Past': Farm Women on the Grasslands Frontier, 1850–1900," *Great Plains Quarterly* 30 (Summer 2010): 203–20.

Thornbury, William D. *Regional Geomorphology of the United States*. New York: John Wiley and Sons, Inc. 1965.

Turner, Frederick J. *The Frontier in American History*. New York: Henry Holt and Co. 1921.

U.S. Bureau of the Census, *Abstract of the Twelfth Census of the United States, 1900*. Washington DC: GPO, 1902.

————. *Compendium of the Eleventh Census, 1890.* Part 1. *Population.* Washington DC: GPO, 1892.

————. *Population of the United States in 1860.* Washington DC: GPO, 1864.

————. *Report on Farms and Homes: Proprietorship and Indebtedness in the United States at the Eleventh Census, 1890.* Washington DC: GPO, 1902.

————. *Report on the Population of the United States at the Eleventh Census, 1890.* Washington DC: GPO, 1895.

————. *Report on the Statistics of Agriculture in the United States at the Eleventh Census, 1890.* Washington DC: GPO, 1892.

————. *The Statistics of the Population of the United States, 1870.* Washington DC: GPO, 1872.

————. *Thirteenth Census of the United States Taken in the Year 1910.* Vol. 6. *Agriculture.* Washington DC: GPO, 1913.

————. *Twelfth Census of the United States.* Part 1. *Population.* Washington DC: U.S. Census Office, 1901.

————. *Twelfth Census of the United States, 1900. Agriculture.* Part 2. *Crops and Irrigation.* Washington DC: U.S. Census Office, 1902.

————. *Twelfth Census of the United States Taken in the Year 1900, Statistical Atlas* (Washington DC: U.S. Census Office, 1903).

U.S. Census Bureau. *2000 Census of Population and Housing Colorado.* PHG-2-7. Washington DC: GPO, 2003.

————. *2000 Census of Population and Housing. Profile of General Demographic Characteristics, Colorado.* DP-1. Washington DC: GPO, 2003.

U.S. Department of Agriculture, Weather Bureau, *Summaries of Climatological Data by Sections.* Washington DC: Weather Bureau, 1926.

U.S. Drought Monitor. http://www.drought.unl.edu.dm/DM_ highplains/html.

Vollan, Charles A. "Hell on Wheels: Community, Respectability, and Violence in Cheyenne, Wyoming, 1867–1869." Diss. University of Nebraska–Lincoln, 2004.

Walker, Francis. *Annual Report of the Commissioner of Indian Affairs, for the Year 1872.* Washington: GPO, 1872.

Weaver, J. E. *Native Vegetation of Nebraska.* Lincoln: University of Nebraska Press, 1965.

————. *Prairie Plants and Their Environment.* Lincoln: University of Nebraska Press, 1968.

Webb, W. E. "Air Towns and Their Inhabitants," *Harper's New Monthly Magazine* 51 (1875): 828–35.

Webb, Walter Prescott. *The Great Plains.* New York: Grosset and Dunlap, 1931.

————. "The American West: Perpetual Mirage," *Harper's Magazine* 214 (1957): 25–32.

Wedel, Waldo R. "The High Plains and Their Utilization," *American Antiquity* 29 (July 1963): 1–16.

"West and East—Debtor and Creditor," *The Nation* 6 (March 19, 1868): 225–28.

White, Richard. "The Winning of the West: The Expansion of the Sioux in the Eighteenth and Nineteenth Centuries," *Journal of American History* 65 (September 1978): 319–43.

Wishart, David J. "Compensation for Dispossession: Payments to the Indians for their Lands on the Central and Northern Great Plains in the Nineteenth Century," *National Geographic Research* 6 (Winter 1990): 94–109.

———. *An Unspeakable Sadness: The Dispossession of the Nebraska Indians.* Lincoln and London: University of Nebraska Press, 1994.

———, ed. *The Encyclopedia of the Great Plains.* Lincoln: University of Nebraska Press, 2004.

Worster, Donald. *Dust Bowl: The Southern Plains in the 1930s.* New York: Oxford University Press, 1979.

Wrobel, David M. *The End of American Exceptionalism: Frontier Anxiety from the Old West to the New Deal.* Lawrence: University of Kansas Press, 1993.

Index